HOW BRITAIN SHAPED THE MANUFACTURING WORLD

I dedicate this book to those skilled and imaginative men who explored new and different ways to make things. Time and again we might admit surprise at the names of those most influential in the story, for many were not 'British'. The peoples of these islands welcomed and offered opportunity to men, for most were men, who had been born elsewhere. Perhaps it was our openness to the world more than anything that resulted in this achievement. So, my dedication extends to those who offered that welcome. Leaders need followers, and this book would fail were it not to honour them, for so many did not follow of their own volition. Slavery and the slave trade provided the muscle for so much of the start of British manufacturing but so too the labour of unnumbered British men, women and children. My dedication embraces them but also the principled men and women who stood up against and put an end to these abuses. Surely they rank alongside those 'fathers' of British manufacturing industries.

HOW BRITAIN SHAPED THE MANUFACTURING WORLD

1851–1951

PHILIP HAMLYN WILLIAMS

PEN & SWORD
HISTORY

AN IMPRINT OF PEN & SWORD BOOKS LTD.
YORKSHIRE - PHILADELPHIA

First published in Great Britain in 2022 by
PEN AND SWORD HISTORY
An imprint of
Pen & Sword Books Ltd
Yorkshire – Philadelphia

ISBN 978 1 39901 515 8

Typeset in Times New Roman 11.5/14 by SJmagic DESIGN SERVICES, India.
Printed and bound in the UK by CPI Group (UK) Ltd.

Pen & Sword Books Limited incorporates the imprints of Atlas, Archaeology,
Aviation, Discovery, Family History, Fiction, History, Maritime, Military, Military
Classics, Politics, Select, Transport, True Crime, Air World, Frontline Publishing,
Leo Cooper, Remember When, Seaforth Publishing, The Praetorian Press,
Wharncliffe Local History, Wharncliffe Transport, Wharncliffe True Crime and
White Owl.

For a complete list of Pen & Sword titles please contact
PEN & SWORD BOOKS LIMITED
47 Church Street, Barnsley, South Yorkshire, S70 2AS, England
E-mail: enquiries@pen-and-sword.co.uk
Website: www.pen-and-sword.co.uk

Or
PEN AND SWORD BOOKS
1950 Lawrence Rd, Havertown, PA 19083, USA
E-mail: Uspen-and-sword@casematepublishers.com
Website: www.penandswordbooks.com

Contents

Foreword

When Phil asked me to write the foreword to his book, I was not prepared for the scale, scope, detail and insights I would gain through this magnificent body of work. Phil covers the changing industrial and manufacturing landscape between the two great exhibitions of 1851 and 1951, the latter being the year I was born. Household names emerge, merge and disappear as the reader is taken on a wonderful journey from our seafaring and exploring past, through a depression and two world wars to the wonderful exhibition of 1951 which displayed the strength and depth of our industrial capability.

I started work in 1967 as an engineering apprentice at Ruston & Hornsby, a name that appears many times in the book, alongside other Ruston names that were the results of mergers or acquisitions over the years. Ruston was established in1857 and, as my career developed, I began to learn that the company had constantly evolved and adapted to the changing world. I was therefore fascinated to read how other great names had transformed themselves over the years.

There has been a long-held story in the industry that the British are great at inventing, but not very good at marketing and selling, citing that as the domain of the Americans. I do not hold this view. I recall stories of Joseph Ruston in the 1800s, embarking upon global sales tours that took months to complete, sending the orders back to his factory, often to be delivered before he had returned. In my career in UK companies like GEC, we were entirely focused and driven to make sales in a global market and this continues to be the case today.

Anyone reading this book will recognize the incredible resilience and inventiveness of the British people, who have adapted, rebuilt and grown through adversity. I hope by the end of this book, the reader will share my pride in British manufacturing.

If Phil were to fast-forward to the mid-twenty-first century, he would record the global nature of our industrial ownership and be able to trace our fingerprints to just about every corner of the globe.

Foreword

What stands out for me in this book is the sheer detail and connectivity of Phil's research, cantering through the decades and linking our industrial evolution and heritage, in a way that captures the reader's imagination. A fascinating read.

Paul Barron CBE D.Sc

Author's Note

Today it seems a brave, or even reckless, assertion to suggest that Britain might have shaped the manufacturing world. Yet, looking back through history, there is a grubby British thumbprint on many of the world's manufacturing industries. In this book I try to explore the assertion by unfolding what is a quite remarkable story. In order to do this, I have drawn on the detailed research of a great many people without whose work this volume would not have been possible. At the outset, I acknowledge my debt to them. A volume of this length cannot be comprehensive of such a broad subject. My aim has been to follow the thread of British manufacturing, pausing at points of particular interest.

I am not saying that Britain alone shaped the manufacturing world, but, as I will explain, it almost certainly started a process that would continue over many decades. The role played by Britain diminished as that played by other nations increased, but it didn't disappear; indeed, it remained and remains strongly influential: British manufacturers are still world leaders.

My interest in the subject was sparked by research I carried out for my books on how the British army was supplied in the two world wars. I was bowled over by the wholehearted commitment of all manner of businesses of Britain in support of the war effort. I had to discover who was behind these companies, where they had come from, but also where they went. It soon became clear that the questions, although related, could not be accommodated in the same volume, so this volume began by research into the first two whence they had come.

I had, through my earlier writing, discovered that my great-grandfather had exhibited at the Great Exhibition of 1851, and so I found a copy of the catalogue and began to thumb through it. Some of the businesses I had come across in my war research were there, but also many others whose names rang bells from my childhood. Those names sent me on voyages of discovery.

I read many books, including David Cannadine's *Victorious Century*, which gave me the context. I devoured Eric Hobsbawm's *Age of*

Revolution which offered a radical view of the industrial revolution. I had studied urbanization as part of my BA, and so turned to Jerry White for his books on London in the eighteenth and nineteenth centuries. It soon became clear that trade was at the heart of the birth of British manufacturing and so I turned to Anthony Slaven's *British Shipbuilding 1500–2010* and Peter Moore's *The Endeavour*. From there it was on to the more familiar coal and iron with Robert Galloway's *A History of Coal Mining in Great Britain*, Eric Hopkins's *The Rise of the Manufacturing Town Birmingham and the Industrial Revolution* and Roger Osborne's, *Iron, Steam & Money*. I had also studied the role of Birmingham as part of my BA. Hobsbawm had directed me to textiles, and so I read *The Lancashire Cotton Industry: A History Since 1700*, edited by Mary Rose, and Robert Poole's *Peterloo: The English Uprising*.

This brought me to individual British companies. I am massively grateful to *Grace's Guide's* wonderful online resource, but also to companies' websites and to writers of articles for their painstaking exploration of subject areas. I thank authors who have devoted themselves to securing for posterity the stories of the companies they explore: Bernard Newman's *One Hundred Years of Good Company* on Ruston & Hornsby, J. D. Scott's *Siemens Brothers 1858–1958* and also his *Vickers: A History*, Demaus's and Tarring's *The Humber Story 1868–1932*, Geoff Carverhill's *Rootes Story: The Making of a Global Automotive Empire*, Carol Kennedy's *ICI: The Company that Changed Our Lives* and Alan Towsin's books on a number of commercial vehicle manufacturers. Books on industries: Aileen Fyfe's *Steam-powered Knowledge*, George I. Brown's *The Big Bang: A History of Explosives*, Alex Askaroff's *A Brief History of the Sewing Machine*, William Manners's *Revolution: How the Bicycle Reinvented Modern Britain*, Steven Parissien's *The Life of the Automobile: A New History of the Motor Car*, Peter Dancy's *British Aircraft Manufacturers Since 1909*, Graham Turner's *The Car Makers*, Keith Geddes's and Gordon Bussey's, *Setmakers: A History of the Radio and Television Industry*. Books on people and families: Henrietta Heald's *William Armstrong, Magician of the North*, Marion Miller's *Cawnpore to Cromar: The MacRoberts of Douneside* and Andrews' and Brunner's, *The Life of Lord Nuffield: A Study in Enterprise and Benevolence*. The *Complete Great British Railway Journeys* by Charlie Bunce and Karen Farrington provided a vivid verbal map which helped me navigate a sometimes-crowded landscape.

I carried out my own research into census returns and published industrial statistics; I had explored industry in the interwar years as part of my BA. My earlier work on supplies in the two world wars proved of enduring value: *War on Wheels* on the mechanization of the British Army in the Second World War, *Ordnance* on equipping the army for the Great War and *Dunkirk to D–Day* which looked at the lives of some of the leaders of the Royal Army Ordnance Corps to whose lot this massive task fell.

This is a book about fathers. Many of the books on industries highlight key individuals, so John Brown is father of Sheffield steel, George Stephenson is father of the railways, Thomas Humber is father of the bicycle and William Preece is father of wireless telegraphy. The British story is not about highly educated people, as it might be in France or Germany, but rather those who learnt their trade on the job.

The story of British manufacturing is not only about the inventors and engineers; their discoveries needed to be sold and financed. As I have already said, and explore further, Britain's export markets were essential; the home market alone would have been wholly inadequate. So, we needed men like Josiah Wedgwood who recognized the commercial potential of manufacturing ceramics of great beauty specifically for the growing community of the wealthy both at home and overseas, Joseph Ruston who would sell his steam-powered machines all over the world and Thomas Brassey who is said to have built not only one-sixth of Britain's railways but half of those in France. It would though be remiss not to acknowledge the role played by William Cecil, Queen Elizabeth I's trusted adviser for he masterminded British patent law which provided protection to those who wished to exploit their inventions here. Many chose Britain in preference to their native land for this reason, although others were attracted by our comparative tolerance.

We needed people who nurtured relationships, so Oliver Lucas, and Harvey du Cros of Dunlop. We needed entrepreneurs, so William Morris and Billy and Reggie Rootes but also those who sailed close to (and sometimes over) the line such as Ernest Terah Hooley and Harry Lawson. The role of managers was crucial, from Richard Arkwright through Seebohm Rowntree and Eric Geddes to Ronald Weeks.

I begin, as it did in my research, with the Great Exhibition in Hyde Park. I then look back at shipping and overseas trade, iron and coal, textiles and the massive role played by steam. I then work my way forward through communication, armaments and the home before spending time on the sewing machine and bicycle, internal combustion engine and electrical power. For me, more familiar territory follows, looking at British manufacturing in the Great War. My first chapter on the interwar years covers the period to the mid-twenties, and is essentially about the impact of the shockwaves from the horrors of the mud of Flanders. I then explore an essentially peacetime economy which had many bright areas. I then argue that for much of British manufacturing the Second World War began in 1935 and lasted ten years with the massive task of rearmament and the insatiable demands of war. Finally, I look at the exhausted nation struggling under the weight of massive debt but with great grit and enterprise, yet still contributing to the shaping of the manufacturing world. I end with a vision of hope as the nation celebrated itself in the Festival of Britain exactly a century after the Great Exhibition.

I am struck by just how much of this story owes a debt to fossil fuels and so carries a share of the responsibility for global warming. Coins, though, have two sides, and on the other are those who harnessed other sources of power not least water as used by Richard Arkwright, William Armstrong, William Siemens and others. Vitally, there are those British engineers whose efforts are now dedicated to net zero.

There are many people to thank. First and foremost, those authors, academics and others who have done such wonderful detailed work, without which I could not even have begun. I include a list of further reading and urge those interested to dig deeper into those books. I am not an engineer although I worked with a good number of manufacturing companies in the course of my career. I am blessed to count engineers among my friends. I am grateful to Gael Lewis and Paul Barron for reading my manuscript and to Paul for also writing such a glowing foreword. Andy Bye, Chairman of the Rootes Archive Centre, also kindly read the passages relating to the motor industry. Should any errors have slipped through the net, they are mine alone. Andy Bye also allowed me to use some Rootes images. I thank him, and also in relation to images, my friend Richard Pullen whose *Landships of Lincoln* tells the story of the tank, but also the Jaguar Daimler archive and the custodians of Salts Mill and Derby Museums. I thank my wife Maggie for her support throughout this quest and Claire Hopkins of Pen & Sword for again showing her faith in my work.

Chapter 1

A Great Exhibition at the Crystal Palace

'The history of the world, I venture to say, records no event comparable in its promotion of human industry as that of the Great Exhibition of the Works of Industry of all Nations in 1851. A great people invited all civilized nations to a festival to bring into comparison the works of human skill. It was carried out by its own private means; was self-supporting and independent of taxes and employment of slaves, which great works had exacted in ancient days.'[1]

This was some of what Sir Henry Cole himself said of the exhibition, as quoted a century later during the Festival of Britain.

On 1 May, 1851, Queen Victoria opened the 'Great Exhibition of Industrial Advances' in Hyde Park to some 20,000 visitors on the first day alone. The exhibition had been promoted from July 1849 by Prince Albert and Sir Henry Cole, President of the Royal Society of Arts, and it went through many and long arguments. Some people, including John Ruskin, had serious reservations about the benefit of industry. Others were writing about its very clear disadvantages in terms of urban poverty. Many, possibly most, saw it as a wonderful expression of patriotic pride.

All strands of industry from both Great Britain and elsewhere were to exhibit their wares. There were 100,000 exhibits from 14,000 individuals and companies from the United Kingdom and overseas, with some 60 per cent from the home nations. The Crystal Palace, erected in Hyde Park to the design of Joseph Paxton, who had created huge hothouses for the Duke of Devonshire at Chatsworth, covered some 900,000 square feet. The six million or so visitors, from all over the UK and further afield, from all sections of society, would have seen the incredible array of objects. Glassmakers would have noticed that Paxton had used handblown glass for the 30,000 panes that comprised the shell of the

1

building. Engineers may have looked at the British exhibits and perhaps have felt uncomfortable when they compared them to the sometimes technically superior products of some European countries and the USA. Overall, though, it was a sense of great satisfaction that prevailed.

1851 was also the year of the most comprehensive census of the United Kingdom undertaken so far. David Cannadine in his book, *Victorious Century*, quotes statistics of the number of people engaged in different occupations in Great Britain. Agriculture came first with just under two million, followed by one million in domestic service. Next came cotton textile workers at half a million; whilst this number was equally split between men and women, men predominated in agriculture and women in domestic service. Next in number came building craftsmen, labourers, and then a third of a million milliners, dressmakers and seamstresses and 300,000 wool workers. There were 200,000 coalminers. Instead of listing the remainder, Cannadine observes that there were more blacksmiths than ironworkers, and more working with horses on roads than with steam on railways.[2] It is worth observing that, drawing these figures together, there were well over a million men and women engaged in textile manufacture.

The Exhibition catalogue gives a sense of the state of the nation's manufacturing through the trades it sought to display. There were four sections: Raw Materials, Machinery, Manufactures and Fine Art; these were then broken down into thirty classes. Just taking the number of exhibitors in each class, the most numerous, at just under 1,000, was 'Machines for direct use including carriages, railway and marine mechanisms', followed by 'General hardware including locks and grates' at just over 800 and 'Philosophical, musical, horological and surgical instruments' at seven hundred and forty. One of my treasured possessions is the signed cover of a copy of the catalogue of the Great Exhibition presented to my great-grandfather, Richard Williams, by the members of the Surgical and Anatomical Committee Class X, 'as a slight token of the services rendered by him as Secretary'.

In Class 1, Raw Materials, there were over 500 mineral and mining exhibits from stone and coal to iron, copper and tin, and then a familiar name, Johnson & Matthey, with 'platinum, palladium, iridium, rhodium and uranium'. Tin and Copper were from Cornwall or South Wales. There were models of mining machinery and of a coal mine.

In Class 2, Chemical and Pharmaceutical products, there was the Washington Chemical Company in Newcastle, and chemical preparations from May & Baker, best known for their malaria tablet made in Dagenham, also Savory & Moore (a chemist shop I remember from childhood, now part of Lloyds Chemists) with kousso and sumbul, both homeopathic remedies. I confess to not recognizing many names in this section, but reading the descriptions its importance is clear. There are chemicals for the dyeing of calico cloth. W. J. Kane of Dublin exhibited bleaching powder (chloride of lime). There is saltpetre, which, when combined with sulphur (the main component) and steam, produces sulphuric acid. J. Wilson of Glasgow exhibited sulphate of ammonium made from a distillation of coal. Interestingly, in the same section, there is Truman & Hanbury with beer.

Among the 150 'Substances used as Food' (Class 3), there were Fry & Son for chocolate and Suttons for seeds, but also Benson, in Oxford Street, and Lambert & Butler, in Drury Lane, with tobacco. Fortnum & Mason in Piccadilly offered preserved fruits. Finally, in Raw Materials, there were, as Class 4, 'Vegetable and Animal Substances used in Manufacture', including Gillows & Co. with furniture, and Heal & Sons with quilts, both in London. There were then suppliers of wood, flax, wool, dyes and glue.

The next section was machinery of all kinds. The exhibition catalogue is fascinating and there are copies in a number of libraries, and it is available online.[3] J. D. Scott in his book, *Vickers: A History*, writes of the leading manufacturers of Sheffield being invited to send a ingot of steel to the exhibition. The ingot was cast in the works of Thomas Turton and weighed twenty-four hundredweight. Naylor Vickers, themselves, exhibited a forged bar of seven hundredweight.[4]

I looked further to find some other names I recognized, and found William Armstrong and his entry, in Section II Machinery, Class 5, 'machines for direct use including carriages, railway and marine mechanisms', which read: 'Armstrong, W. G. Newcastle-upon-Tyne – Model of hydraulic crane, steam-engine, accumulator, corn-lift, and hydraulic machine for unshipping coals.' On the same page as Armstrong, I found: 'Watt, James & Co – 18 London St., London and Soho, Birmingham – Des. And Manu. Marine Engines, of the collective power of 700 horses, designed for driving the screw propeller by direct action. Models made in 1785, showing the early application of steam power to locomotion.'

Moving down the list there was: 'Maudslay Sons & Field, Lambeth, Des. And Manu – A small double cylinder direct-acting high-pressure steam-engine. Connecting-rod adapted to marine steam engines, of the collective power of 800 horses. Models of patent marine steam-engines for driving screw propellers, &c. Model of a patent gun-metal screw propeller.' The visitor is then referred to Class 6, No. 228 (Machine Tools, Coining Press).

I also noted Butterley & Co. of Alfreton in Derbyshire with an eight-horse oscillating steam engine (Butterley was where Thomas Humber, of motor car fame, first worked); Clayton, Shuttleworth & Co. of Lincoln is listed also with an oscillating steam engine but with 'arrangements simple and compact, suitable for working corn mills, sawing machinery etc' (Claytons produced many aircraft in the First World War); there is then Siemens, C. W. Birmingham Inv. – with a 'working model of a patent chronometric governor. Model of variable expansion valve. Model of a surface condenser. Water-meter. Regenerative condenser. Working model of a regenerative evaporator'. William Siemens was born Carl Wilhelm Siemens near Hanover in 1823, and came to England twenty years later as a trained mechanical engineer.[5] Siemens Brothers was most emphatically a British company, and I write more of it in subsequent chapters.

Central to the industrial revolution was cotton and in particular machinery for making vast quantities of cloth. The section shows a good number of companies exhibiting power looms.

Scrolling further down the list, I noted J. R. Napier of Glasgow with a portable forge and H. Bessemer of St Pancras, with 'a centrifugal pump for draining land, discharging 20 tons per minute'. Napier is the name of a famous engineering family which included both the shipbuilder, Robert Napier, and two of his cousins, both named David. One was a fellow Scot shipbuilder, the other a precision engineer in London. Bessemer is eternally associated with steel-making, as, indeed, is William Siemens.

There were then a number of railway companies which provided a great deal of detail:

Gt. Western Railway Co.:

> Locomotive engine and tender, constructed at the company's works at Swindon. One of the ordinary class of engines constructed by this company for passenger traffic since 1847.

It is capable of taking a passenger-train, of 120 tons, at an average speed of 60 miles an hour, upon easy gradients. The evaporation of the boiler, when in full work, is equal to 1,000 horse-power, of 33,000 lbs per horse – the effective power as measured by a dynamometer is equal to 743 horse-power. The weight of the engine empty, is 31 tons; coke and water 4 tons – engine in working order 35 tons.

There is then much more technical detail until the entry arrives at fuel consumption: 'with an average load of 90 tons, at an average speed of 29 mph including stops [an ordinary mail train] it [uses] 20 lbs of coke per mile'.

The London & North Western Railway had a much pithier entry, 'narrow-gauge express engine, the "Cornwall" designed by Mr. Trevethick'. There then comes a name of a locomotive manufacturer that can be traced right through to the British Railways era, R&W Hawthorn, Newcastle upon Tyne, with a 'first-class patent passenger locomotive engine'.

I had been looking for non-railway operators supplying the railways, and so was pleased to find Ransomes & May of Ipswich manufacturing 'Barlow & Heald's railway turntable. Wild's railway turntable and switch. Barlow's iron sleeper. Registered water crane and patent compressed treenails and wedges for railways'. Ransomes, I recognized because the chairman of the company in 1916, Wilfred Stokes, invented the Stokes mortar. I also remember the name from my grandparents' lawnmower.

Looking ahead to the motor industry, it was interesting to find H. Mulliner of Northampton producing a 'four-wheeled carriage, commonly called a Brougham', and Thrupp of Oxford Street also with a 'Landaulet Brougham and shamrock car'. Importantly, in Class 2 Chemical and Pharmaceutical products, there was James Young in Manchester producing mineral oil and paraffin. I explore the whole history of the oil business and its related applications, not least the internal combustion engine, in Chapter 11.

Moving to the section on machine tools, Napier & Son of Lambeth caught my eye with their 'compass which registers on paper the compass course which a vessel has steered for 24 hours and "perfecting printing machine"'. This company, run by David Napier, would go on to manufacturer motor cars in the 1900s and, after the Second World War, the famous Deltic diesel engine. There was also, of course, J. Whitworth & Co. of Manchester – 'self-acting lathes, planing, slotting, drilling and boring, screwing, cutting, and dividing, punching and shearing machines. Patent knitting machine. Patent screw stocks, with dies and taps. Measuring machine and standard yard'. Bryan Donkin, who was the first to manufacture a tin can, exhibited an improved paper-making machine.

In the Building section (Class 7) I noted Finch & Willey of Liverpool who had made a model of the railway bridge over the Wye to Isambard Kingdom Brunel's design, a name my children will always associate with his railway bridge over the Tamar, for my insistence on asking for his name every time we crossed into Cornwall on holiday. There is a long entry for the Commissioners of Northern Lighthouses, with models of lighthouses and related equipment designed by Robert, Thomas and Alan Stevenson of that remarkable Scottish family of engineers. There is also G. Naysmith with iron girders.

Class 8, Naval Architecture, Military Engineering, Guns and Weapons had the Wigram shipyard at Blackwall on the Thames and also Ely cartridges.

Class 9, the Agricultural Machinery section is relevant, not only to show the extent to which agriculture was being mechanized, but also because the challenge of driving powered vehicles across rough muddy terrain would become very relevant in military terms, some sixty-five years later, with the invention of the tank by Lincoln engineer, William Tritton. Clayton & Shuttleworth are listed in this section as well in Machine Tools (above). Claytons were exhibiting an 'improved portable steam engine for agricultural contractors' purposes, an improved registered grinding mill for all grain and an improved combined threshing, shaking, riddling and blowing machine'. Ransome & May are there, again, with 'patent iron ploughs; double breast or moulding ploughs; West Indian, double furrow, universal, broad share and subsoil ploughs'. Richard Hornsby & Sons of Grantham listed a 'six-horse power patent portable steam engine and an improved portable threshing machine'. Charles Burrell of Thetford in Norfolk exhibited a steam engine specifically designed to drive agricultural implements.

In Class 10, Philosophical, Musical and Horological instruments, there is the name Elliott & Sons exhibiting 'drawing instruments, theodolites, transit instruments slide-rule, azimuth and altitude instruments'. Their premises were at 56 The Strand, close to that of my great-grandfather at Weiss & Son. Their name will recur in this story in connection first with Siemens, but then in the aircraft industry and GEC. They began business in 1800. Class 10 also has entries for makers of electric telegraph equipment including the British Electric Telegraph Company exhibiting 'Highton's patent electric telegraphs and apparatus, Morse's arrangement of telegraph worked by secondary power, and a series of indicating and pointing telegraphs worked by various descriptions of coils and steel magnets'. Based in St John Street, near the Adelphi, there is F. Whishaw with a 'gutta-percha telephone and railway trains communicator' (gutta-percha was a naturally occurring insulation material akin to rubber). I also noticed J. P. Joule of Salford, because I recognized the name as a brewery I had seen from the canal. This was correct since Joule was the son of the brewer; he was rather more famous having invented Joule's law. He was one of the founding fathers of the electricity industry. I noticed Smiths as clockmakers of Clerkenwell in London, thinking ahead to Smiths Industries. It was a different Smith, but a significant clockmaker. Smiths Industries also originated in London, but, somewhat later, in 1876.

Moving to manufactured goods, it is worth observing that the manufacturing industry employing the most people, Cotton (Class 11), only had sixty-five exhibitors, whilst wool manufacture had 500 and silk and linen 170 (Classes 12 to 15). I explore this intriguing industry in Chapter 4. In terms of exhibitors, under cotton there is William Hollins of Mansfield in Nottinghamshire exhibiting both cotton and wool; they later combined the two into Viyella.

Under Wool, there is Fox Brothers of Wellington in Somerset which is still in business and which welcomes visitors. A large advertisement by Hyam & Co. of Manchester tells much more. They were tailors, clothiers and manufacturers for gentlemen and children, and also had branches in Liverpool, Birmingham, Leeds, Hull, Bristol, Glasgow and Dublin. They claim a 'pre-eminence, being the first house in the kingdom for fashionable clothing'. Under Silk, there is Samuel Courtauld one of the most famous names in British textiles. There are also the names of two significant London haberdashers, Marshall & Snelgrove and Swan & Edgar.

In Leather (Class 16), I noted the London leather goods shop, Swaine Adeney, but also the Hudson Bay Company displaying furs. In

Printing (Class 17) there was Spicer Brothers who printed the catalogue and who gave my father his first job in 1907. There was J. A. Novello printing music, De La Rue with an envelope folding and gumming machine; De La Rue would go on to print banknotes. I then noticed Pitman presenting a chart of phonographic and phonotypic alphabets; we later know Pitman shorthand for use by secretaries. In many sections there were presentations by Societies for the Blind. In printing it was the Edinburgh school with an ink that would raise letters on the page. In Lace and Other Cloth (Classes 18 to 20) Nottingham features with R. Birkin who also exhibited under lace-making machinery. In clothing, I noted Corah in Leicester which is still in business.

Class 21 was Cutlers. The second largest class (22) 'General Hardware including Locks and Grates' has some well-known names. Spear & Jackson, with saws rather than the garden tools with which they are associated today. Mappin Brothers in Sheffield with cutlery; they would later merge with Webb. The famous foundry at Coalbrookdale is in the catalogue with a large range of castings. Chubb & Sons is there with locks and Taylors of Loughborough with bells. There are a good number of manufacturers of domestic stoves, including some using gas and gas lights for home use. A good number of local gas companies had become established producing gas from heating coal; the gasometer, which readers may remember from childhood, began to appear from which gas was taken in cast iron pipes to light the streets but also some homes. Gas cooking would be the preserve of the rich for some years yet.

Another entry in this second largest category was J. Reynolds, or John Reynolds, nail maker of Birmingham. John's grandson, Alfred Milward Reynolds, joined the business in 1884, and significantly in 1897 filed a patent for a tube butting process. This would provide a strong joint between two steel tubes and was of great relevance to the bicycle industry. Reynolds set up a company, Patent Butted Tubing Co., which in 1923 changed its name to Reynolds Tube Co. Ltd. which would later become part of Tube Investments.

Looking through some of the other sections, I noted Windsor & Newton for paints, and Rowney for pencils. Some thirty years after the invention of the game, there is W. Gilbert of Rugby with footballs. For the sake of balance there is Lilleywhite of Islington with cricket balls and bats.

In the section on Glass (Class 24) there is Chance Brothers near Birmingham, Powell & Sons with the famous Whitefriars Glass Works in London and St Helen's Plate & Sheet Glass Works from where, later, the business of Pilkington Brothers was carried on.[6] It was Chance who made the glass for the Crystal Palace. This is followed by the section on China in which I recognized Minton and Wedgwood. Then in Class 27, Manufactures in Mineral Substances, for Building and Decoration, is Doulton & Co of Lambeth offering glazed stoneware drain and water pipes. This company would become the manufacturer of Royal Doulton. Drainage would become of major significance with London's great stink only seven years later and the construction of the London sewers.

Hidden in Class 29, Miscellaneous Manufactures and Small Wares we find soap, which in 1851 was becoming more popular as the atmosphere became dirtier. Two names jump out, both in London, Knight and Pears, the latter exhibiting their transparent soap.

To the many visitors one question surely must have been how had Britain come to be the hive of industry that the exhibition portrayed, but, even more so, how did it gain such a lead over other nations? I try to answer this question in the next three chapters looking first at trade, shipping and the growth in the urban population, then at coal and iron which this growing market demanded and finally at textiles which satisfied needs at home and experienced explosive growth overseas. The growth demanded power and I explore the potent combination of steam and steel. To the mind of a twenty-first-century time traveller would come the question, what happened next, and that I seek to address in the remainder of the book.

Chapter 2

Trade, Exploration and Shipping

Quinquireme of Nineveh from distant Ophir
Rowing home to haven in sunny Palestine,
With a cargo of ivory,
And apes and peacocks,
Sandalwood, cedarwood, and sweet white wine.

Stately Spanish galleon coming from the Isthmus,
Dipping through the Tropics by the palm-green shores,
With a cargo of diamonds,
Emeralds, amethysts,
Topazes, and cinnamon, and gold moidores.

Dirty British coaster with a salt-caked smoke stack
Butting through the Channel in the mad March days,
With a cargo of Tyne coal,
Road-rail, pig-lead,
Firewood, iron-ware, and cheap tin trays.

John Masefield

John Masefield's poem, *Cargoes*, does, I think, hold the key to beginning of British manufacturing. Eric Hobsbawn, in his book, *Age of Revolution*, observes that, toward the end of the eighteenth century, the conditions were right for industrial revolution, not least, he says, because 'private profit and economic development had become accepted as supreme objects of government policy'.[1] Key to private profit was trade, and in this chapter, I explore quite what this meant.

We might start by recognizing features of this island nation. Seafaring was a way of life for a sizeable minority, and this involved exploration of foreign lands as well as the more obvious fishing and coastal transport. John Masefield's poem paints the vivid scene. The British were an adventurous people. They were also a trading people, and foreign lands offered opportunities for buying and selling.

It is this spirit of adventure that in many ways is the key to how Britain evolved from being a country driven by the rhythm of the seasons to one of much greater prosperity. For, in many coastal towns, alongside the blacksmith and wheelwright, there was also the shipbuilder and sailmaker; this was particularly true in the case of the major ports of London, Bristol and Liverpool, but of many other smaller ports too. As an island nation, the sea had for centuries beckoned the adventurous, whether it be for fishing or for exploring other shores.

Some forty years of research have been brought together in Anthony Slaven's *British Shipbuilding 1500–2010*; shipbuilding, like wool, is fundamental to our island story. Slaven suggests that, all around our shores, there were many carpenters who turned their hand to the building of small boats. Their use was restricted to coastal waters, and, perhaps, as far as the Low Countries, France and possibly Portugal and the Mediterranean. Trade with the Far East was conducted overland, as evidenced by the Silk Road. The late fifteenth and early sixteenth centuries saw the 'great voyages of discovery', and much longer voyages to the spice islands, Africa and China.[2]

At this time, it was not the British who ruled the waves, but rather the Spanish and Portuguese. Britain's, or rather England's response was a catalyst for shipbuilding. Slaven tells that, when Henry VIII came to the throne, the fleet comprised five ships. Henry set about with gusto the task of creating a navy, 'building forty warships and creating dockyards at Deptford and Greenwich'. This was the first activity on the site of what would become the Woolwich Arsenal, and was the construction of the *Grace à Dieu* in 1518, a vessel very much larger than its predecessors at 1,400 tons. [3] Slaven describes how men 'from Exeter in the west to York in the north' had to be pressed to provide the necessary workforce. Alongside this naval activity, the mercantile fleet was also growing as a result of protective measures to ensure that English goods were transported on English ships. The Crown granted monopoly trading rights to the Muscovy Company in 1555 to promote trade with Russia, and the Levant Company in 1581 for Mediterranean trade. Shipyards on the Thames and Medway provided the ships. It wasn't just this distant trade, the western ports built ships for fishing, whilst Hull and Newcastle built whalers and coalers. The defining moment came when the English, under Sir Francis Drake, defeated the Spanish Armada in 1588.

The exploration of foreign lands led to the discovery of exotic delights such as spices, wines, tea, tobacco and sugar, but also the more seemingly commonplace cotton. Trade in these commodities was brisk in the later Middle Ages, bringing prosperity to ports such as London, King's Lynn, Bristol and Liverpool. Wealthy landowners would enjoy these foreign delights but also imported handcrafted china, textiles and metal goods . Those who traded in them, in turn, prospered, as did those providing professional services to them, such as lawyers, bankers and land agents.

The Thames was packed with ships: those from the East Indies laden with spices, tea and cotton; those from the West Indies heavy with sugar; but also many from other countries bringing a huge variety of produce, and, of course as Masefield reminds us, from Newcastle laden with coal. The ships were owned by merchants who stood to make great fortunes from their risk-taking; by the same token many were hit with disaster when cargoes were lost. Overall, though, great prosperity was enjoyed by this adventurous group of men, and of course their families. It was largely these who provided the customers for the increasing numbers of shops and, of course, British manufacturers of 'toys', those metal objects of delight made by craftsmen.

It wasn't just metal: Josiah Wedgwood, using clay from the area we now know as Stoke-on-Trent, combined art with mass production to manufacture ceramics of both beauty and utility as British-made alternatives to those imported from China. He created a factory employing division of labour and an early example of cost accounting. He also built a village, Etruria, for his workers, a model that others would follow. He lived on the site with his large family in Etruria Hall which he had built. He was a distinctly hands-on entrepreneur, experimenting with clays and glazes and personally throwing the first vases to be made at the new factory.

Jerry White, writing about eighteenth-century London, identified particular shipowners who put their wealth to other uses; these are names we readily recognize: Barclay, Baring, Hoare. For, from this merchant activity, an infrastructure of banking grew, but also an insurance market, both of which would be essential as the overall economy grew in size and complexity. What is interesting is that all this grew away from industrial activity but also, fortuitously, in preparation for it. Alongside this, what Hobsbawn calls social overhead capital was being created in the form of shipping, ports, and improved roads and waterways. The first English canal was promoted by Francis Egerton, the third Duke of Bridgewater, to transport coal from his mines in Worsley to Salford on the northern side of Manchester. On him rests the title, 'Father of the Canals'. He had witnessed the canals of central France and was convinced that similar routes could be used in England where inland transport was dire. The Bridgewater canal was followed by many others including the Trent and Mersey canal which provided Wedgwood with transport both for his production and his raw materials.

The existence of overseas markets was fundamental to the coming revolution in industry. A great many of these markets were to be found in what was fast becoming the British Empire, not yet the one on which the sun never set, for a great many colonies were added during the nineteenth century. David Cannadine writes that in 1792 the Colonial Office in Whitehall had oversight of some twenty-six colonies. We need to go back further, certainly before 1772 when the American colonies gained their independence. *The Oxford Companion to British History* points to 1607 when the first American colony of Virginia was established, and Slaven suggests that some 100,000 people crossed the Atlantic between 1630 and 1643. From these beginnings grew colonies along the American eastern seaboard and those in the Caribbean, 'the West Indies'.

As Rebecca Fraser tells in her account of one emigrant family in *The Mayflower Generation*, the first exodus to the 'new world' was not to seek trade, but rather freedom to practise religion.[4] It was only much later that the American states became significant in Britain's trade, but, when they did, they did with a vengeance in the dark shape of the slave trade. In 1672 a charter was granted to the Royal Africa Company giving it a monopoly over trade on the West African coast. It was succeeded by other companies, but their purpose was the trade in human beings, to become slaves, on the sugar estates of the West Indies and the cottonfields of the southern states of America.[5] This scar on our history has been written about elsewhere and cannot be addressed adequately in this volume, with its focus on manufacturing. So, I will note it without in any way dismissing either its huge significance or horror.

Looking eastwards, the first East India Company was established in 1599 to compete with the Dutch for the spice islands. This was all about trade from the outset: how to satisfy the growing moneyed classes at home. The company's influence and eventual control of the Indian subcontinent grew in fits and starts up to the mid-eighteenth century when it was finally complete and offered the mother country a market of dazzling proportions. At the beginning, David Gilmour in his book, *The British in India*, writes that, the company's settlement, or factories as they were called, were just three (Madras, Bombay and Calcutta) among a considerable number of other European settlements.[6] All had the same objective: making money. The word factory was as opposed to the manu-factory, and was a place of trade – the factor was the chief trader.

The growth in trade required shipping to transport it, and the mercantile fleet grew to perhaps 420,000 tons by the mid-eighteenth-century. It wasn't steady growth, for the three major wars in the century between Britain, France and Spain switched attention to military building, and the more commercial yards on the Thames became recognized as fit to build to naval specification. The Thames provided most naval tonnage, with further yards in Essex and Suffolk and Hull. A standard third-rate warship was 1,500 tons. The Thames also held the monopoly for building East Indiamen at between 800–1,200 tons. It was therefore building to a much larger scale than the other yards around the coast.

The Napoleonic Wars in effect gifted to British shipbuilders a growing and captive market as British influence spread; the merchant fleet grew from 1,132,517 tons in 1776 to 2,478,000 tons in 1815. However, these figures hide a vital point: much of the increased tonnage came from prizes of war rather than from British yards. The shipbuilding that was undertaken focused mainly on the north-east. There was of course naval construction, not only in the Royal Dockyards and elsewhere on the Thames, but as far north as Leith and, significantly on the Solent. At the end of the Napoleonic Wars, some 25,000 men were employed in shipbuilding. We also see the emergence of large yards: Bulmer in South Shields with 181 men, Perry, Wells & Green's Blackwall Yard in London with 173, F. Hurry at Howden Docks with 155 and Scott's at Greenock with 151. There was still further shipbuilding activity, with the south-west and north-west ports building fishing boats and coasters, but more ominously larger ships for the slave trade. Scotland and Ireland built for fishing, but there were signs of the Clyde emerging as a shipbuilder for the West Indies slave trade too. The north-east was fast becoming the main merchant shipbuilding district.

The building blocks were beginning to fall into place. There was a small but growing home market of increasingly wealthy people hungry for delights. Agriculture was able to meet the nation's needs, whilst releasing large numbers of people hungry for work. As I tell in the next chapters, coal and iron were beginning to be available to power and make machinery. Adventurers unlocked markets many times larger than Britain to supply raw material and to consume many thousands of cheap goods. British shipyards were making merchant vessels able to cross any ocean and a navy was beginning to show its teeth.

The population was growing, largely in the absence of epidemics and civil strife, yet there is no evidence of any great shift in population numbers until the latter part of the eighteenth century when circumstances came together in such a way as to break the traditional agrarian cycle. This we now know as the industrial revolution.

Chapter 3

Coal and Metal

'Coal had "tentacles in every part of this changing society". Landowners loved it for it lay under their land; farmers benefitted from its use in burning lime for fertilizer; textile manufacturers used its heat in bleaching and dyeing; houses were built from brick and glass both made by the heat of coal; many small workshops across the land, as we shall see, used it to enhance their productivity.'
Roger Osbourne, *Iron, Steel and Money*[1]

As wealth began to spread, those newly monied joined those with inherited land in wanting things, whether in terms of building materials for homes, decorative items or gadgets, and this demand was met by coal and metal. The Great Exhibition catalogue shows clearly, from the sheer number of companies making them, that this small but growing middle class wanted metal gadgets, but also that the phenomenal growth of both textiles and shipping demanded metal tools and machines.

Mankind had been making things from metal for millennia. In Medieval England, in every large village and small town, there were blacksmiths and wheelwrights; there were also wainwrights, for carts were vital in transporting supplies. Wherever metal-bearing ore was found, it would be smelted using charcoal which, it had been discovered, was more suitable than wood, having fewer impurities, burning more steadily but more importantly at a much higher temperature. Coal was there for the picking in a number of places by the sea, particularly in Northumberland, and was found to be a useful source of heat, although, because of impurities, not as well suited to smelting as charcoal; it was known as sea-coal (as opposed to char-coal). In 1882, Robert Galloway wrote a remarkable history of coal-mining in Great Britain, and, from this, it is possible to map its growth but also that of metal.[2] It is fundamental to this story.

Over the centuries, men had sought out further sources of sea-coal, and, where it was evident on the surface, they would dig and extract what lay not too deep beneath. By the thirteenth century, the quantities became significant. Newcastle, which was the centre of much of the early mining, would send sea-coal by ships, known as keels, to London where it was used in dyeing, brewing and lime-burning for building. Attempts were made at using it for domestic heating, but it was totally unsuited to the traditional open hearth, giving off smoke and noxious fumes. A portable chimney became a popular means to prevent rooms from being smoked out. In time, the design of houses changed to accommodate it. The smoke from burning coal was an undoubted nuisance; a proclamation in 1306 prohibited artificers from using sea-coal for their furnaces, and, so, many returned to traditional charcoal. Britain had been a country covered in woodlands, and so the use of wood for heating and much else was in the national DNA. By the time of Elizabeth I, the continual felling of woodlands and the demand for wood for the building of ships resulted in a scarcity of wood and charcoal, and so coal became the fuel of choice. The digging of mines increased in what are now, or rather were in the twentieth century, the coalfields. Coal was also being exported to the continent and used increasingly in all parts of Britain. Osborne offers some figures: 'coal production increased from 227,000 tons in 1560 to 3 million tons in 1700.'

Prosperous urban dwellers and landowners were becoming hungry for more comfortable places to live and so for bricks, glass to make windows and iron for other aspects of building, but also, for example, for ceramics from which the fashionable could drink tea . With the continued shortage of wood, the need to use coal rather than charcoal for smelting presented an urgent challenge. The original patent for the production of glass using coal was taken out by Robert Mansell, Vice-Admiral of England, much to the amusement of King James who opined that, 'Robert Mansell, being a seaman, whereby he had got much honour, should fall from water to tamper with fire, which are two contrary elements'. The impurities in coal presented major challenges, but Mansell persevered and eventually found that coal mined near Newcastle was suitable, thus, in effect, founding the British glass industry.[3] It was the presence of plentiful and suitable coal, combined with nearby clay deposits, that encouraged Wedgwood to set up ceramics production, first at Burslem and then his creation at neighbouring Etruria.

Iron presented a yet bigger challenge, and Galloway tells of repeated attempts to produce iron in suitable quantities and quality. A good number failed, until a patent was taken out on 21 February 1621, in the name of Lord Dudley, 'for melting iron ore, making bar iron, &c, with coal, in furnaces with bellows'. The patent may have been in the name of Lord Dudley, but the ideas and skills were those of his son, Dud, who had come down from Balliol College, Oxford, to manage his father's iron furnace and forges. Dud was met with huge opposition, and was unable to bring his project to fruition. Many others tried similar techniques, but they too were met with failure. Attempts were made using coke, but still with no success. The Civil War intervened and Cromwell himself became involved, but also without success. On the restoration, Charles II came to the throne and Dud re-emerged to make yet another unsuccessful attempt. All the trial and error by so many at last produced the desired result and by 1700, Leigh, writing the *Natural History of Lancashire*, could say that 'iron was being made 'by means of cakes of pit coal', i.e. coke.

This is perhaps the point at which to introduce another thread into the story, that of Birmingham and that part of England essentially bordering the River Severn down through the Forest of Dean, a country punctuated with smoking forges in every village. The picture that Galloway paints of mining is of a thousand flowers blossoming, or ideas being hatched and developed in many pits rather than as any organized process. Birmingham was perhaps a hatchery of engineering ideas. It was home to key elements of the industrial revolution with men pursuing trades such as metal-smelting, iron-forging, shipbuilding, chemicals, pottery, glassmaking, brewing and construction. Osborne suggests that by 1700 this sort of industry accounted for 30 per cent of the economy, with only agriculture ahead at 40 percent.

Birmingham's industry began with forges, the working of metal, mainly iron. During the Civil War Birmingham had been on the side of Parliament and the output of the forges in the shape of pikes, swords and guns must have been a most welcome contribution. With the Restoration came a new confidence among the 'middling types' and a new prosperity. Birmingham was ready and waiting to serve this by supplying, not articles of war, but trinkets, pins, buttons – those things that were essential to the aspiring family. In doing this, Birmingham had discovered two of the keys to industrialism: the division of labour and the use of small machines.

An issue faced equally by the craftsmen of Birmingham, builders of bridges, the inventors of machinery for use with textiles and the engineers of the coalfields, was the need for a significant increase in the volume of iron produced. By 1700, the techniques of smelting iron ore with coke and copper and tin with coal had been discovered. Galloway, though, tells how 'the total make of pig-iron in England in 1740 is set down at 17,350 tons', a figure wholly inadequate for the demands which were growing. He points his reader to Coalbrookdale Foundry in Shropshire where the Darby family were using a blast furnace powered by water. At Coalbrookdale, the Darbys cast the first iron bridge, which lent its name to the town where it was built. The Darbys, being members of the Society of Friends, declined to cast cannon, the other major growing use for iron. It was the foundry at Carron which under took this military work. Skills of working with iron were developing all the time.

The Darbys produced cast iron; a much more difficult challenge was bar or wrought iron. Traditionally bar iron was produced by heating cast iron with charcoal and working it to make it malleable. The problem was the dependence on charcoal, but also the time the process could take and the small volumes that could be produced. The initial solution was to import bar iron from Russia and Sweden. The challenge for the British was to discover how bar iron could be made from British cast iron using coal rather than charcoal. Osborne writes of the great many patents filed as iron masters experimented with different methods. The man acknowledged as the inventor of a much more streamlined process was Henry Cort, of Gosport in Hampshire, who filed his patent in 1783. His method involved a combination of puddling and rolling. Interestingly, Cort also had a naval connection, in that his business was run in partnership with Admiral Adam Jellicoe. Sadly, for Cort, it didn't end well with his patents confiscated by the government on the discovery of fraud by his partner. For the users of iron, it was a revelation.

Iron was now being worked in many more parts of Britain. In 1759, at Dowlais near Merthyr Tydfil, an iron works was founded by a group of iron masters. Eight years later, John Guest joined the company as works manager.[4] Guest would later join with Keen & Nettlefold in what became one of Britain's largest industrial companies, GKN.

It wasn't only iron; tin had been mined in Cornwall and South Wales for centuries. In 1831, William Llewellyn founded the Aberdulais Tinplate Company where iron ingots were rolled into flat plates and a thin protective layer of tin attached. It was one of hundreds of tin mills which grew up around the country. Tin was reasonably readily available, easy to work and very effective in coating iron and steel to prevent rust. Aberdulais is now owned by the National Trust.

Back in Birmingham, the latter part of the eighteenth century saw the establishment of larger factories alongside the traditional small workshops. Boulton & Watt, at their Soho works, were one of the first manufacturers of the equipment needed to extract gas from coal. In the early days of coke production, waste materials, essentially gas and tar, were simply dumped as being of little use. The ingenuity and natural inquisitiveness of those producing coke encouraged them to explore all that was being wasted. Coal damp, or the gas that leaked into many coalmines, was in a few cases being piped and used for lighting. The gas released in the making of coke, likewise, was in time captured in cast-iron pipes and used for lighting. It was, however, full of impurities, some injurious to health as well as unpleasant to the nose. Processes were developed for first the removal of impurities and then their use. The same was true of tar, the most basic use of which was it application to wood as a preservative. Tar, though, is richer than this, and a whole range of substances could by appropriate processes be isolated. Turning back to gas itself, by the 1800s, a whole range of plants for gas production began to appear around the country. Large country houses would have dedicated plants, sometimes also supplying estate villages.

Another major Birmingham trade was brass. Made from copper and calamine, imported from Cheshire and Bristol, Birmingham worked in brass by initially by casting, but, after 1769, by stamp and die. As demand grew, the brass itself was made in Birmingham, for example by the Birmingham Metal Company off Broad Street, in 1781. In 1790, brass manufacturers combined to found their own companies to produce copper in Redruth and Swansea. It is hard to think it now, but during the nineteenth century, Cornish copper and tin dominated the world. The number of works increased from fifty in 1800 to 280 in 1830 and 421 in 1865. Size also increased and this shift from the small workshop enabled both efficiency and more control. It also won its plaudits: 'What Manchester is to cotton, Bradford in wool, and Sheffield in steel, Birmingham is in brass,' said W. C. Atkin.[5] Birmingham minted coins and other brass fittings were used worldwide.

Sheffield had long been home to cutlers, who would take the output of the many small iron founders and, in small workshops in the town, manufacture knives, forks and spoons, but also swords and cutlasses. The iron for these purposes had 1.5 per cent of carbon added to make it into steel. It was thus stronger than wrought iron and less brittle than cast iron. Its manufacture can be traced back many centuries to Japan and India, and from India to Toledo in Spain, known for its extremely sharp sword blades. In England, as early as the fourteenth century, steel was being produced in small quantities in Sheffield where it was then fashioned, using the available water power, into cutlery. Up until the eighteenth century, most British iron was considered unsuitable to use in making steel and so iron was imported from Russia and Sweden. Osborne explores early steelmaking and tells how Benjamin Huntsman, a clockmaker in Doncaster, began to experiment to find more suitable steel for springs and pendulums. A theme through Osborne's book is that many innovations were made by Quakers. He suggests that non-conformists were outside the established trade and other bodies and so much freer to try new things. Hunstman was no exception. In order to make steel, great heat was needed and could be provided by the burning coke, but this had to be kept separate. Huntsman experimented with crucibles made of clay from Stourbridge mixed with local Sheffield earth. The result was a hard steel which attracted customers from across Europe. In the late eighteenth century, his process was being copied by an increasing number of steel refiners in the Sheffield area, but Huntsman was regarded as the best. As Osborne puts it, 'Sheffield had been a centre of steelmaking before Hunstman, but afterwards it became a world powerhouse.'[6] Incidentally, the first trace of the Vickers family in Sheffield comes in 1750 when they were millers at Mill Sands. One son, William, was in the steel business and his brother, Edward who ran the millers, married into the steel family of George Naylor. I tell more of the Vickers family in Chapter 5.

Metal and coal production were growing hand in hand. As mines were dug deeper and deeper, dangers and difficulties multiplied: coal catching fire underground, coal emitting inflammable gasses, and water flowing into shafts from the land through which they were sunk. There was also the not insignificant issue of how to transport such bulk from underground to the place where it would be used. Galloway tells the story of how these dangers and difficulties were overcome by the application of science and engineering through a great deal of trial and error. It was a story that would become one of the threads on which the industrial revolution grew, not of itself sufficient but in every sense necessary, as will become apparent.

This indeed was an age of invention. Osborne tells of the trials and tribulations of the patent system which we might think of as an inventor's protection. The origin of the granting of patents dates back to the sixteenth century and, more than anything, was designed to protect the economy. He traces the system back to William Cecil, the trusted adviser to Elizabeth I. Cecil wanted to attract foreign manufacturers to England, which he saw as far behind in the development of manufacturing techniques. So, he granted to such men setting up in England what in effect were twenty-one-year monopolies. Much later, when inventors needed to protect their inventions, they had to go through a cumbersome process of applying for the grant of a patent, but, once it was granted, it was up to them to enforce it. Imperfect though the system was, inventors did use it and the number of patents granted is perhaps a measure of the nation's collective inventiveness. Osborne offers some numbers: 'between 1700 and 1740 the average number of patents awarded annually was fewer than five; from 1740 to 1780 the average number was nineteen; from 1780 to 1800 this increased to fifty-two.'[7] It is interesting to note just how many later inventors and innovative manufacturers were not native to these islands, but had been attracted by a benign social and economic environment.

Invention wasn't restricted to those applying for patents; it went on quietly but effectively in blacksmiths shops around the country. One such was in the village of Barrowby just off what is now the A1 outside the Lincolnshire town of Grantham. It was worked by Mr Seaman who, so the story goes, one day received a visit by a young man from Elsham in north Lincolnshire by the name of Richard Hornsby. Seaman put Hornsby through his paces and found a man of exceptional ability. Soon they set up in partnership together as Seaman & Hornsby in Grantham itself as agricultural engineers producing anything from ploughs to threshing machines powered by horses. They also served the domestic market, producing a washing machine.[8] The name, Hornsby, will appear again a number of times in this story.

In the next chapter I explore the application of invention to the textile industry which would emerge as one of the key drivers of industrialization.

Chapter 4

Textiles

And was Jerusalem builded here,
Among those Dark Satanic Mills?

William Blake

At the Great Exhibition, the number of exhibits relating to the textile industry was not great, but the census of 1851 had pointed to the huge number of people the industry employed. It was highly significant, but where had it come from, not least those dark satanic cotton mills?

In the sixteenth century, the British economy was still agrarian and would prosper and decline in tandem with good and failed harvests. In villages and towns around the land, there were bakers and brewers, weavers and bootmakers. It was an economy where, except for the privileged few, only needs were being met. Clothing for the wealthy was of wool and linen; that for the poor of wool but also leather. Particularly in poorer families, clothing would be passed down from one generation to the next; it couldn't be washed.

When cotton cloth began to be imported, it started a clothing revolution, but really much more. Cotton would have so many uses, 'from bandages and belting for machinery, and sheets and pillowslips, to exquisite ballgowns'. It had only been available for the rich, until 'the first chintzes were unloaded from the East India Company ships in the early seventeenth century'.[1] For the rich, it added variety to the wardrobe; for the poor, it meant clothing that could be washed. The importing of finished cloth was followed by the importation of raw cotton which would be spun and woven here. The port of entry was, certainly to begin with, London, but this was followed by imports into the other major ports: Bristol and Liverpool, and the spinning and weaving took place nearby. Liverpool, with its hinterland of Lancashire, would soon rise to prominence because Lancashire's damp climate was particular suited to cotton and its rivers could provide power from water wheels as processes became more mechanized. That, though, was for the future, for none of this would have happened had there not been in these islands a long tradition of spinning and weaving, and, of course, this began with wool.

The spinning and weaving of wool had been an industry in most parts of our island since the loss of manpower from the plagues had encouraged landowners to move away from arable farming in favour of raising sheep. The best sheep were said to be English and Welsh, but the best weavers were Flemish, and so fleeces were exported in vast quantities, so vast that they became an easy target for taxation. This encouraged the growth of local spinners and weavers, aided by an influx of Flemish wool workers fleeing persecution.

As a result, wool cloth markets developed around the country, in Norwich, Bristol, Gloucester and Kendal.[2] More importantly, the country gained a great many skilled spinners and weavers. As was the case with many trades in the Middle Ages, tradespeople gathered together in guilds for mutual support and to protect their interests. In the case of wool, these were found in towns such as Exeter, Honiton, Norwich and Beverley, and, by the sixteenth century, they became an obstacle to growth. The response was for the trade to establish itself in the West Riding of Yorkshire which had no such controlling bodies and where wool families could prosper. The importance of the wool trade to the economy was underlined in 1614 by an Act of James I which prohibited the export of raw wool. For the next two centuries all wool 'clipped in England was processed in England too'.[3]

The skills in spinning and weaving wool and also flax were equally applicable to cotton, which had been spun and woven for an equivalent number of centuries in the countries where the cotton plant thrives. In the seventeenth century, high on this list was India that was well under the cosh of the East India Company which was all too happy to make money from the export of wonderfully coloured Indian cotton to the fashionable British and European markets. Cotton fabrics, and indeed those from wool, were produced in many parts of India, in Bengal and the city of Cawnpore which would become known as the Manchester of India.

In time, British merchants saw a moneymaking opportunity if, rather than importing finished goods, they could import raw cotton and manufacture it in Britain. So, alongside finished products, raw cotton began to be imported. The early sources were the Levant, essentially what we now know as Turkey, as well as the West Indies and Brazil.[4] These would soon extend to the southern states of America, and India. This trade was not unopposed, for cotton textiles were stiff competition for native wool and linen. The Calico Acts were introduced in 1721 to prohibit the import of printed fabrics, and this soon extended to a prohibition of the wearing of calico prints. Production thus shifted to heavier fustian fabrics, woven from a mix of cotton and wool or flax, used as outerwear for men. The repeal of the Calico Acts opened the floodgates for more and more cotton. Mary Rose, in her *History of the Lancashire Cotton Industry*, offers some figures for millions of pounds of raw cotton imports. In 1720–29 it was fourteen, by 1780 this had grown to forty-eight.[5] The import of finished cotton goods by the East India Company was banned in 1813. Imports of raw cotton increased to 934 million pounds by 1820 and by 1850 it would rise to 4,072.

In eighteenth-century Lancashire, cotton was predominantly a cottage industry with the weaver and his family working together. For many, the cottage would be on a smallholding where crops would be grown and animals kept. This would not occupy all the family's time, and so cotton could be taken and processed. It would involve the whole family: father, mother, children and grandparents if they lived that long.

The way in which the industry was organized was based on merchants, not manufacturers. Taking the case of wool, the Cloth Hall in Huddersfield, for example, was home to some 2,000 merchants who would take production from a large number of individual spinner or weaver families. Towards the middle of the eighteenth century, the evidence is that this kind of life offered a reasonable living. The business of cotton, to a degree, followed that of wool. Raw cotton was being imported cheaply, and fabric and cotton goods sold to the increasing number of relatively well-paid artisans and others in the home market, but also exported to growing markets at good prices.

The growing demand for cotton fabrics provided the incentive for inventive weavers and spinners to explore better ways of working. This brought into play the skills of artisans used to working with metal whom I discussed in the previous chapter. For the purposes of this story of the textile industry, I shall stick with the key people and the advances they made. The first name is of a Bury man, John Kay, who, in 1733, patented the flying shuttle. Osborne tells how Kay had already patented a cording and twisting machine for use in the worsted trade; clearly, he was man of many gifts. However, as is so often the case, his invention was initially resisted by many weavers. Once it was accepted, though, it kicked into play a momentum that would prove irresistible, as weaving accelerated, the spinners simply could not keep up.

The spinning jenny was invented by James Hargreaves in Stanhill, Lancashire, in 1764/5 and massively increased the amount of yarn available to weavers. Hargreaves was followed in 1769 by Richard Arkwright whose water frame, run from a central power source, became the core of the new factory system. Arkwright, like Hargreaves and Kay, came from Lancashire, and like them was met with opposition. He moved closer to Nottingham and patented his device in 1770. He installed it in a new mill at Cromford in Derbyshire, which had a plentiful supply of water to provide power.[6] The Cromford Mill became the model from which the factory system of production developed. Arkwright was followed in terms of invention by Samuel Crompton's mule, which, in effect, combined the 'jenny' and 'frame' and which would be used well into the twentieth century.

So far, I have made no mention of silk, which has its own important role in this story. At Derwent Mill in Derby in the 1720s a mill was established to produce silk, adopting a method that had been used in Italy.[7] It is suggested that Arkwright may well have taken his inspiration from this. It is perhaps yet another instance where methods were developed in an unseen collaboration between people of many nations and regions. Derwent Valley Mills are now a UNESCO World Heritage Site and house an exhibition of making and weaving silk.

Across the Channel a significant development in weaving silk took place just after the turn of the nineteenth century. Joseph Jacquard invented a machine that would control the weaving process by the means of punched cards. I recall punch cards from my first encounter with computers in the 1970s; Jacquard's cards were not only similar but were very much the forebear of computer input devices. The hole in the card would tell the machine which thread to use and at which point. There is a portrait of Jacquard produced by his machine that needed some 22,000 punch cards to contain all the necessary instructions; once the cards were created, the pattern could be perfectly reproduced many times over.[8]

Thus, alongside the cottage textile industry, mechanization came in more and more. Names which we now recognize were emerging.

John Smedley, now known for its fine woollen garments, set up at Lea Mills in Derbyshire close to Cromford, in 1784, producing simple muslin fabric and spinning cotton.[9] The term long johns is attributed to John Smedley. William Hollins set up its mill in Pleasley that same year, attracted by the availability of water and a climate kept damp by the number of trees. Labour was provided by a workhouse; many of the workers were children.[10] We begin to see the context for Blake's words.

Technical developments alone could not account for the growth of the textile industry; markets too were needed. The French Revolution and the Napoleonic Wars that followed provided a catalyst that would trigger a step change in cotton production. Cannadine suggests that cotton had become the nation's largest export by 1815. This shift from satisfying the increasing demand for cheap cotton fabrics in the home market to exports is significant. Whilst the importance of the home market and the impact the availability of cheap textiles had on the lives of poorer people was significant, the industrial 'revolution' came when production exceeded that which was 'needed' and for which new markets had to be found. The markets were those found by the merchant adventurers, mainly in the colonies, but also European countries before and after the Napoleonic Wars, and, importantly, Latin America. This gives the date which, for the beginning of the revolution, Eric Hobsbawm sets at around 1780. Osborne offers a further very telling statistic. In 1790, 4 per cent of the clothing in Europe was made of cotton; by 1890, it had grown to 73 per cent and the population had roughly doubled to 400 million.

Underneath the headline figures, the position was rather more complex. European countries had provided good markets for British-made textiles and these markets were closed by the Napoleonic Wars. The resulting fall in demand for cloth led to reduced prices and dramatic reductions to family incomes. The merchants, who had operated this cottage industry, too were squeezed. Something had to be done. Costs needed to cut and volumes increased if the merchants were to maintain their standard of living. The answer was to hand in the shape of the manufactory. If suitable buildings could be equipped with machinery capable of doing the same work as a man, the industry could continue to thrive. Richard Arkwright's time truly had come.

The nation's merchants thus benefitted from the Napoleonic Wars, but its poorer population most certainly did not. Peterloo, that very English rebellion, was set in cotton-trading Manchester. A recent detailed investigation of the contemporary accounts of the massacre of 1819 reveals much about the cotton industry of the time, in particular that, notwithstanding the strides made toward mechanization, it was still predominantly a cottage industry with the weaver and his family producing cloth and then selling it to one of Manchester's many warehouses.[11] Toward the end of the eighteenth century, this had provided a relatively good living. With the Napoleonic Wars and the consequent restriction on exports, prices tumbled. Weaver families found themselves with less income, but also facing higher food prices as a result of bad harvests. Hobsbawm quotes a figure of 500,000 handloom weavers starving. Petitions were made to Parliament, but fell on deaf ears and this eventually led to the peaceful gathering at St Peter's Field which ended so tragically. It wasn't just the north-west; the East Midlands hosiery industry suffered, and there were riots in Nottingham and London; 'there were 20,000 unemployed weavers in the London District of Spittlefields alone'.[12]

The industrial revolution that began to emerge from this also was far from benign, with scandalous working conditions for men and women, and children as young as 7 in the new factories. I have already mentioned the case of William Hollins. There were exceptions such as Quarry Bank Mill in Lancashire and New Lanark in Scotland (which can both be visited today), where children were given a rudimentary education, but it would be many years before conditions improved. At Quarry Bank, which was one of the largest cotton manufacturers in the world, the children still worked long hours in dangerous conditions.

It wasn't only spinning and weaving: the finishing branches of the industry witnessed major technical advances. Traditional open-air bleaching took several months. In his paper, *Textile Bleaching and the Birth of the Chemical Industry*, Klaus Wolff describes what was in effect a three-stage process.[13] He looks at linen and cotton together, not least because the early introduction of cotton was as combined with linen. Linen tended to be a dirty green and so was more in need of bleaching than generally white cotton. The first part of the treatment was for the woven fabric to be repeatedly washed and boiled in alkali detergent. The residual alkali was then removed by a washing in acid. Until the mid-eighteenth century this would be lactic acid, essentially soar milk. The washed material would be laid out in the sun (and rain) for a number of months. The Dutch were said to be the masters of this bleaching process, as evidenced, for example, by the famous landscape painting by Jacob van Ruisdael, *The Bleaching Fields*. Once bleached, the cloth would be stretched into shape and then often starched.

Lactic acid was more readily available in Holland, with its extensive dairy industry, than Britain, and so it was here that alternative acids were sought. The solution came with sulphuric acid, the bulk production of which had been developed by John Roebuck in 1747.[14] Sulphuric acid had been known to alchemists for centuries, and also the more powerful nitric acid known as 'aqua fortis' for its ability to dissolve all metals other than gold. Sulphuric acid was being made in relatively small quantities from burning mixtures of sulphur and saltpetre. Roebuck replaced glass vessels with lead boxes, enabling him to produce it on a scale sufficient to supply the growing chemical industry. George Brown was a former chemistry teacher, who, some fourteen years after his retirement, wrote a very engaging book on explosives, entitled, *The Big Bang: A History of Explosives*. In it he also explores acid and alkali. He quotes Lord Beaconsfield as observing, 'there was no better barometer to show the state of an industrial nation than the figure representing the consumption of sulphuric acid per head of population.'[15]

The alkali detergent was derived from potash, mainly 'barilla' from the Spanish salt marshes. This supply was supplemented by burnt vegetation from Britain, Europe and North America. The key was salt from which sodium and chlorine could be separated. Wolff writes of the lack of integrated thinking. Chemists would process common salt to separate sodium and leave the chlorine as a waste product, but a very polluting one given that it combined to created hydrochloric acid. It took time before the bleaching qualities of chlorine were recognized. It was a Frenchman, Nicolas Leblanc, who was first to develop a process for making alkali from salt, even though he died before exploiting his invention. British chemists took up his process. Interestingly, one James Watt had earlier been working on such a project but had turned his attention to steam, joining up with Matthew Boulton. Returning though to salt, the chemists faced a major economic barrier in the form of the Salt Tax until it was eventually abolished in 1825.[16] Salt reserves in both Cheshire and Northumberland were used, and those areas became centres of the chemical industry. An influential exponent of the Leblanc process was Tennants of Glasgow.

The introduction of chemicals (sulphuric acid) cut the bleaching time in half, but then the coming of chlorine-based bleaching powder at the end of eighteenth century reduced the months to a single day. Dyehouses also employed mechanical power, as evidence by Livesey, Hargreaves & Co. near Preston.[17] The British textile industry was moving into its prime.

Alongside the growth of the Cheshire chemical industry came increases in soap manufacture. Growing industrialization resulted in towns and cities becoming dirtier from factory chimneys and at the same time the burgeoning middle classes were more able to afford what had hitherto been the luxury of soap. We can look at London to find the proponents of soap for the better off in the names of Knight and Pears, the latter later gaining fame through their advertising using Millais' painting of *Bubbles*.

For soap for wider use, the north-west towns of Warrington, Bolton and Wigan were home to rather larger manufacturers: Crosfield in Warrington and Gossages in Widnes. In the neighbouring town of Bolton in 1851, William Lever was born and, at age 16, entered his father's grocery business whose offering included soap. William became increasingly frustrated at the reliance on others for the soap they sold and so he began making his own in Warrington. William was a founder of Lever Brothers which would go on to become Unilever.[18]

The time was now right for a quantum leap, if only a source of power could be found.

Chapter 5

Steam and Steel

Faster than fairies, faster than witches,
Bridges and houses, hedges and ditches;
And charging along like troops in a battle,
All through the meadows the horses and cattle:
All of the sights of the hill and the plain
Fly as thick as driving rain;
And ever again, in the wink of an eye,
Painted stations whistle by ...

Robert Louis Stevenson,
From A Railway Carriage

No one visiting the Great Exhibition could have been in any doubt of the fundamental importance of steam; indeed, many would have travelled to the exhibition in a carriage pulled by a steam railway engine. Some may well have come on a Cook's Tour. In the early nineteenth century, the production of coal and iron and indeed textiles had been held back by the power then available, that of running water and horses. Something more was needed and steam was to be the answer.

Steam made its first serious appearance in the coalmines. As I told in Chapter 3, the depth to which mines were being sunk uncovered, in addition to rich seams of coal, both dangers and difficulties for the miners. One significant difficulty was that mines filled with water from the surrounding rock formations, and this needed to be pumped away continuously for coal to be extracted. Galloway describes a whole host of different mechanical methods employed until the use of the steam engine became a reality in the first decade of the eighteenth century. There has been a number of attempts before, not least by Savery, but it was the 'atmospheric engine' invented by Newcomen that brought about a revolutionary change. His engine was described as

> a machine capable of draining with ease the deepest mines;
> applicable anywhere; requiring little or no attention;

31

so docile that its movements might be governed by the
strength of a child; so powerful that it could put forth
the strength of hundreds of horses; so safe that, to quote the
words of a contemporary writer, 'the utmost damage that
can come to it, is it standing still for want of fire'.[1]

The Newcomen engine did not rotate in the way we think of steam engines
on railways, for example; it was static and relied on the production of a
vacuum, under a piston sliding in the cylinder, to raise the water using
atmospheric pressure. These engines were soon employed in many
mines which previously had been drained by mechanical means using
the power of horses or running water. Osborne asks us to pause at this
point and to marvel at Newcomen's technical achievement, writing,
'Newcomen had got his engine moving a sixteen inch diameter piston
through a stoke of eight feet once every four and a half seconds.'[2]

The engine was further developed, often, by those engineers building
and installing them. William Brown, working as a colliery viewer near
Newcastle, turned his skills to the building of Newcomen engines, but,
also and importantly, casting the cylinders in iron, rather than copper.
Brown was also casting, in iron, the pipes feeding the steam engine.
Newcomen came from Devon, and was clearly aware of the mining
challenges faced in the Cornish tin mines. It was through a Cornish
connection that the first Newcomen engine came to be installed in the
United States. It was often said that anywhere in the world where there
was mining, the Cornish accent would be heard. By the mid-nineteenth
century, Cornwall was the largest producer in the world of tin and
copper, as is evidenced today by the many disused mine chimneys along
the Cornish coastline as well as inland. The ability to pump water out
of mines had made mining under the sea possible. It was said that in
stormy weather the miners would hear the rumble of rocks moving on
the seabed above.

Problems remained to be solved. Coal was transported underground
by men, or indeed women and children, pulling trucks; these trucks were
then raised to the surface, often by the power of horses or waterwheels,
and then transported by carts to the ships which would take the coal to
its destination. The first mechanical improvement was the running of the
trucks on wooden rails which enabled much greater loads to be pulled.
It was still horse or human power that was used.

The Watt steam engine, which, unlike Newcomen's, used power rotation using a single cylinder and heavy flywheel, was of massive importance to the coalmining industry. Newcomen engines were often used to pump water to turn wheels used to raise coal up the pit shaft to the surface. These, in turn, had replaced the former lifting gear powered by teams of horses. In 1794, the Watt double-acting steam engine was first applied to the pit lifting gear and soon replaced all those driven by horse or water.

James Watt has already been mentioned in the context of his famous partnership with Matthew Boulton, and also his work on sulphuric acid with John Roebuck. Watt came from just outside Glasgow and had started out as a mathematical instrument maker. He began, with the sponsorship of Roebuck, to explore ways in which to improve the efficiency of the Newcomen engine, interestingly, using the ironworks at Carron to cast cylinders. The lack of necessary precision attracted Watt to Birmingham, where, with Boulton, he began a revolution in manufacturing. No longer did factories have to be near sources of water to power machinery; they could be set up anywhere.

A yet farther-reaching development was emerging from the forges where steam engines were made. In the coalmines, railways were increasingly being used to transport coal both underground and on the surface, but still by using horse power. The substitution of steam for horses was a clear objective for many engineers; the question was how. Watt had invented an engine which could power a rotation. A first and obvious application of this to railways was in effect to copy a mine's lifting gear, but on the horizontal plane, and so have a static steam engine pulling trucks with ropes or chains. A number of such systems involved counterbalancing full and empty trucks with the assistance of steam power. Mine owners were soon largely convinced by the effectiveness of railways, although there was debate about the type of rail; more significantly, a good number still favoured horse power over steam. The goal for the adventurous few was, though, a steam locomotive that could move, and so pull trucks along rails without the means of a rope. The challenge was how to achieve sufficient power, and also a sufficient connection between wheel and rail, to move a heavy weight, but also to tackle an incline.

Galloway introduces names much loved by rail enthusiasts. In 1804, Richard Trevithick attempted locomotion on the Merthyr Tydfil railway in the South Wales coalfield. He used a single piston and flywheel, but found that the power produced was insufficient to cope with the weight of the engine. In 1811, John Blenkinsop patented a mechanism something akin to a rack and pinion. He engaged the engineering firm of Fenton, Murray & Wood, and used steam engines with two cylinders working cranks at right angles to each other. It was a success. Blenkinsop wrote that, 'an engine with two eight-inch cylinders weighing five tons, drew twenty-seven waggons, weighing ninety-four tons, up an ascent of two inches in the yard; when lightly loaded, it travelled at ten miles an hour, did the work of sixteen horses in twelve hours, and cost £400'.[3] Blenkinsop was followed by other inventors exploring variations on his theme, and Blenkinsop himself installed his engines at a number of collieries.

The problem with Blenkinsop's mechanism was the need for the rack rail; the ideal was seen as a locomotive with drive wheels running along parallel rails. That an engineer by the name of George Stephenson was involved in this will come as no surprise. To me, what is more surprising was that the railway, as opposed to the steam locomotive, had by then been in use for 150 years, almost all on private land. For example, in Yorkshire, the Middleton colliery had been connected to neighbouring Leeds by a four-mile rail track along which trucks were pulled by horse power. Galloway tells of public lines at Loughborough in Leicestershire built in 1789, and a line from Mersham to Wandsworth in Surrey which opened in 1803. In 1823, an Act of Parliament was passed for the construction of the longest railway line to date, between Stockton and Darlington to open up the South Durham coalfield, with Stephenson appointed as engineer. It seems, first, that his locomotives were not sufficiently powerful to cover the whole distance, and that a static engine was needed for the steepest incline. Horses were also used alongside locomotive engines; indeed, in 1827, serious thought was given to going over 100 per cent to horse power given the lack of satisfaction with steam.

A name now comes into the story, which is perhaps lesser known, that of Timothy Hackworth, 'an ingenious mechanic'. He was manager of the works department of the new line and persuaded the directors to allow him to develop an engine 'after his own design', which was, inevitably, a variation on the existing themes. The new engine soon made those of Blenkinsop and Stephenson redundant, but still did not satisfy demands. The final twist in the early story of steam railways came with the Liverpool and Manchester railway, and it was the demands of cotton traders, led by corn merchant Joseph Sandars, that brought George Stephenson back into the picture. Manchester mills were transporting tons of cotton goods to the port of Liverpool by canal which took some thirty-six hours and which was expensive. What was needed was a steam railway.

George Stephenson planned the rail route to Liverpool, which included sixty-four bridges and viaducts along thirty-five miles of track. It was, though, more likely that his son, Robert, designed and built his *Rocket*, 'by the happy combination of the multitubular boiler and the steamblast, Mr Robert Stephenson succeeded in producing an engine far superior to any previously built in point of speed and efficiency'. Heavy rails were laid at considerable cost and, with heavier locomotives, 'the superiority of the railway system to every other mode of conveyance was placed beyond question'.[4] By 1850, the line was carrying two million tons of cotton a year. It also carried passengers to ships leaving Liverpool for the new world with emigrants seeking a new life, in place of their previous cargoes of slaves. It was the first twin track line in the world that carried paying passengers and so may rightly lay claim to be the birthplace of modern passenger railways.[5]

David Cannadine places this development in the context of his *Victorious Century*. He points to massive population growth between 1801 and 1831 with those of Birmingham and Liverpool doubling and those of Glasgow, Merthyr Tydfil and Manchester almost trebling. Between 1815 and 1830 the number of cotton mills in Manchester increased from sixty to ninety and coal production increased from sixteen million tons to just under thirty million. He writes of the 1830s as a period of great railway building. 'In 1835 there were only 338 miles of railway open in Britain; but by 1841 the figure had risen to 1,775 miles.'[6] Places were being connected: London to Southampton, Portsmouth, Brighton and Dover; to Bristol and on to Exeter, to Birmingham and on to Liverpool, Manchester and towns in the north-west; to Hull, York and Newcastle. But also cross-country: Carlisle to Newcastle, Liverpool to Leeds, Derby to Bristol. This was becoming a connected country, indeed the first country in the world to connect its cities by rail.

Within London, on 14 December 1836, the earliest of the metropolis's sixteen railway termini opened on the southern side of London Bridge at the end of a four-mile stretch of track running eastward to Greenwich. White tells how, 'in the first eighteen months, it carried 650,000 passengers mainly pleasure-seekers for Greenwich's whitebait dinners and riverside pubs, its fine park and observatory, its uproarious fair'.[7] This was followed by a Bishopsgate terminus for the Eastern Counties line to Romford and later East Anglia, and the London and Blackwall Railway to the new East India Docks. The first city terminus at Fenchurch Street came in 1841.

The late 1830s and early 1840s were years of depression, but recovery of exports in 1841/2 meant that investors were ready for further railway mania. Between 1844 and 1847, 442 new Railway Acts were passed and 2,000 miles of track were opened. Cannadine suggests that a quarter of a million navvies worked on the railways with a wage bill of £16 million, some half of the total investment made in those years. Robert Stephenson built the bridge over the Menai Strait connecting London to Dublin by train and sea. He followed the wrought-iron and stone suspension bridge built by Thomas Telford in 1826 as part of the post road linking the two capitals. Robert Stephenson also built the Royal Border Bridge at Berwick, connecting London and Edinburgh. Isambard Kingdom Brunel extended his Great Western Railway across the Tamar bridge into Devon and Cornwall. In terms of speed, you could travel from London to Bristol in four hours and London to Manchester in eight.

The growing 'railway mania' resulted in requests for permission for nineteen projects in London. 'There were so many proposals, threatening to carve up the metropolis like some brick and iron cat's cradle, that a Royal Commission was established to consider how best the schemes might be adapted to some rational plan. One option favoured by many was a grand central station to which several companies might run their lines.'[8] The Commission rejected all but two schemes which sought to run lines south of the river, and, in effect created a rail-free central zone. The displacement of people, by the lines built thus far, had been in many thousands, with viaducts cutting through swathes of slum dwellings.

Railway mania had another side: people were making and losing a great deal of money as one speculation followed another. Entrepreneurs like George Hudson were lauded and vilified in equal measure. Hudson ended up controlling 1,000 miles of railway and in particular had linked to the rest of the nation York and Sunderland which he also represented in Parliament.

The question of who manufactured the locomotives for the increasing number of railway companies is interesting. The entries in the catalogue for the Great Exhibition had the Great Western Railway, and its iconic engineer Isambard Kingdom Brunel, producing locomotives from their works at Swindon. It then had R&W Hawthorn in Newcastle manufacturing its first-class patent passenger locomotive engine. There was also Robert Stephenson's own company which focused on railway locomotives. Another was the Vulcan Foundry which had been established by a Liverpool engineer, Charles Tayleur, in 1830. Hawthorn also made marine engines, and I write more on these below. It was a mixed economy. Later in the century, more and more of the larger rail companies produced their own locomotives in their workshops and so we can add the famous railway towns of Crewe, Derby, Doncaster and York. It made sense, for they repaired locomotives and so knew the good and bad features of the engines. Also, when repair work was in short supply, the workforce could be usefully engaged on new engines.[9]

It is impossible to overstate the importance of the railways in driving the growth of the iron and steel industries. The Great Western Railway is associated with the Dowlais Ironworks in Merthyr Tydfil, for it supplied the iron for bridges and rails. Dowlais went on to supply the iron for Brunel's ship, the SS *Great Britain,* and it also exported rails to America, Germany and Russia. In 1840, it employed 7,300 people and by 1845 was the largest ironworks in the world. The Ebbw Vale ironworks supplied rails for the Stockton–Darlington railway.

Rolling stock and carriages were also needed by the rail companies. They made many goods wagons in their own workshops, but the carriagemaker Joseph Wright features when it came to passenger carriages. Wright began as a London coachbuilder and operator; he owned most of the stagecoaches operating between London and Birmingham. With the coming of the train, he redirected his efforts towards railway carriages and, in 1845, moved out of London to a new site at Saltley conveniently situated close to Birmingham and four of the large railway companies' routes. The new factory produced carriages for just about all the British rail companies as well as exporting them to Egypt, Sweden, Norway, Denmark, Holland, Spain, Italy, South America, India and Australia. In 1862, the business was transferred to the Metropolitan Railway Carriage & Wagon Company Ltd., a company which will reappear in a number of subsequent chapters. Britain had taken its place as the world's railway workshop.

Progress was also being made with steam-powered ships, but also of ships, however powered, with iron hulls. Slaven records the first successful use of steam power in a ship in the USA in 1797. This was followed, on 28 March 1803, by the fifty-six-feet *Charlotte Dundas* in Scotland, which covered the eighteen-mile trip from Grangemouth to Glasgow in nine hours. Whilst these were not major successes, indeed the canal proprietors abandoned trials fearing damage to the canal bank, the idea had taken hold, and, by 1820, steamships were in service on all major British rivers, save for the Wear. A major issue was both the space that the engine would occupy in the ship, and their inefficiency; Slaven quotes the consumption of ten pounds weight of coal per horse power hour. The agile hands and minds of a number of engineers, such as David Napier, John Penn and Maudslay Sons & Field, explored alternatives, and, by 1830, engines were capable of powering ships for long sea voyages. In 1838, the SS *Serius* just beat Isambard Kingdom Brunel's SS *Great Western* to the first all-steam westbound crossing of the Atlantic. SS *Serius* was powered by an engine built by Robert Napier on the Clyde; Robert Napier, at the Fairfield Shipyard, would later be known as the father of Clyde shipbuilding, of which I write more below. These ships were followed, in 1845, by Brunel's SS *Great Britain* which was both iron hulled and steam powered through propellers.[10] I mentioned R&W Hawthorn in relation to railway locomotives; from 1850 they became much involved with marine engines and, in 1885 amalgamated with the shipbuilder A. Leslie & Co., to become R. & W. Hawthorn, Leslie & Co. This latter company, in its capacity of manufacturer of railway locomotives, can be traced through to the English Electric Company of the 1950s, but that is rather leaping ahead.

Brunel's was not the first iron-hulled ship. Experiments had been made in the use of iron for barges, and Slaven quotes the Shropshire ironmaster, John Wilkinson, having in 1787 built his barge, the *Trail* for use on the Severn. In the development of iron-hulled ships, particularly in conjunction with steam engines, David Napier comes to be mentioned again as does John Laird and the firm Maudslay Sons & Field, the latter, in 1832, building an iron steamer for the East India Company. Up until 1850, the major yards producing iron-hulled steamships were split fairly evenly between the Thames and the Clyde, but the latter's proximity to both coal and iron would enable it to take an unassailable lead.

The massive growth in trade provided a much-needed spur to the shipbuilding industry such that, between 1815 and 1883, there was a seven-fold increase in ship production. Ships powered by steam were being built alongside those powered by sail. Once again, growth was far from steady, and came in peaks and troughs.

The first half of the century was once more dominated by sail, but with advances in technique. The Tonnage Laws encouraged builders to minimize length and width, but to make hulls deep to maximize tonnage. As with so much tax avoidance, this was counter-productive, making ships slow and difficult to sail. The Tonnage Laws were relaxed, and builders such as Green, Wigram's & Green at their Blackwall Yard built fast three-masted, full-rigged ships for eastern routes. The Americans, who were outside the Tonnage Laws, developed faster clippers, in time copied by English builders such as Maudslay Son & Field at Greenwich.

I have already mentioned the growth in the number of cotton mills in Manchester. Soon dozens of coalmines around Wigan and Bolton were supplying coal via the Bridgewater Canal for the increasingly mechanized cotton industry. Steam engines had been installed in many mills, greatly increasing production. The cotton industry was now massive, and its economic significance to Britain huge. In 1833, it employed 1,500,000 people. Hobsbawm offers some other numbers. In terms of exports versus home consumption, in 1814 exports had only slightly exceeded home demand, but by 1850 exports were over 50 per cent greater than home sales. Looking at the midpoint, 1820, he gives the split of exports: Europe 128 million yards, America (outside the USA), Africa and Asia, 80 million, and compares this with figures for 1840 where Europe took 200 million and 'under-developed' areas 529 million. It was the ability of the British to sell into these undeveloped markets that really spurred economic progress. Latin America was a massively important market, but so too India, the former king of cotton goods, which became a huge importer: in 1820, it took 11 million yards, but in 1840 this had grown to 145 million. In terms of British imports of raw cotton, this grew from 11 million pounds in 1785 to 588 million in 1850, and total cotton production grew from 40 million to 2,025 million yards in the same period.[11]

Hobsbawm makes the point that none of the inventions which enabled the industrial revolution thus far was really high tech. He is scathing on the subject of the English education system, which in his view was only saved by the presence of Scots from their schools and universities, and he lists James Watt, Thomas Telford, Loudon McAdam and James Mill. The French had their Ecole Polytechnique and the Germans

Bergakademie, but the English stuck fast to classical education at Oxford and Cambridge, fearing, he suggests, the genie of science. Osborne is full of praise for the English inventors who discovered their advances through years of practical experience. In the 1820s, 1830s and 1840s the new patents in cotton spinning numbered fifty-one, eighty-six and 156 respectively. A further aspect can be seen in groupings such as the Lunar Society in Birmingham. Here manufacturers like Wedgwood, Boulton and Watt came together with scientists including Erasmus Darwin, Joseph Priestley and, on occasions, Benjamin Franklin and Richard Arkwright to explore new ideas.

Cotton was also producing for its factory owners, massive profits and surpluses which were being reinvested in railways, capital goods and investments overseas. They also found their way into the great houses of the period, with master craftsmen such as Chippendale and Adam and forward-thinking manufacturers such as Josiah Wedgwood.

If it had been cotton that started the revolution, it was the railways and shipyards, and their insatiable demand for iron and steel which powered it onward. The Stockton–Darlington railway had opened the South Durham coalfield and was bringing coal to Stockton, and, by 1830 onward, to Middlesbrough which was producing iron on a small scale from ore brought from Whitby. It would become massively important in the production of steel.[12] Iron had been produced in other parts of the country for centuries, principally where there was a good supply of wood, so the Weald in Kent and the Forest of Dean in the south Midlands. With the development of smelting with coal and coke, blast furnaces appeared on the coalfields where there was also local mining and quarrying for iron ore, most particularly where there was also fast-running water to power the wheels necessary to create the blast of air for the furnace, so, principally in and near Sheffield, explaining its strong association with iron and steel. The coming of the steam engine to pump water needed to turn wheels opened up the other deposits of iron ore amongst the coal, so in South Wales and on the Clyde. Hobsbawn gives some figures. 'In the first two decades of the railways, the output of iron increased from 680,000 to 2,250,000 tons and that of coal from 15 million tons to 45 million tons.' He adds that each mile of railway required 300 tons of iron simply for the track.[13] This massive increase in production brings me to names and places very much at the heart of iron: John Brown and Vickers and Sheffield, Armstrong and Newcastle, Guest and Merthyr

Tydfil, Dorman Long (which took over John Vaughan and Bell Brothers) and Teeside.

In Sheffield, following a break-up of a previous partnership, in 1829 William Vickers went into partnership as Naylor, Hutchison, Vickers & Co. The business was substantial, having in 1837 an inventory made up of 'water and steam-power machinery, rolling mills, tilt forges, steel houses, sheds and furnaces and steam engine'. In the late 1830s, William began spending his time on the Sheffield and Rotherham railways, and it was his brother Edward who, more and more, was running Naylor Vickers, as it had become. Edward had four sons, George, Thomas, Albert and Frederick, and sent Tom and Albert to Germany to receive a technical education.

The Low Moor Ironworks, just outside Bradford in Yorkshire, was another pioneer and an example of a company combining both iron production and coal mining. In 1843, a Naysmith steam hammer was built for the works which produced a massive gun for the Great Exhibition. It then shifted its focus to civilian production, making railway tyres, railway boilers, water pipes and heavy industrial components. The steam hammer invented by James Naysmith revolutionized aspects of heavy construction. A steam hammer was used by Robert Stephenson to drive piles into the River Tweed for his Royal Border Bridge at Berwick.[14]

Steam was not the only power. William Armstrong was a native of the hills surrounding Newcastle where he had become entranced by the power of water. He was by training a solicitor. His biographer, Henrietta Heald, tells how he followed this, rather than his first love of engineering, to please his father.[15] Engineering, though, was ever present. Walks in the hills of his native Northumberland had sown seeds of how the power of water may be employed in industry. This led to experiments in hydraulics and eventually the setting up of W. G. Armstrong & Co. to manufacture hydraulic cranes.

James Rendel, a civil engineer who had studied under Thomas Telford, was reputed to be one of the foremost hydraulic engineers of his day, and he encouraged William Armstrong to follow his passion and set up a manufactory for the production of hydraulic machines, which he did at Elswick near Newcastle. Heald describes the well-ordered site, the men who worked with Armstrong and the worry the economics of the business placed on him. He had no trouble getting orders for his machines, but worried greatly at the need to raise capital to finance the business. Fortunately, associates with the relevant financial expertise and connections were to hand. It seems to be all about connections. James Rendel had been in partnership with Nathaniel Beardmore. I immediately thought of William Beardmore, the Glasgow engineer, but could find no close family connection. Another of Armstrong's associates was Thomas Sopwith, who was the grandfather of the pioneering aviation engineer who produced the Sopwith Camel in the First World War. In exploring Armstrong, I looked at hydraulics more generally and encountered Joseph Bramah, the machine tool manufacturer who invented the hydraulic press which took the place of the steam hammer in heavy engineering. He had begun life as a carpenter, but then applied his skills to develop a more secure lock; the company that bears his name is still trading. One of Bramah's associates was Henry Maudslay, who had been a storeman at the Woolwich Arsenal, of which I tell more later. Cyril Mausdlay wrote an account of Henry's life; Cyril was one of the founders of the Maudslay Motor Company. Henry had set up shipbuilder Maudslay Sons & Field after he left Bramah. It is all connected.

One of Armstrong's first orders was to the Manchester machine toolmaker, Joseph Whitworth & Co. I would say that anyone who has used a screwdriver has almost certainly driven a screw with a Whitworth thread. Joseph Whitworth, its inventor, was the son of a Stockport loom-frame maker. He started work in a cotton mill, but soon showed an aptitude for engineering. He began work as an engineer in the London workshops of Henry Maudslay, and worked briefly for Charles Babbage on his calculating machine. He set up on his own in 1830. Among his successful projects were the screw-cutting machine, but also a machine for the production of pottery of standard sizes and a massive brass cast screw of a steam ship.

The Great Exhibition, where both Whitworth and Maudslay exhibited, had followed one year after a highly significant discovery in the north-east of a very substantial source of iron ore on the northern flank of Cleveland Hills near Middlesbrough, roughly parallel with the River Tees. Middlesbrough ironmasters had already been smelting ore from Whitby. This discovery encouraged them to set up blast furnaces close to the River Tees, with transport routes from the ironstone quarries, Durham coalmines, Yorkshire deposits of limestone and onward routes for iron to market. In a paper written in 1929, John Frey, writes that the first such ironmaster, John Vaughan, built his blast furnace on 'virgin soil on the banks of the Tees and two years later the "Clarence" furnaces were built by Bell Brothers'.[16] Within twenty years, the three blast furnaces had grown to 130, placing this new area fourth in the league of UK iron production behind South Wales, the Midlands and Scotland.

The ore was particularly suited to the new open-hearth production of steel and for me this brought in a surprising name, that of William Siemens, whom I mentioned in the first chapter as an exhibitor at the Great Exhibition. J. D. Scott, in his book, *Siemens Brothers 1858–1958*, explores the career of this remarkable engineer, but also the related career path of his older brother, Weimer, and the parallel stories of Siemens Brothers, which was emphatically English, and Siemens AG which was equally German. Carl Wilhelm (he later changed his name to William) had come to England to earn enough to keep his eight orphaned brothers, but also to amass sufficient wealth to enable him to work full-time on his passion of science. One application of this passion was in the development of steelmaking, but, as Scott makes clear, this was not his core business and I write about this in Chapter 6. Core business it may not have been, but the Siemens open-hearth system was of massive importance, and opened up steelmaking areas that previously had been held back by impurities in ore. The Clyde in particular would see rapid growth in its steel production as a result.

Interestingly, in the Middlesbrough area, attention was given to the use of the spoil, with the slag transformed into fertilizer, road metal and cement, and the flue dust used for potash recovery. The Teeside iron and steel industry was massively important, not least for the production of rails and plates for the ever-expanding railways.[17]

Alongside Siemens' open-hearth system, there was the better-known system, patented by Henry Bessemer in 1855, whereby air was blown through molten iron to oxidize impurities. The Dowlais Ironworks, like others in the industry, faced great changes in the 1850s and it was the first British company to acquire a licence to use the Bessemer process; over the next ten years, it worked under the guidance of William Menelaus to make bulk steel production economically feasible. In 1871, they were producing 26,000 tons per annum and in 1884 118,000.

John Brown was known as the 'Father of the South Yorkshire iron trade'. He was born in Sheffield in 1816 and, in 1844, following an apprenticeship in the emerging steel industry, founded his own company John Brown & Co., manufacturing steel from a small foundry in

Sheffield. Four years later, he had developed a conical spring buffer for railway carriages. In 1856, he moved all his operations onto the Atlas Works in Brightside and, three years later, was producing steel rail using the Bessemer process. Possibly one of his most important discoveries was that of rolled armour plate. Previous ships had been clad with cast-iron plates, Brown found that, by rolling steel, far more effective armour could be produced. By 1867, three-quarters of Royal Navy ships had Brown's armour plating on them. He was knighted in 1867.

Vickers was one of the first Sheffield firms to introduce the Siemens method of steel production. It is perhaps no coincidence that, in her biography of William Armstrong, Henrietta Heald notes the development of open-hearth steel production by William Siemens and Pierre Emile Martin and the huge impact that had on the manufacture of guns by such as Armstrong and, of course, the Arsenal at Woolwich.[18] A major 'civilian' company to adopt the Siemens-Martin steel was Dorman Long, which began life in 1876 at the West Marsh Ironworks in Middlesbrough. In the 1880s it adopted the new steelmaking technologies at both West Marsh and the recently acquired Britannia Works. Steel for railway rails transformed railway economics for the previously used wrought iron had needed replacement every six months. Steel rails could last more than a decade.

Vickers had grown out of the Mill Sands Works and had begun work on what would become the River Don Works, with technical innovation introduced by Tom Vickers who was emerging as the technical partner. Benzon, their US agent, stepped in to provide the finance that was needed. The partnership became the limited company Vickers, Sons & Co. on 17 April 1867, with Benzon as chairman and holding half the shares and with Edward Vickers and his sons holding the other half. Benzon had become well known in Sheffield and was also a director of John Brown & Co. Vickers, Sons & Co. went from strength to strength and was acclaimed by a visiting American expert as 'the best specimen of mechanical engineering at present in existence'.[19] It was making a great success out of the production of crucible steel for 'railway tyres, straight and crank axles, and general castings and bar steel'.

Sheffield was also home to many firms of cutlers. One such, George Wostenholm, took on as an apprentice a young lad from Chatteris in Cambridgeshire named Joseph Ruston. Ruston's ambitions soon outgrew the cutlery trade, and he bought into a Lincoln firm of millwrights and general smiths trading as Burton & Proctor. On 1 January 1857, this company began to trade under a new name, Ruston, Burton & Proctor, with Joseph Ruston taking charge of the commercial side. Burton couldn't cope with the speed with which Ruston wished to advance the business, and, so, left Ruston & Proctor which then developed all manner of portable steam engines. There is lovely book, *One Hundred Years of Good Company*, by Bernard Newman published on the centenary of Ruston's company, which seeks to tell its story through a combination of straightforward history interlaced with some fictional dialogue.[20] I have drawn on its history in a number of places in this book because Ruston, his successors and collaborators were remarkably influential in a number of crucial developments.

Ruston developed machinery principally for agriculture, Lincolnshire being one of the main farming counties in Britain. As the new urban areas demanded more and more food for their growing populations, so farmers had to mechanize both to meet demand, but also to replace labour lost with the movements of people to towns and jobs in industry. The most popular use of steam power on farms was for the powered threshing machine, but experiments were also made for steam power to pull ploughs. Perhaps following the lead in the early railways, these tended to be static machines pulling the plough across large fields by means of ropes. The use of traction engines on land was problematic, given their weight and the quantities of mud in Lincolnshire fields.

With Joseph Ruston, it is important to remember that his horizons were a good deal wider than those of his adopted county. He wanted to be wherever farmers were looking to mechanize their work and this was the case in the vast wheat-growing regions of Russian, Canada and Argentina. I write later of a particular sales trip Ruston made to Russia.

The name Ruston would later combine with that of Hornsby in neighbouring Grantham. Hornsby had traded in partnership with Mr Seaman, the Barrowby blacksmith, until 1828 when the latter retired; thereafter, it was R. Hornsby's Agricultural Machine Manufacturing and Iron and Brass Foundry in Spittlegate, Grantham. It was not long before Hornsby was manufacturing portable steam engines, and, indeed, one such was exhibited at the Great Exhibition which also won prizes at exhibitions at St Petersburg and Gothenburg. As Newman says, 'he didn't invent the portable steam engine, but he developed it so successfully that, for some years, he had a virtual monopoly in its manufacture.'

The discovery of steel was also fortuitous for the shipbuilding industry, which now entered a period of great output of steel-hulled, steam-powered ships. The building of sail ships continued to grow relatively modestly in the years 1815 to 1850, from 102,100 tons to 119,100 tons. The building of steamships grew much faster, but from a much lower base of 800 tons in 1815 to 14,600 tons in 1850. The next twenty years would see an explosion in steamship building to 225,700 tons alongside a small contraction of sail building to 117,000.

Shipyards in 1850 were generally still small and many came and went in time with the economic cycle. Some were more firmly based, and began a process that would see substantial yards at Blackwall on the Thames and at Greenock on the Clyde. The common pattern was for shipyards to buy engines and boilers from specialists such as Hawthorne in the north-east, Robert Napier on the Clyde and Maudslay on the Thames. This changed in the 1860s as the first integrated yards appeared, such as Palmer's on the Tyne which linked 'iron mines, blast furnaces, engine and boiler shops and a shipyard at Jarrow'. Slaven adds that this made it more like the largest enterprises on the Thames.[21]

With the development of larger, integrated yards, names, which we recognize today, begin to appear. For example, Harland & Wolff is mentioned as having received a capital injection of £87,500 in 1873. Iron ships had taken over the Clyde, Tyne and Tees. The Clyde had the largest yards, some twenty-seven with an average workforce of 889 men. The north-east had twenty-eight yards with 12,416 men, and the Thames eighteen yards with 9,110 men. Most of the leading companies were comparatively new, but there were still some of the older ones: Laing and Pile in the northeast, Denny and Stephen on the Clyde and Rennie, Penn and Maudslay on the Thames. William Hillman, of whom I will write more in relation to the bicycle and motor car, trained with John Penn.

Looking at some figures, the merchant fleet had grown from 2.5 million tons in 1815 to 6.6 million in 1880; within these figures, steam tonnage had grown from nothing to 2.7 million tons. This represented one-third of the world's tonnage and one half of the world's steam tonnage. Technical innovation and specialization was key, with the Clyde taking the lead in fast packets, passenger and cargo lines, the Tyne, Wear and Tees focused on tramp cargo and bulk carriers. Competition started to become regional between the Clyde, the North East, the Mersey and Belfast.

The market for shipping expanded with the Atlantic passenger lines, the subsidized mail routes and ships for the mass migrations of Europeans to North America, Australia and New Zealand. Slaven mentions, in particular, Samuel Cunard who, with partners, set up the British and North American Royal Mail Steam Packet Company with ships built by Robert Napier on the Clyde, thus beginning a long and fruitful relationship.

Naval orders to private yards had been fairly minimal following 1815, with what there were going mainly to yards on the Thames. 1860 saw the first British ironclad, HMS *Warrior*, built by the Thames Ironworks, clad with armour by John Brown and armed with guns from Armstrongs. Following the end of the American Civil War, orders increased to 235,500 tons between 1869 and 1878. This time, the Thames only managed to bag one-fifth with a further fifth going to the Clyde. It was the Tyne which took the lion's share, with the majority split between Palmers and the relative newcomer, Armstrong Mitchell.

Heald tells how Charles Mitchell had helped with the sea testing of Armstrong's guns, of which I write about this in Chapter 7, and it was for this reason that Armstrong chose to go into business with him, rather than the larger Palmer's at Jarrow.[22] Mitchell was from Aberdeen, and had worked with a London-based marine engine builder before joining John Coutts's yard on the Tyne. Setting up on his own account, he supplied ships to Russia. He had married Anne Swan and had taken on two of her brothers as apprentices. Charles would later found Swan Hunter. Armstrong's Elswick works were six miles upstream from Mitchell and it was only after the Tyne Commission dredged the river that he could use the river to transport between the two sites. It was also necessary to replace an eighteenth-century bridge. Armstrong rose to the challenge and built a hydraulically operated swing bridge of 1,450 tons. This transformed access to Elswick, and Heald recounts how in 1876, an Italian ship, the *Europa,* steamed up to Elswick to collect a 104-ton gun which was lifted on board by an Armstrong hydraulic crane – an incredible feat. It delivered the gun to La Spezia in Italy where it was unloaded by another Armstrong hydraulic crane, thus cementing a business relationship with Italy which would boost Armstrong's production for the next twelve years.

Coal and the production of coke for use in iron smelting was also producing gas which was increasingly being used to the light the streets of growing urban areas. However, streets newly lit by this gaslight could no longer hide the dreadful poverty. In the mines and the factories, safety was featuring, following damning reports on the condition of working people in the industrial areas. The first Factories Act had been in 1833, with two more in 1844 and 1847. In 1853, Prime Minister Palmerston steered through a further Act essentially blocking loopholes in earlier statutes, but, in particular, made it illegal for young people to work between 6 p.m. and 6 a.m.[23] In 1874, the new prime minister, Disraeli, inherited a Factories Bill from the outgoing Gladstone government, which further reduced working hours. A further Act followed two years later, consolidating previous legislation.

There were far-sighted employers taking a stand for better conditions of employment. One such was Titus Salt who had made his fortune in the Bradford textile industry. He conceived, not only a state-of-the-art mill, but also a village, named Saltaire, where his workers could live away from the squalor of the crowded town. 'Housing was provided of the highest quality. Each had a water supply, gas lighting, an outdoor privy, separate living and cooking spaces and several bedrooms. This compared favourably with the typical worker's cottage.' [24] Salt Mill is now home to a permanent exhibition of David Hockney's paintings. It is a UNESCO World Heritage Site for its place in the story of town planning.

The early excesses of industrialization were becoming a thing of the past. In the mines, Sir Humphrey Davy had invented his safety lamp as far back as 1815. Serious accidents continued, often resulting from the build-up of dangerous gases underground. For decades ventilation had been effected by lighting furnaces at the bottom of mine shafts, this creating an upward flow of air. In the 1860s, work was undertaken to find better mechanical means of ventilation; interestingly, one such, the Guibal system, was introduced with great success at the Elswick colliery and was replicated elsewhere many times over.[25]

For all this, it had been the railway that had transformed the country. The railway was a key driver of improved communication, but it would soon be followed by others.

Chapter 6

Communication

'The influence of the postcard and telegram has so completely metamorphosed the spirit of our letter writing that it would need a keener insight than many of us could boast to read a man's nature through his letters.'
Elizabeth Baumer Williams in
Macmillan's Magazine,
August 1891

The railway had linked a previously disconnected country. It would make further advances over the coming years, but, in terms of communication, it would be joined by two vital lieutenants: widely available printing and the telegraph. Sir Henry Cole had, with Sir Roland Hill, introduced the postage stamp, making communication by letter much simpler. Letter writing by hand was seen as the courteous form of communication, and Elizabeth had, with her husband, custody of some one hundred letters Charlotte Brontë had written to Elizabeth's father-in-law, William Smith Williams. It is no wonder she treasured letter writing. The world, though, was moving faster, and, to keep pace, needed to communicate more widely and quickly.

Printing, in the modern sense, had been invented some three centuries earlier, and had caused its own revolution, not least in opening the Bible to those other than clergy who walked a life of faith. However, the book was the preserve of the wealthy. They were objects of beauty to be treasured as any great art, and so not available to the common man or woman. Literacy was the preserve of the few. The publishing world was dominated by a few highly respected firms producing fine volumes of great beauty – and price. Aileen Fyfe, in her book, *Steampowered Knowledge,* suggests that, in the 1820s, a copy of Walter Scott's novel *Kenilworth* would have cost 31s 6d.[1] She puts this into context, by quoting weekly wages for lower ranking professionals at 40s. Even for a skilled compositor, buying a new book would be beyond dreams. There were reasons for this high cost.

Paper was a byproduct of cotton and, at the beginning of the nineteenth century, was still made by hand. There were hundreds of paper mills around the country, but their processes were laborious. Pulped linen and cotton rags would be poured onto a wire mesh where they would be pressed onto felt and then left to dry for as long as a month. The prodigious growth in cotton production meant that shortages of earlier periods were a thing of the past by 1830. Nevertheless, it was an expensive and tedious process. Print was still composed by hand with letters being set in a frame, ink applied and the whole pressed carefully onto the paper sheet. The process would be repeated on the reverse side of the paper. The sheets would then be folded, cut and stitched before being bound. The cost of printing was thus significant. It was a highly skilled trade and one where the skilled compositors were well paid, even if their weekly wage of 25s couldn't stretch to the price of a single novel. Also, in relation to cost, the French Revolution comes to be quoted once more, since, even after the defeat of Napoleon, the government was fearful of too much news and comment reaching too many people; accordingly, taxes were levied on paper, advertising and publication. The tax on paper was 3d per pound weight, and a stamp of 4p was required on each newspaper. The tax on advertisements put them beyond the reach of most businesses. It was only in time that the taxes reduced, but they would not disappear until the 1860s.

Things though were to change. In the latter part of the eighteenth century, the descendants of those same people, who had had the Bible revealed to them through printing, began to see it as their duty to open books, principally the Bible itself but also improving religious tracts, to the masses. The Sunday School movement and the evangelical churches were encouraging reading by many more people and, once able to read, these people formed a growing market for the printed word. Their demand was in part satisfied by reprints of the classics for which copyright no longer applied, but also by tracts and pamphlets. Cheap 'hack' writing came out of Grub Street and the first of the 'penny dreadfuls' began to appear, building on the popularity of the gothic novels of the late eighteenth century. More and more people were able to read and so hungered for any printed material they could lay their hands on.

The publishing world responded in a number of related ways: the mechanization of the production of paper, which came to a large degree as a result of the efforts of one man, John Dickinson.[2] Dickinson embraced the science of papermaking and perfected a cartridge paper suitable for use with artillery. The idea of a commercial papermaking machine had been conceived in 1803 by Henry and Sealy Fourdrinier, using a continuous wire mesh on which the pulp was poured. Aileen Fyfe suggests that these two had given insufficient attention to securing their patents which meant that others could take and then develop their ideas. The *John Dickinson* history suggests that these early machines also had drawbacks only overcome by later techniques, such as those patented by Dickinson himself in 1811. Essentially, the Dickinson process involved a wire mesh cylinder immersed in liquid pulp. A reliable supply of clean water was vital and Dickinson found his at Aspley Mill near Hemel Hempstead in Hertfordshire. Another ingredient for certain papers was china clay. In the mid-eighteenth century, huge deposits were discovered near St Austell in Cornwall and an industry began extracting the precious clay for papermaking but also, and more so, for the making of porcelain by companies such as Wedgwood. The invention of steam-driven printing presses by Koenig in 1810, using a cylindrical plate to roll paper over the flat typeset, enabled faster printing, particularly suitable for newspapers.

The mention of steam-driven printing presses brings again into the story the engineering dynasty of Napier, for David Napier, who had worked with Henry Maudslay, moved to Fleet Street and developed a number of machines for the printing industry.[3]

London was where most such people worked, and it boomed in the wake of the Great Exhibition. Fenchurch Street railway station passenger traffic doubled in 1851 to 3.5 million a year. Traffic into London Bridge increased from 5.6 million in 1850 to 10.8 million in 1854 and 13.5 million in 1859. However, the city's population began to fall from 128,000 in 1851 to 113,000 in 1861 and 76,000 in 1871 as people moved to the new suburbs. The city, though, was busier than ever with an estimated 400,000 workers walking in every day in 1854, with a further 54,000 coming by rail, 30,000 by steamer, 88,000 by horse bus and 52,000 by other vehicles crowding the city streets.[4] This crowding prompted road-building, although insufferably slowly because of the lack of any coherent local government.

In London, a scheme for an underground metropolitan railway was conceived connecting Paddington to Farringdon along the line of what was still called the New Road, which, half a century earlier, had linked the village of Paddington with the city. Building began in 1859 despite concerns at the smoke a steam engine would produce in an enclosed space, a concern partly overcome by attempts at smokeless fuel. This line triggered an upsurge in railway activity, with Victoria Station opening in 1860, Charing Cross in 1864, Blackfriars in 1865 and Cannon Street in 1866. St Pancras, then the largest enclosed space in the world, opened in 1868, designed by George Gilbert Scott to overshadow the neighbouring King's Cross.

The bigger London problem was the stink, and its solution became inextricably linked with improvements to communications within the metropolis. The summer of 1858 was hot, and so the stench of the Thames, which had long been an open sewer, was unbearable. That was the least of Londoners' worries for much of the London water supply came from the Thames and outbreaks of cholera were rife and terrifying. The whole conurbation must have been foul, with cesspits under most buildings often overflowing between visits from the night-soil men. The invention, or rather development, of the water closet only added to the problem since they drained into sewers which ran into streams flowing down to the Thames. We can recall from the Great Exhibition catalogue that Doulton & Co. in Lambeth were producing glazed stoneware drain and water pipes.

As has been the nature of almost every development described in this story, the process of the creation of a sewerage system for London was one of delay and procrastination. The concept was clear. As all sewage made its way to the Thames, the most obvious solution was to run major sewers from west to east along the line of the Thames, both north and south to take it to where the currents of the Thames estuary would disperse it. Key to the solution was the creation of local government for London in 1855 with the Metropolitan Board of Works. The newly created board engaged Joseph Bazalgette as its engineer who put forward a scheme based largely on this thinking already in place. It stumbled, before the Chancellor, Benjamin Disraeli, pushed through a necessary change in the law and found the required £3 million. The result was a brilliant achievement which still stands today as the Thames embankments. Under the northern side the Metropolitan Railway was able to extend the route into what is now the Circle Line, and in this way the great stink provided the vital connection between the railways emanating from all sides of the capital.[5] It was many years in the making but, by the end of the 1860s, London was functioning with far greater efficiency and comfort, but still not for anywhere near all the population.

The building of both the Metropolitan Railway and the London Sewer drew on much human muscle. Ben Pedroche has written on this in his book, *Working the London Underground from 1863 to 2013*.[6] He pays tribute to the tens of thousands of navvies who dug the trenches which the railway and sewers would follow. There was some use of steam-powered diggers, but the overwhelming majority of the work was done by hand. The steam diggers were probably American, following the invention of the steam shovel by William Otis in 1839. Ruston & Proctor of Lincoln were manufacturing steam diggers, but their time would come later and in Manchester rather than London. Whitaker & Sons of Runcorn was the first company to produce a 360-degree steam digger, but this was not until 1884 and Whitakers was acquired by Ruston & Proctor in 1911. British manufacturing industries did, however, flex their muscles in support of the project. Over 300 million bricks were required, also cast-iron girders and ceramic and iron pipes. It was a massive undertaking.

The nation's infrastructure was taking shape. The railways continued to expand and British railway companies were building railways around the world. Another champion of railway expansion was George Hudson whose questionable methods were something of a precursor to those employed by motor industry financiers about whom I write in Chapter 10. He was well connected, an MP for Sunderland and friend of the Duke of Wellington;. He was the son of a Yorkshire farmer and clearly devoted to the north. He invested in railways and eventually controlled 1,000 miles of track.[7]

Clothing production, as distinct from textile manufacture, was growing and becoming mechanized employing the sewing machine of which I write in Chapter 9. Different means of travel were becoming more important and I write also in Chapter 9 of the development of the bicycle. With travel comes communication more generally and we have Sir Henry Cole's introduction of the postage stamp to thank for the growth in that incredible resource for biographers: letters. As well as these improvements in connectivity, the activity of the City of London increased with new banks and insurance companies all needing new office accommodation. In support there was more work for printers, engravers and trade and other newspapers.

Almost hand in hand with the development of the railways had come another vital means of communication, the telegraph:

> On 25 July 1837, William Fothergill Cooke, an English inventor, and Charles Wheatstone, an English scientist, made

the first electric telegraph communication between the station rooms at Camden Town – where Cooke was stationed, together with Robert Stephenson, the engineer – and London Euston, where Wheatstone was situated. The directors of the London and Birmingham Railway were their audience, and their goal was to improve safety on the railways.[8]

Two years later a second telegraph cable was run by the Great Western Railway from Paddington to Slough and this was made available for public use in 1843. Samuel Morse sent the first telegram in the USA in 1844. The telegraph had come about through the explorations being made into electricity from the discoveries of Benjamin Franklin through to the invention of the battery by Volta in 1800. The discovery of electromagnetic induction by Michael Faraday in 1831 enabled the generation of electricity by magneto-electric machines.[9]

The mention of the telegraph brings the name William Siemens back into the story. William had come to London in 1843 to sell his and his brother's invention of 'an improved form of gilding by means of electro-deposition using a "thermo-electric battery"'. He was able to sell this for £1,600; with half going back to his brother, he was now set up for some years. His time was taken by his work on heat recovery, but his brother focused on telegraph with the help of a young mechanic called Halske. Their experimentation bore fruit and they formed the German company Siemens & Halske, appointing William as their London agent. The business prospered and a third brother, Karl, set up in Russia. One issue they had overcome was that of insulation which they did by the use of gutta-percha, which was a natural thermo-plastic obtained from guttiferous trees throughout the Pacific rim. Cables were being laid over distances of some miles over land, but the challenge was to lay them under the sea. Armouring was needed to protect the cable through currents and rocks but there was also huge risk of losing the cable during laying. Werner and Halske worked on improvements, as William worked on heat recovery. They were not alone in the use of gutta-percha: the India Rubber, Gutta Percha & Telegraph Works Company was manufacturing insulated cables. This latter company would become BTR plc also manufacturing motor vehicle tyres, sports equipment, waterproof clothing and industrial hoses.

In the 1860s, submarine cables had succeeded railways as the fashionable speculation of the day. In England cables were being made by companies whose main business was the making of steel ropes. One such, Newall & Company, entered into partnership with Siemens & Halkse and William Siemens to act as the UK base for Siemens & Halske. The very risks involved in cable-laying attracted William, and he built a factory in Woolwich to manufacture cables capable of surviving the toughest of conditions. The first significant Woolwich cable laid was of 116 miles, from Cartegena to Oran. Five years later they were invited to tender for a cable running from Lowestoft to Teheran where it would link to the existing Indian government line. Scott says, 'the laying of the Indo-European line was an outstanding achievement of civil engineering even in an age of great achievements.'[10] Five years further on again and the task was the laying of the Direct United States Cable, some 3,060 nautical miles. When tested by Sir William Thomson (later Lord Kelvin), it was found to be in 'perfect condition ... a very remarkable as well as valuable achievement'. The next significant move was the design of a purpose-built ship, *The Faraday*, which would significantly reduce the risk of deep-sea cable-laying. The Siemens business was also broadening in scope.

The transmission of telegraph messages was massively influenced by the work of Charles Wheatstone at King's College, London, where he contributed significantly to the thinking on the whole subject of electricity; many of us will remember the Wheatstone Bridge from school physics lessons. The Wheatstone automatic telegraph was perhaps singularly important. The Morse code could put into transmittable form alphabetic symbols. Earlier apparatus could enable the recipient of a signal to read from an alphabetic dial the letter being transmitted and, from there, to transcribe words and sentences. Both were slow and labour intensive. Wheatstone's automatic machine, and its subsequent developments, enabled the printing out of messages from the telegraph itself.[11] The machine was widely used, not least by newspapers who could thereby transmit copy with comparative ease.

Reuters were an early user of the telegraph which they used to provide a commercial news service to their company clients. Paul Julius Reuter had moved from his native Germany in 1848, the year of revolutions, and settled in London in 1851 when he set up the Reuter Telegram Company.

It may seem odd to someone typing this book on a laptop, but the makers of the first typewriters had serious concerns about just who might wish to take advantage of their invention: it was a matter of courtesy for a man or woman to take the trouble of writing a well-composed and neatly set-out letter. To offer such a thing in printed form seemed almost an insult, a suggestion that the recipient had trouble reading. Nevertheless, in America Christopher Lathan Scholes did produce the first typewriter with a QWERTY keyboard in 1874.[12] There had been writing machines before, but none had taken off. There are images of typewriters made by Charles Wheatstone, we assume en route to the automatic telegraph, but none was patented. The American invention did not take off immediately for the very reason of an absence of a ready market. This changed once office managers began to think through the implications of developments on shopfloors of the division of activities into defined tasks – and so the typist was born. The typewriter eventually found a manufacturer in the Remington Company, but others soon followed. In England, in 1908 Imperial Typewriters was set up in Leicester by Hidalgo Moya, an American-Spanish engineer.

The Remington Company was also one of those exploring other aspects of office mechanization. This was taking place in the USA, perhaps because, with a larger domestic market for goods and services, the need was greater. So, we have William Burroughs, a bank clerk who became frustrated by the laborious mental arithmetic involved in adding column after column of numbers. He moved to St Louis where, in 1888, he linked with metal manufacturer Joseph Boyer and developed his mechanical adding machine. A UK operation was established in Nottingham in 1895.

In 1890, again in the USA, a mammoth task presented itself in the need to collate the results of the census of some sixty-three million people. Herman Hollerith, an engineer from Columbia University, developed the punch card system for use both in recording and sorting the data. The system was a technical success, but Hollerith failed to convince the commercial market. He met Thomas Watson, who was working for the National Cash Register Company (NCR), and persuaded Watson to join the Computer-Tabulating-Recording Company which would in 1924 be renamed International Business Machines.[13]

The developments in communication outlined in the chapter would equip Britain for further steps forward in the development of manufacturing in which she would again take a lead. They would also equip British industry for something a great deal more sinister.

Chapter 7

Armaments

'Armstrong and Krupp and the French arms manufacturer Schneider came to be known as "Europe's deadly triumvirate" ... over the next eighty years they were to be celebrated first as shields of national honour and later, after their slaughtering machines were hopelessly out of control, as merchants of death.'

William Manchester, Krupp's biographer [1]

In 1852, with only fifty field guns remaining in the United Kingdom from Waterloo, 300 new guns with 200 ammunition wagons were ordered to be dispatched to the Crimea. These were for use by the Horse and Field Artillery, mainly nine-pounders and a few six-pounder guns. Wellington had belatedly accepted that the rifle could be a better alternative to the musket, and, in 1851, the Board of Ordnance ordered a number of Minié rifles from Liège, and the Royal Ordnance Factory at Enfield manufactured what would become known at the Enfield Rifle. The School of Musketry had been formed at Hythe to provide training.

In 1805, the Ordnance Factories at Woolwich, which supplied the army and navy with cannon, were redesignated The Royal Arsenal, and also began supplying muskets but 'the work was confined to rough stocking and setting up barrels bought from private firms in Birmingham'. In 1807, a factory was acquired at Lewisham to provide barrels and locks, which was moved four years later to Enfield.[2] At about the same time, the barracks at Weedon were taken over for the storage and inspection by armourer sergeants of Birmingham-produced muskets. The ironworks at Dowlais in South Wales, run by John Guest, supplied cannonballs to the army. A brief glance at the Royal Navy brings up the name of Marc Isambard Brunel and his contract in 1803 to manufacture pulley blocks for the navy. Significantly, in this story, this was one of the very earliest examples of mass production with individual workers performing the same single task only in a multitask process on a standardized product. Marc Isambard Brunel was the father of Isambard Kingdom Brunel and, like so many who made England their place of work, was not of British descent, but French.

The Arsenal was under the control of the Board of Ordnance, of which the Duke of Wellington was Master General from 1818 to 1827. A gunpowder factory had been set up at Waltham Abbey in 1787, whilst most armaments were then stored at the Tower of London. The making of muskets had originated in the narrow streets surrounding the Tower of London. The iron had come from the smelters in the Weald where there had been accessible quantities of iron ore and plentiful wood for charcoal. The shortage of wood in Elizabethan times had largely killed off the Weald as a source of iron, and supplies were had from elsewhere. Birmingham, originally, had taken its iron from smelters in the Forest of Dean, but coal was readily available in the Black Country as an alternative means of smelting, and so the manufacture of guns naturally gravitated there.

The troops who set sail for the Crimea were armed with a mixture of smoothbore muskets and Minié and Enfield rifles, each requiring different ammunition. Very few had received the necessary training. It was an ominous start to a campaign and soon the shortcomings became clear. News from the front brought to public attention the gross inadequacy of cannon, which, with cannonball, had traditionally been used to breach defences, or, with a red-hot ball, to set fire to them. For the army, explosive shells were being used with howitzers and mortars, but over very limited ranges. There was also the shorter low-velocity carronade firing a sixty-eight-pound shot, used mainly for the armament of forts. Experiments had been made with firing shells from cannon and significant distances were achieved, but without significant damage to the enemy. Major-General Shrapnel had introduced the practice of filling the shells with ball shot. These, when fired from cannon, would explode, spreading the shot all around. If the shell hit the target, and if the shell exploded on landing, great damage would result. The 'ifs' were important, not least since fuse technology was very basic and cannon could fire with only limited accuracy.

J. D. Scott makes the point that there is no evidence that Armstrong had any previous intention of manufacturing armaments; that was the business of the Royal Arsenal. However, spurred by the news from the

Crimea, William Armstrong set to work to develop the better cannon that was needed, using the techniques of rifling. Existing guns were colossal. Armstrong conceived a gun that was in effect a larger version of the rifle.[3] He was not alone in this: Joseph Whitworth explored alternative methods to produce the smaller accurate weapon that was needed. Heald suggest that Isambard Kingdom Brunel was also involved. It seems that Armstrong's designs pipped at the post those of Joseph Whitworth and kicked into play a rivalry that would last decades. The development of the gun was far from simple, and demanded many hours of test shots to perfect accuracy, but, more so, a great deal of metallurgy to find the right material to withstand intense pressures as guns became more powerful. Armstrong was assisted in his test programme by Mitchells, the Newcastle shipbuilder.

Armstrong was encouraged to develop his ideas, which he did to the satisfaction of the War Office. In a patriotic act, he presented the patents for the new gun to the nation, and was appointed to the government position of Engineer to the War Office of Rifled Ordnance. The government then awarded a contract to the Elswick Ordnance Company, which had been set up by Armstrong but in which Armstrong no longer had any financial interest.

Guns to Armstrong's design were produced at both Elswick and also at the Royal Arsenal at Woolwich, where Armstrong was appointed superintendent of the Royal Gun Factory with John Anderson, later general manager, as his assistant.[4] In 1854, Anderson undertook a major programme of modernization and expansion. He introduced steam power into the Foundry and the Royal Carriage Factory. Similar building and modernization programmes were undertaken at the Royal Small Arms Factory at Enfield and the Royal Gunpowder Factory at Waltham Abbey. Much of what Anderson created remained in use until the Royal Ordnance Factory closed in 1967.

Another key appointment was made in 1854, when Frederick Abel took the office of Ordnance Chemist which had fallen into disuse in 1826. Under Abel, the technology of ammunition took major strides with Woolwich as a centre of excellence. At this point I need to pause, for explosives, for which Abel was responsible, were part of a much broader picture which also covered their use in mining and civil engineering, of which a great deal was going on, not least with the building of the railways. The name of Abel thus needs to be coupled with that of

Nobel, not because they collaborated, but because they were rivals, each championing a different, newly invented high explosive.

I pick up Nobel's story mid-nineteenth century, once more with the help of George Brown, when he was working in Sweden with his father exploring how nitroglycerine could be used. Nitroglycerine was a combination of glycerin and nitric acid. Brown quotes Nobel as saying, 'the real era of nitroglycerine opened with the year 1864 when a charge of pure nitroglycerine was first set off by means of a minute charge of gunpowder.'[5] This was the first high explosive, as Brown goes on to explain, 'whereas rapid burning gun powder produces pressures of up to 6,000 atmospheres in a matter of milliseconds, the decomposition of nitroglycerine needs only microseconds and can give rise to pressures of up to 275,000 atmospheres.' This was a ground-breaking discovery that had the potential to make the life of the miner and civil engineer a great deal easier, but also to unleash weapons of previously unimagined ferocity. Nobel worked with Vickers, Armstrongs, Whitworths as well as Krupps.[6]

The problem was that nitroglycerine was very unstable and many lethal accidents were the result. Nobel relished a challenge, and so sought means to increase both stability and safety. The result was perhaps his greatest invention: dynamite, a combination of nitroglycerine and a soft, white, porous substance called kieselguhr. The demand for the new explosive was 'overwhelming' and Nobel built factories in some twelve countries. In England the Nitroglycerine Act forbade 'the manufacture, import, sale and transport of nitroglycerine and any substance containing it'. Nobel was not put off, but did clash with Frederick Abel who was trying to do at Woolwich, with nitrocellulose, what Nobel was attempting with nitroglycerine. The net result was that Nobel failed to raise the money he needed for a factory in England. Fortunately for him, Scotland, with its separate legal system, welcomed him. A factory, his first joint venture, the British Dynamite Co. Ltd., was built at Ardeer on a desolate area of the Ayrshire coast in 1871.[7] Nobel's fellow investor in the British Dynamite Company was Sir Charles Tennant, the British champion, through his company Tennants of Glasgow, of the Leblanc process for producing soda ash.

Frederick Abel championed the use of Nitrocellulose and worked to make it safe. Nitrocellulose was the result of treating cellulose with hot concentrated nitric acid and sulphuric acid. The cellulose used was cotton, and the product took the popular name of gun cotton. It was a high explosive, but also apt to explode unintentionally. It was manufactured by the Royal Explosives Factory at Waltham Abbey.

By the 1870s, high explosive was being made using either nitroglycerine or nitrocellulose, but, in each case, the shell or bullet still needed to be propelled by gunpowder. The answer was smokeless powder, and, once again, both Nobel and Abel came up with their own solution. It was not long before the next major development, the invention of cordite, again with Nobel and Abel vying for position. By the end of the nineteenth century, cordite was being manufactured by Kynoch & Co. and by the National Explosives Company as well by Nobel's factory at Ardeer.

Yet, more was happening at this birth of the UK arms industry. The name, David Napier, again enters the story, for he had added to his printing machine manufacture, the making of machines for the Royal Arsenal for bullet-making and gun-boring. Birmingham had been home for many years to many gunsmiths, and, in around 1854, they came together in a loose grouping they called the Birmingham Small Arms Company. The grouping was incorporated into a limited company in 1861, and, a year later, a twenty-five-acre site at Small Heath was selected for their factory. The company converted muzzle-loading Enfield rifles and then produced Martini-Henry rifles. The name BSA will appear many times in the story.

Birmingham was growing as crucible of engineering skills. 'In 1834, in Birmingham, John Nettlefold had opened a woodscrew mill. And in 1856, just down the road, Arthur Keen had founded the Patent Nut & Bolt Company (PNB) with his American partner, Francis Watkins, and which had become a major manufacturer of fasteners.'[8] Keen was not only an engineer, he was a director of the Birmingham and Midland Bank, and it was through this connection that the name Guest re-enters the story. Keen had heard that Lord Wimborne, now head of the Guest family, was looking to sell Dowlais ironworks and, whilst PNB was many times smaller, Keen made an approach and a deal was done for the purchase for £1.5 million. The press were intrigued. The *South Wales Daily News* of 20 July 1900 observed the good value to the purchaser adding, 'As to Guest, Keen & Co, I look on it as a second Consett; repetition of the Nut and Bolt; an industrialist at the top of the list.' Keen had done well, and a year later he added Nettlefold, making the company we now know as

Guest, Keen & Nettlefold.[8] In 1905, GKN was Britain's fifteenth largest company and even now a leading defence contractor.

Another early nineteenth century invention of massive importance, particularly to the navy, was the tin can. For centuries, sailors had grown hungry and often died on their diet of salt beef and dry biscuits. Napoleon set a challenge to inventors to find a way of preserving meat for long sea voyages. Nicolas Appert accepted and devised a way of preserving meat in sealed glass jars placed in boiling water. Glass was thought too fragile, and a British merchant, Peter Durand, was granted a patent for preserving using tin-plated cans. An engineer called Bryan Donkin bought the licence for £1,000, and began to produce cans from his premises in Bermondsey. On 30 June 1813, he demonstrated his product before King George III to much acclaim. Donkin's engineering skills were much wider than just the tin can, as evidenced by his presence at the Great Exhibition with an improved papermaking machine.

The return of the victorious British army from the disaster of the Crimea had been met almost immediately by an even bigger threat to the Empire than Waterloo. The Great Rebellion or First War of Independence, or Indian Mutiny as the British press preferred, was vicious on both sides. The East India Company had its own army paid from its trading profits and reinforcements were sent from the UK. The Manchester of India, Cawnpore, was the place of a massacre of hundreds of British men, women and children, and the retaliation which followed saw the British killing anyone who was suspected of being a rebel.

The rebellion was eventually quashed, the East India Company abolished and India became part of the Empire with an Indian civil service 'whose high-minded and disinterested ethos was very different from that which had prevailed before'. There was an Indian Army with a high proportion of British troops and a viceroy answerable to the new post of Secretary of State for India. Thus began a new chapter in Anglo-Indian relations.

Cannadine recounts an event which took place shortly after the rebellion. Isambard Kingdom Brunel had begun in 1854 to design a ship, the *Great Eastern*, which would be capable of steaming to India via the Cape of Good Hope with enough coal for the journey plus room for enough troops, horses and artillery to reinforce the Indian Army so substantially that any future rebellion would be 'crushingly supressed'. It was due to be launched in November 1857, but, in view of delays, did not get to the water for another year. It was then beset by endless difficulties. It crossed the Atlantic a number of times, but never made it to India. At 700 feet, it was the longest ship to enter service for the next fifty years.[9]

Looking at the British economy as a whole in 1880, Cannadine notes the relative decline of textiles in favour of heavy industries. Textiles still made up one-half of exports, with a further quarter being made up of coal, steel and engineering. The industrial areas were the Midlands, the North West and North East, but also the lowlands of Scotland, South Wales and that part of Northern Ireland surrounding Belfast. In terms of employment, coalmining which had employed 216,000 in 1851, now employed 495,000 with even greater increases in iron and steel and shipbuilding.[10] In 1881, Britain was still the workshop of the world, with nearly a quarter of the all the world's manufacturing, and 44 per cent of the world's exported manufacturing goods. It was also exporting people. 'From 1880 to 1893 the number emigrating [annually] would never fall below 200,000 and would peak at 320,000 in 1893.' Most went to the USA, followed some way behind by Canada, the Antipodes and South Africa. It wasn't just people, it was money, with investment pouring into infrastructure in India and elsewhere. Cannadine points to the improvements in living standards among the middle classes, and also to the wealthy landed families becoming ever wealthier. Disraeli had made Queen Victoria Empress of India, and she reigned supreme. For all this, the underlying economy was slowing down; the years 1873 to 1896 would later be known as the Long Depression, and there was clear evidence of continued suffering by the poor. The trades union movement began to grow and industrial unrest bubbled up. In spite of these domestic issues, successive governments would see, often reluctantly, that the continued protection of Britain's Indian Empire was not only vital for trade, but that it demanded 'the urgent acquisition of vast new tracts of territory across the length and breadth of Africa'. This would need military muscle which resulted in the Boer wars, for example, but also further developments in the armaments industry.

The second Boer War (1899–1902) first saw the extensive use of wired telegraph and telephone, although the telegraph had been used to a limited extent in the Crimea. In the Boer conflict, experiments were also made with Marconi's wireless telegraph equipment about which I write in Chapter 11, but it was found to be too bulky. Telegraph and telephone on the other hand were used extensively, with some thirteen million messages handled by the 2,500 officers and men of the Telegraph Battalion who laid 18,000 miles of cable which linked to the submarine cable to London. In terms of equipment, it was Wheatstone's automatic telegraph that was introduced to great effect.[11] At Waterloo, Wellington had used the three arms of the army – infantry, cavalry and artillery – together at close quarters. With artillery achieving ever longer ranges, such close control would no longer be possible and demanded a different style of command: the use of electric telegraph to aid communication with the on-field commanders became vital.

For Britain, the growing volume of trade demanded an ever-increasing fleet of merchant ships (the British fleet made up 40 per cent of the world fleet in 1913) with a navy to protect it, and this large fleet needed to be built. Slaven offers some numbers, looking at the two decades before the outbreak of the First World War. In this period British shipyards constructed an astonishing 60 per cent of the world's tonnage. The nearest rival was Germany with a quarter and then the USA with 18 per cent; the American Civil War had dramatically disrupted American shipbuilding. The British were not only making ships for their own fleets, but also the fleets of other countries, where some 30 per cent of production for non-British registration came from British yards.[12]

The huge level of activity offered to British yards great advantages, as did their long heritage. With the growing dominance of steam, iron and steel, the Thames yards and those on the south coast declined. However, the yards of the North East, the Clyde and Belfast grew in size and number. Within the yards, there was no great number of formally trained engineers or naval architects, but rather men who had learnt their trade on the job and continued to learn. This continuous learning, facilitated by a constant and substantial flow of work, enabled practical technical invention.

The design of engines was crucial, as was the introduction of steel into shipbuilding, which offered greater strength and greater flexibility. Slaven recalls the development by Howden of the Scotch boiler, 'which, combined in a cylindrical tank, raised pressures to 80 lb psi'. The American Babcock & Wilcox developed the design with a water-tube boiler aimed at increasing temperatures and pressure further. It seems that the water-tube system did not catch on with the British, and the full potential of the Scotch boiler would only be realized somewhat later, when combined with the triple-combustion engine. Babcock set up a manufacturing facility in the UK at Renfrew in 1895.

Engine design would be taken a leap further in 1884 with Charles Parson's steam turbine. Watt and Boulton had developed the piston engine from Newcomen's original atmospheric engine, but, in spite of further developments, it didn't run smoothly or produce the amount of power that Parsons saw possible. He had been an apprentice at Elswick, and in 1884 became a partner in another Newcastle engine builder, Clarke, Chapman & Co. It was there he invented a steam engine that would cause rotation, not by the operation of a piston, but by rotating blades driven by steam. He established his own company, C. A. Parsons & Co., to manufacture steam turbines. Allison Marsh relates the story of the ship, SY *Turbinia*, Parsons built to demonstrate the power of the steam turbine. She tells how he gate-crashed the parade of naval vessels to mark Queen Victoria's Golden Jubilee, and how his ship, at thirty-four knots, outpaced all the naval vessels. He was rewarded by an order from the navy a year later in 1898. In 1905, the Admiralty decided that all new vessels should be powered by steam turbines.[13]

The shipbuilding industry was also taking on a recognizable form in terms of names. Larger yards and armaments were beginning to dominate. Slaven provides two tables, one of the shipyards in order of size of production, and one of shipbuilding companies in order of capitalization. Looking at the first table for 1911/12, Swan Hunter on the Tyne is top with 6 per cent of gross tonnage production. Second is Harland & Wolff of Belfast whose story shows yet again how the developments of the industrial revolution linked. Belfast was becoming increasing prosperous with developments in the textile industry. William Durgan, known in Ireland as the king of the railways, saw the potential for growth, not only in railways, but also shipping and he undertook the excavation of the harbour.[14] This made the docks perfect for shipbuilding, something clearly seen by Edward Harland and Gustav Wolff.

Armstrong had combined with the Mitchell shipyard on the Tyne in in 1883 and, building on the success of Armstrong's rifled cannon, the Elswick works was fast becoming an 'arsenal complete in itself'.[15] Heald tells that, in 1896, Armstrong was becoming concerned that Vickers, fast catching up with both themselves and Krupp, would present serious competition to Elswick, particularly in the field of armour plate.

Vickers was still at heart a steel company, but, towards the end of the 1890s, the directors made the decision to shift their focus to armaments. The Vickers family were already involved with inventors, Maxim and Nordenfelt, developing the machine gun and submarine; they had already manufactured guns and armour plate for naval ships. In 1897, they took the plunge and purchased the Barrow Naval Armaments Co. shipyard at Barrow-in-Furness. The Barrow yard had been founded by the Dukes of Devonshire, one of a number of examples of landed wealth becoming involved in manufacturing. With the purchase of the yard by Vickers, the duke became one of its major shareholders.[16] The completion of the railway from Carlisle to Furness had opened up this hitherto backwater which became a hive of industry. Vickers also bought Maxim-Nordenfelt and soon secured major naval orders for the Barrow yard.

Whitworth, in Manchester, had been producing quantities of armour plate at their Openshaw works, and were well regarded by the Admiralty. Armstrong feared that Vickers would buy them, and so he made his own bid which was successfully concluded in 1897, when the company became Armstrong Whitworth.[17] Armstrong, once combined with Whitworth, ranked seventh in Slaven's table. Another combination, Cammell Laird, at Birkenhead came tenth in the table with Vickers at Barrow eleventh. One of the key developments of these two decades was this marriage of shipbuilding and armaments. In this regard, John Brown & Co. on the Clyde, with its Sheffield armour plating production, ranked fourteenth out of twenty.

The second table from 1910, ranking by capitalization, demonstrates the growing strength of armaments, placing Vickers top, followed by Armstrong Whitworth, John Brown & Co., William Beardmore and Cammell Laird. In 1902, Vickers had taken a 50 per cent holding in Beardmore which 'with their 12,000 ton press had placed themselves second to none in Great Britain for armour plate'. Scott suggests that Vickers may have been motivated by a desire to keep Beardmore out of ordnance; alternatively, that they owned Vickers a lot of money.[18]

William Beardmore junior founded William Beardmore Limited on the Clyde in 1886. It succeeded the partnership of William Beardmore senior and Robert Napier which owned the Parkhead Forge, acquired by Napier in 1841 and which had built the second Royal Navy ironclad HMS *Black Prince*. Beardmore became a giant of Scottish industry and will appear often in this story.

The inclusion of the names Cammell Laird and John Brown brings in yet another strand in the web of armaments manufacture, that of the Coventry Ordnance Works. Cammell and Brown's both wanted to be able to arm their ships without having to go to their competitors, Vickers, Armstrong or Beardmore for guns, so they, with Fairfield Shipbuilders, invested in a business begun by carriagemaker H. H. Mulliner & F. Wigley. The result was a massive and advanced factory in Coventry bordered by both railway and canal.[19]

In the closing decade of the nineteenth century, naval production received a boost from the 'two-power standard' that the Royal Navy should be kept at a size at least equal to the navies of the next two largest nations. The Naval Defence Act of 1889 had been brought to Parliament to maintain the dominance of the Royal Navy against those nations who had formed alliances in Europe: the Dual Alliance of France and Russia and the Triple Alliance of Germany, Austria-Hungary and Italy. All these countries were seeking dominance to further their economic interests. Britain's economic interest was clearly the protection of her overseas markets, and hence the importance of a large and well-armed navy.

One-half of the ships ordered to meet the target set for the 'two-power standard' came from private yards, and, with the addition of production for foreign navies, British yards produced over two million tons a year between 1889 and 1913. The Clyde shipyards supplied 45 per cent, with 21 per cent from the north-east, essentially Armstrongs, and 24 per cent from Vickers and Cammell Laird.[20] Scott writes of the development of ever more heavily armed and armoured ships, ultimately the *Dreadnought* class. He tells how Krupp patents were used by both Vickers and Armstrong in armour-plating, and how Krupp was found to have used Vickers high-carbon armour plate in their projectiles, an idea quickly copied by Vickers.[21] Politically, Britain and Germany were heading for a clash; industrially Vickers, Armstrong Whitworth, Beardmore, Cammells and Brown's were shaping up for an almighty confrontation with Krupp.

If this wasn't enough, in the late nineteenth century, the production of a metal, that would be very much the darling of the twentieth century but also crucial to the armaments industry, was begun in western Scotland by the British Aluminium Company.[22] Aluminium had been first named by Sir Humphrey Davy, although he never succeeded in extracting the metal from alum. A good number of people had tried to extract it for it is very common, making up 8 per cent of the earth's crust. Early methods were very expensive, making it, in effect, a precious metal costing as much as £50,000 a ton. However, people believed that its uses were likely to be many, not least because it was both very light and very strong. The breakthrough came in a period of two months when Hall discovered electrolytic reduction in the USA, and, only a little later, Heroult did the same in France.[23] The method was to dissolve the alumina in a bath of molten cryolite at a temperature of 982°C. The aluminium would separate and sink to the bottom of the iron, carbon-lined cell. The challenge was to find an economical way of heating to the required temperature. The answer was hydroelectric power, as first generated by Siemens in Guildford, but on a much grander scale. The place chosen by the newly formed British Aluminium Company was Foyers on Loch Ness in Scotland, and this began production in 1895. This was followed by Kinlochleven in 1909. The same technique was in use in others countries, most particularly Canada and Norway with even better capacity of hydroelectric power.[24]

The pieces were falling into place for the most murderous conflict the world had ever known. Three yet more significant manufacturing developments would take place before the first shot was fired: the bicycle, the internal combustion engine and the massive growth in electrical power. Before looking at these, I want first to look at manufacturing for the home.

Chapter 8

The Home

'It presents the eye an interesting spectacle of numerous vessels floating to and from the port of Hull: while that opulent and commercial town in its low situation close to the banks and surrounded by the masts of the shipping in the docks seems to rise like Venice from amidst the sea, the whole comprising a scene which for beauty and grandeur can scarcely be exceeded.'

This quotation from *Bradshaw's Guide* had, behind it, a profound change in the lot of the British home. The railway had opened up the hinterland but had also made accessible the shore to inland dwellers, and, in particular, had brought to the tables of ordinary people food never previously dreamed of. Hull, which had been a home of whaling, became the home of the British fishing fleet, landing vast quantities of cod and haddock which would be whisked away by train to all parts of the country.

Chains of stores began to appear on the high streets. Flour, from grain mainly imported from the USA, was milled in large mechanized plants.[1] It may have been progress, but it wasn't all rosy. Flour was of variable quality and so too, therefore, was bread. Eggs were really only fresh when eaten close to the farm producing them; any making it into the cities could be as much as four weeks old, and some much older, imported from as far afield as Russia.

In relation to food production, one striking statistic was that, notwithstanding its long agricultural heritage, in the late nineteenth century Britain imported three-quarters of its foodstuffs. Research by the University of Hertfordshire reveals that 80 per cent of wheat, 40 per cent of meat and nearly all sugar was imported.[2] Wheat would come from the USA, meat from Australia and New Zealand, but also South America, the USA and Denmark. Sugarcane was imported from the Caribbean.

69

Looking further into these numbers, the National Farmers' Union (NFU) has published a helpful piece of research by Laura Stearman.[3] She argues that the issue goes back to the agricultural depression of the 1870s, when government in effect decided to take advantage of developments in refrigeration and transport to import food from lower-cost countries, rather than supporting farmers at home. The British had more than enough shipping to secure steady supplies and a navy sufficiently well equipped to defend the merchant fleet.

My father, Leslie, was born in 1891 in a semi-detached house in Dulwich in South London. He left some memories of childhood; however, he never told me what toys there may have been for him and his younger brother: perhaps a horse tricycle from G&J Lines, but more likely a wooden toy bought from a street trader. After 1900, they may have had a *Mechanics Made Easy* set and accompanying instruction manual. Frank Hornby, a Liverpool office worker, had been making perforated metal strips for his sons which could be connected by means of small bolts and nuts to make anything from model trains to bridges and cranes. The adoption of the name Meccano came in 1907, by which time Leslie had started work. One toy I am uncertain about is Harbutt's Plasticine which was first manufactured in 1900. My doubt stems from my memory of my father's extreme concern that my sister and I might walk it into the carpets; it is very difficult to extract from the carpet pile. For wealthier families, the main source of toys was Germany with manufacturers such as Steiffe for teddy bears and Marklin for tinplate. The British firm Bassett-Lowke designed and supplied clockwork trains, but which were often manufactured for them in Germany. Kenneth Brown in his wonderful book, *The British Toy Industry*, suggests that the comparatively poor provision for British children was the result of the absence of childhood for so many working from an early age, but also the lack of disposable income on the part of so many parents. Both of these reasons reduced in influence as the century drew to a close.[4]

My father recalled a washerwoman who came each week; of course, washing machines were for most a luxury for the future. She may have used Sunlight Flakes manufactured by Lever Brothers. William Lever had moved to a 300-acre green field site near Birkenhead which he named Port Sunlight.[5] In 1888 he began production of Sunlight soap at the new factory and soon began to build a neighbouring village for his workers, recognizing the benefits of green space and fresh country air on his workers and their productivity. Another Lever Brothers product was Lifebuoy soap, which I always remember my father using. Yet another was Vim scouring powder, which his mother, Mildred, may have used for the dishes. The washerwoman was rewarded, in addition to her pay, by a glass of beer to quench her thirst. This could have been produced in Burton, where the town's breweries were responsible for a quarter of the beer consumed in England; more likely it would have been one of London's breweries.

At the rear of the house was a conservatory which brings glass back into the story. At the Great Exhibition, Chance Brothers of Birmingham made the panes for the Crystal Palace; could they have made the panes in the conservatory? There were many other glassworks, perhaps most notably James Powell & Sons also known as Whitefriars Glass.

My father told stories of drinking ginger beer with a spoonful of ice-cream floating in it. Schweppes had provided carbonated water at the Great Exhibition, and was producing tonic water in 1870. Ginger beer had been alcoholic until the mid-nineteenth century to address the issue of dirty water. With improved water treatment, the ginger beer Leslie drank would have been bottled and carbonated, but non-alcoholic, as would be lemonade. Ice-cream would have been made from eggs, or powdered egg, and milk.

In the late nineteenth century, many urban dwellers had moved away from baking their own bread or brewing their own beer, the latter because of the improving quality of water.[6] Bread remained a core element of diet, and I remember my father's fondness for it; it would be bought from the local baker. It is possible that the bread would have been made with Smith's Patent Process Germ Flour, which was renamed Hovis, following a national competition. Hovis flour was milled by S. Fitton & Son in Macclesfield and was soon made into both Hovis bread and Hovis biscuits, which, in 1896, were being supplied to Her Majesty the Queen. It wasn't only Hovis; Joseph Rank had been milling flour for use by local bakers since 1883 when he introduced milling by rollers rather than the traditional millstone.[7] The London docks was home to a good many flour mills, which made sense given the percentage of grain that was imported.

Leslie's mother may have used powdered milk to feed her young sons, from Cow & Gate or perhaps Glaxo, which would become better known for pharmaceuticals.[8] The name Glaxo derives from the name given to a patent dried milk powder (*lacto*) by New Zealand milk producers, Joseph Nathan & Co. In terms of other foods, Mildred may have bought items like Bird's custard, which had been manufactured in Birmingham since 1837, later, along with baking powder, blancmange powder, jelly powder, and egg substitute. Mildred was a Scot, and so may have been attracted by Baxters tinned fruit or even tinned soup. She may have obtained her sugar, tea and coffee from Home & Colonial Stores. Cutlery would be from Sheffield and crockery for use on special occasions perhaps from Crown Derby or Royal Doulton; Wedgwood might have provided her ornaments.

The reference to egg substitute brings into the story the butcher J. H. Dewhurst, because I noted, in an article on the butcher and its owners, the Vestey family, a reference to poor availability of eggs and how the Vesteys imported them from China in particular for use in Lyons cakes. In relation to Dewhurst, the business began with the importation of meat from Argentina, taking advantage of the developments in cold storage. The Vesteys set up the Union Cold Storage Company in 1890, although the main development of the Vestey empire would happen in the interwar years with the growth of the Dewhurst chain of butcher shops. The article also mentions Fray Bentos in Uruguay; Leslie may well have eaten Fray Bentos tinned corned beef.

The mention of Lyons cakes shines a light on a company that would in the 1930 be the world's largest catering company, J. Lyons. It was founded in 1894 by Joseph Lyons, Montagu and Isadore Gluckstein and Barnet Salmon (the maternal grandfather of Nigella Lawson) to address the poor catering offering at trade exhibitions. By the coming of the First World War the company employed 20,000 people and was the largest baker in London and the largest tea broker and restaurant operator in the world. [9]

Another visible sign of manufacturing activity was the growth of the retail sector, bringing to an ever-hungry public the fruits of the manufactories. The London department store Lillywhites opened in 1865, and Newcastle's Fenwick in 1882. J. Sainsbury first opened in 1869 and Marks & Spencer in 1884.

In terms of their suppliers, we need to go back further. Cadbury first opened a grocery shop in Birmingham in 1824, but by 1831 was manufacturing chocolate.[10] It wasn't until 1878 that they moved production to Bourneville, four miles from the city centre, conceived as a place where employees could live near their work, but away from the overcrowding of the city. As George Cadbury put it, 'no man ought to be condemned to live where a rose cannot grow.' In 1822, Joseph Huntley opened a shop in Reading, Berkshire, selling biscuits. He was joined by his cousin George Palmer nineteen years later. In 1846, Huntley & Palmers built their factory which, by 1900, employed 5,000 people. In 1859, Henry Tate went into partnership with John Wright, in Liverpool, refining sugar. Their business thrived, with Tate's sons joining him in ten years later. It wouldn't be until 1929, that Henry Tate & Son merged with Abram Lyle & Son to form Tate & Lyle.

I write in *Dunkirk to D-Day* about my grandfather, Alfred Williams' career and inventions. If he smoked, he could buy cigarettes made by John Player. There were of course many others, for example W. D. & H. O. Wills in Bristol. He would have bought his suits from a tailor or perhaps from one of the growing number of off-the-peg gentlemen's clothing manufacturers, many of whom were in Manchester. Hyam & Co, advertised in the Great Exhibition catalogue, was one of the first to utilize machinery to produce clothing in large quantities.[11] There were haberdashers and milliners for smaller items. Boots and shoes would probably be had from the local cobbler, although C&J Clark were marketing their hygienic range designed to fit the shape of the foot.[12]

Alfred's shirts may well have been made in Londonderry, in Northern Ireland. Derry had been a centre of linen production in the early nineteenth century, but, with the decline in that industry, it rose to the challenge and redirected the skills of its people to shirt-making. In the 1850s, the factory system of production had been introduced with the new sewing machine, about which I write in Chapter 9, and which would dramatically increase productivity. There were five shirt factories in Derry in 1850 and this had grown to thirty-eight in 1902, plus a whole host of outworking. Companies of note included William Scott & Sons, Hogg & Co., Welch Margetson and Tillie & Henderson. It was the Glaswegian, Tillie, who saw the benefit in bringing all shirt-making activity together under one roof, and it was he who introduced the first sewing machines, but also a steam-powered cutting machine in their five-storey factory with 1,500 employees. The factory was significant enough for Karl Marx to reference it in *Das Kapital*. Shirts were supplied to the British market but also overseas.[13]

In Britain, as probably elsewhere, medicine had been largely herbal until the so-called quacks began to peddle their 'patent products' of questionable value with some manufacturers spending huge sums on advertising. There is a wonderful nineteenth-century advertisement for 'Morison's Pills – a cure for all curable diseases'. That is far from the whole story. The Pharmaceutical Society was formed in London in 1841, and one of its founding members was William Allen who was a partner in the Plough Court pharmacy, whose origins can be traced back to 1715. In 1856 Allen, joined his nephews in Allen & Hanbury which grew particularly through its renowned cod liver oil (not one of my favourite memories of childhood). Much later Allen & Hanbury would be bought by Glaxo Laboratories.[14]

In 1849, John Boot opened his first herbalist shop in Nottingham 'as an alternative to traditional medicine drawing on the American Thomsonian system of healthcare'.[15] One year later, his son Jesse was born and so began a company that would transform the health of the nation: Boots Pure Drug Company.

The development of synthetic medicine was taking place mainly in Germany and the USA, and the British were importing German products such as aspirin.[16] E. M. Tansey, writing in the *Journal of the Royal Society of Medicine*, suggests that one British company formed by two young Americans was engaging seriously in pharmaceutical research. The young Americans were Silas Mainville Burroughs and Henry Solomon Wellcome, and the company was called Burroughs, Wellcome & Co.[17] They set up the first office to be lit by electricity, and a factory in Wandsworth to manufacture compressed medicines. Marketing to the medical profession was important, as were efforts to distance themselves from the peddlers. Wellcome set up research laboratories and recruited scientists to explore the benefits of natural products. The path of progress was not without it challenges. For example, the use of horses in the development of vaccines led to a stand-off with government over licensing, and, with the medical profession, over the thought that a commercial concern could be approved to carry out animal research. Tansey suggests that government approval eventually came when they recognized the risk of valuable research activity going abroad.

Beechams were another force in pharmaceuticals which had progressed from making patent medicine in 1848 to adoption of scientific research.[18] Thomas Beecham developed a recipe for laxative pills and by 1887 had built the first factory in Britain to have electric power.[19]

There was a significant crossover between pharmaceuticals and the broader chemical industry. The role of America and other countries in satisfying UK domestic demand was significant. Looking at the companies which set up substantial subsidiaries in the UK, famous names emerge even before the First World War. Many more would set up here in the interwar years.[20] The chemical and, in particular, the dyestuffs industry had major overseas involvement. The German Hoechst Elsmere Port plant produced nearly all indigo dye. The same factory produced anti-syphilis medicine. One of the few British dye manufacturers, Clayton Aniline, was bought by the Swiss Ciba in 1911.

The native British chemical industry grew with the textile industry's hunger for soap and dyes. The industry was made up for forty or so small companies operating on the Cheshire salt-field and neighbouring Merseyside, producing industrial chemicals such as soda ash, chlorine, sulphuric acid, bleach and explosives. Taken together, they comprised the largest heavy chemical industry in the world. The largest company, Brunner Mond, took on a licence from the Belgian Solvay to produce soda in bulk and became part of the Solvay Group which loosely drew together users of the process in a number of countries. The competing Leblanc process was embraced by Tennants of Glasgow which brought together the other Leblanc companies into the United Alkali company.[21] The final decades of the century saw these two groupings seeking to embrace new competing technologies alongside chemical companies in Germany and the USA. In 1911, Lever Brothers was the major customer of Brunner Mond for soda and this set in motion a conflict which drew Brunner Mond into the business of soap production. In a story of great skill and diplomacy, it was a situation that had seemed disastrous for Lever, but had by 1914 put the company in a position of great strength.[22] It would be a British company to watch.

The chemical industry as a whole would become a powerhouse of British manufacturing in the interwar years, alongside the motor industry to which I turn by first looking at the bicycle and its elder sibling, the sewing machine.

Chapter 9

The Sewing Machine and Bicycle

*'No useful sewing machine was ever invented by one man;
and all first attempts to do work by machinery, previously
done by hand, had been failures. It was only after
several able inventors had failed in their attempts, that
someone with the mental powers to combine the efforts of
others, with his own, at last produced a practical sewing
machine.'*[1]

James Gibbs, the son of a Shenandoah farmer

It is the story of this book: the way one idea builds on another, until finally
an answer is found. The sewing machine was ultimately an American
invention, vital to the textile industry but also to many homes across the
land. It brings in another aspect, how more and more inventions were
crossing borders, with people of different nations building on the work
of others. It is also the story of how one invention leads to another: first
the sewing machine, next the bicycle.

In the case of Britain, I want to take one step back, for things mechanical
had been made by skilled and inventive people for centuries. The clock
and watch are perhaps the most visible, but there also many tools used in
the workshops of Birmingham, for example, which meant that in Britain
there were skilled 'mechanics' aplenty. The story of British clockmaking
is told in a lovely short book by Kenneth Ullyet, *British Clocks and
Clockmakers*.[2] It is a story of craftsmen, taking an idea which came from
Italy and developing it in a very British way. He tells of the City Livery
Company of Clockmakers, aimed at keeping foreign craftsmen at bay, but
also of the famous clockmakers, not least Harrison and his chronometer
which mastered the calculation of longitude. Whilst Britain had many
skills, it didn't have a watch or clock manufacturing industry of any
magnitude. The same was true of the sewing machine. As I shall show, it
was in the bicycle that British manufacturing once again came to the fore.

In Class 6 of the Great Exhibition catalogue, I came across an entry for C. T. Judkins of Manchester who was displaying a sewing machine capable of sewing 500 stiches per minute. The relevance of such a machine shouts loud and clear when we look back at the 1851 census and the 'third of a million milliners, dressmakers and seamstresses'. A sewing machine would have transformed their lives, but also massively have increased capacity for making clothes. The story is, of course, not that simple. We have seen with iron production that many failures come before, eventually, someone succeeds. This was very much the case with the sewing machine. Alex Askaroff has written a number of books on the subject and in his *Brief History* quotes one of the sewing machine pioneers with the words with which I began this chapter.

Askaroff traces the development of the sewing machine back to England and a German named Charles Weisenthal who took out a patent for a needle to be used for 'mechanical sewing', but nothing else is known. There followed a series of uncoordinated attempts and repeated failures as testament to just how difficult it was to transform the result of a skilled movement of fingers into a mechanical process. However, in 1844, a Massachusetts farmer, Elias Howe, finished his sewing engine and, in 1846, patented it. This machine did the job, and many of its features are present in modern-day sewing machines. He failed to find interest in the machine in the USA and so took it to England, where, again, it seems no one was interested and so he returned home only to find that a number of sewing machine companies had begun production, including a man named Singer, and they were using aspects of Howe's design.

Askaroff then describes how Howe embarked on a series of lawsuits against the companies who were using his design, not least Isaac Singer. Singer took out his own patent on 12 August 1851: 'his machine was reliable and factories soon started using it to increase their production.'[3]

This began a frenzy of sewing machine production, not only in the USA but also in Germany and Britain, and indeed many other countries. Looking at Britain, a website called sewmuse.co.uk attempts to bring together the many sewing machine companies in Britain which manufactured in the second half of the nineteenth century. The author of the site cautions that many companies imported American machines which they merely distributed in Britain. Some though certainly did manufacture and I have already mentioned C. T. Judkins of Manchester.

However, there is some doubt whether they just designed and sold machines which other manufacturers produced for them.

Hillman and Herbert was a company that caught my eye, and I went to the Hillman car owners' website where they set out the history: 'During the 1860s Josiah Turner and James Starley formed the Coventry Sewing Machine Company and recruited skilled engineers from the London area to join them, one of these was named William Hillman.'[4] William Hillman was born in Lewisham in South London and had worked with the marine engine builder John Penn before his move to Coventry. Another engineer, who joined the Coventry Sewing Machine Company having worked for Penn, was George Singer. George and Isaac Singer were not related!

William Hillman had become friends with William Herbert, who was working as an engineer in nearby Leicester. In 1875, Hillman invented a roller skate and, through Herbert's good offices, sold it successfully to the Leicester skating rink. Herbert was the brother of the machine toolmaker, Alfred Herbert. Hillman and William Herbert decided, from this experience, that they had complementary skills and the set up the Premier Works in Coventry.[5] This business manufactured sewing machines and soon, using Hillman's skills both as a cyclist and in engineering, produced a Premier bicycle and a tricycle. They were both great successes and sold in good numbers. A few years later, they brought out the Kangaroo bicycle which was the first, or one of the first, safety cycles with a chain drive. A. E. Harrison suggests that the first safety cycle was produced by John Kemp Starley, the son of Hillman's former employer, trading as Starley & Sutton. Manners supports him in this, adding that the cycle was named the Rover. It was later improved by Woodhead, Angois & Ellis of Nottingham, which would later become the world-famous Raleigh Company.[6]

These men were not alone in the development of the bicycle. Harry Lawson was a Londoner, son of a modelmaker, who began his working life in an Islington ironworks. In the 1870s, he made a number of bicycles and his efforts were described as the 'first authentic design of [a] safety bicycle employing chain-drive to the rear wheel which was actually made', and he has been ranked alongside John Kemp Starley as an inventor of the modern bicycle.[7] In the 1880s, he joined the Rudge Cycle Company as sales superintendent. Rudge-Whitworth was a Coventry company formed in 1894 from the merger of Charles Pugh's

Whitworth Cycle Company, based in Birmingham, and the Rudge Cycle Company of Coventry. Lawson is recorded as having been involved in a number of ventures until, in 1897, he entered the motor car business, as I tell in the next chapter.

Another very significant bicycle name is that of Thomas Humber, who was born in Sheffield in 1841, and began his career as a blacksmith before moving to the Butterley Ironworks, following which he set up on his own as a blacksmith working in Nottingham. His obituary in the *Dundee Evening Telegraph* of 28 November 1910, tells how he was regarded as the father of the British cycle trade. It tells the story of how he was reading a copy of the *English Mechanic* and came across the description of a velocipede, a French invention. From this and an image which was also in the magazine, he made a velocipede of his own and rode it around Nottingham. This attracted passersby to ask him to make one for them. This he did, with each order taking two months. Business grew and the bicycle was refined. In due course, he moved to a factory in neighbouring Beeston and, in 1878, went into partnership with Marriott and Cooper. The company also produced tricycles and, in 1884, Humber patented a 'safety bicycle': 'it was one of the first to use a "diamond" frame, which was stiffer than the single tube backbone used previously. Humber was one of several makers who exhibited bicycles at the Stanley Shows featuring a small front wheel connected to a long sloping fork (unlike Lawson's earlier Bicyclette with large front wheel).'[8] The Stanley Shows were held annually in London by the Stanley Cycle Club.

On 17 June 1887, a prospectus appeared in the newspapers seeking investors in Humber Limited. Thomas Humber had left the partnership with Marriott and Cooper and had agreed to sell his business to a William Horton. Humber Limited was to acquire the Humber business from Horton together with the other cycle businesses Horton owned. Thomas Humber would become general manager. The company would go on to become a major manufacturer of motor cars as I tell in the next chapter. One of the many engineers who worked for Humber was John Siddeley, who worked there as a draughtsman but who also managed their racing department.

Another company to enter the bicycle business was the Birmingham Small Arms Company which, in 1880, was approached to make the Otto patent safety cycle. The cycle business, however, had to make way for rifles when these were demanded by the government.

An essential and related development was that by Scottish-born John Boyd Dunlop who, whilst living in Belfast, developed the pneumatic tyre which both greatly improved the comfort of riding a bicycle but also its speed. With Harvey du Cros, he set up, in 1888, what would become the Pneumatic Tyre Company.[9] It began producing tyres in Dublin but then moved to Coventry and in 1896 taking new premises and also premises vacated by the Singer Motor Company.

E. T. Hooley was an entrepreneur whose name will reappear in the story of the early motor car. His biggest claim to fame, or infamy, was the purchase of the Pneumatic Tyre Company for £3 million and its immediate floatation as the Dunlop Pneumatic Tyre Company for £5 million of which *The Economist* of 30 July 1898 wrote:

> On the strength of the Dunlop deal, Mr Hooley came to be regarded as the Napoleon of Finance. At his word, Capital could be created by the million and fortunes could be made as if by a magician's wand. There have been many successful company promoters, but Mr Hooley was to eclipse them all alike, in the variety of his schemes and in the gigantic profits provided by them not only for the great financier but that everybody connected with him.[10]

Ernest Terah Hooley was remarkable by any standards. He was the son of a lacemaker from the Derbyshire town of Long Eaton. He began his career in his father's business, but moved into stockbroking and, from there, into company promotion. In his 'golden years' he floated and made a personal fortune out of two other household names: Bovril and Schweppes. He died in 1947 in a small house in College Street, Long Eaton. The obituaries tell of a man who rubbed shoulders with royalty and the good and the great of his time. They also tell of a man bankrupted more than once, and imprisoned for fraud, again, on more than one occasion. The *Derby Daily Telegraph* of 12 February 1947 said this: 'From earning 30 shillings a week in his father's lace mill, he became one of the most powerful financiers of the century, and so wealthy that it was said he owned £10 million worth of land in Great Britain.' He owned Risley Hall in Derbyshire and, of more relevance to this story, developed Trafford Park Industrial Estate in Manchester, the first such estate in the country. I write of Trafford Park in Chapter 11.

John Siddeley had moved from Humber to work for Dunlop in 1893, but, in 1896, set up his own Clipper Tyre Company (which became Continental Tyres). He clearly understood the value of promotion and promoted his tyres on Humber cycles, before turning to motor car tyres.[11]

Another essential development, alongside the bicycle and the pneumatic tyre, was the cycle lamp, and, once again, Birmingham played its part with its workforce skilled in working tin. One of these was named Joseph Lucas.[12] Roy Church tells how Joseph Lucas had set up business in the distribution of oil lamps, but, with the coming of the bicycle, saw the opportunities available to manufacturers. He was joined by his son Harry and, in the late 1870s, they set up in partnership manufacturing bicycle lamps. It was Harry who had the business brain, although self-taught. He believed that quality was vital, that orders should only be accepted if they could be delivered, and that price mattered. They produced their famous King of the Road lamp in 1880, and also the Lucas 90 Plus cheaper lamp for what was a fast-growing market. Harry also wrestled with finances as he focused on cashflow and just how difficult it was for a young company to grow. They acquired additional premises in 1895 and, as the workforce grew, mercifully so did demand, and profits began to come through in handsome numbers – some £23,000 per year on average in the three years to 1897 when the partnership became Joseph Lucas Limited.

A. E. Harrison, in an article from 1969, paints a picture of the growth and geographical distribution of bicycle companies in Britain at the turn of the century: 'There were two manufacturers of complete cycles in Coventry in 1874, fourteen in 1882, twenty-two in 1890 and thirty-five in 1892. Birmingham had six makers in 1875, forty-three in 1880, fifty-four in 1886 and one hundred and fourteen in 1891. Nottingham had eight manufacturers in 1878, thirteen in 1886 and thirty-three in 1892.'[13]

The mention of Nottingham brings Raleigh back into the story as probably the best-known British make.[14] In 1888, Frank Bowden bought the workshop on Raleigh Street where Woodhead, Angois & Ellis had been developing the bicycle. In 1895, E. T. Hooley invested in Bowden's company. By 1896 Raleigh had the biggest bicycle factory in the world, covering seven and a half acres with 850 employees producing 30,000 bicycles a year. Six years later Bowden bought Sturmey-Archer gears.

The increase in road usage demanded better roads. Ruston & Proctor's catalogue now included steam road rollers along with steam diggers. It wasn't just England: their records include orders from Bulgaria for road rollers. By the same token, Britain's roads were benefitting from mechanization from other countries. Notwithstanding these improvements, government viewed roads as dangerous places and so restricted the speed at which powered vehicle could travel. As I tell in the next chapter, this held back the development of the British motor vehicle industry but only briefly, for it would go on to be the industrial powerhouse of the next century.

Chapter 10

The Internal Combustion Engine

'He was probably no less scrupulous than many of the other remarkable characters who used other people's money to amass vast fortunes for themselves in the City of London at the turn of the nineteenth century. On the credit side, those who worked for him said that he was both fair and generous. He was certainly not a greedy man who loved money for its own sake.'

'Bunty' Scott-Moncrieff on H. J. Lawson[1]

The name Harry Lawson brings us pretty close to the beginning of British motor manufacturing, but not quite. I need to dig further back, helped by that catalogue of the Great Exhibition and the name James Young.

In 1847, Scotsman James Young noticed an oily fluid in the Riddings coalmine, and distilled a quantity of it to produce a thin oil which could burn in lamps and a thicker oil for lubrication. He went on from this to enter into a partnership in Manchester manufacturing oil and paraffin wax from coal. Just one year earlier, a Canadian, Abraham Gesner, had also refined a liquid from coal which he called kerosene, and which he produced commercially to light the neighbouring town of Halifax.[2] Kerosene was also being distilled in Poland and Russia. The Russian enterprise led to the first oil tanker, the Murex, built by William Gray in West Hartlepool for Marcus Samuel & Company, the founder of Shell Transport & Trading. Samuel's previous business had been as a dealer in seashells.

The discovery of oil in Russia brings the name Joseph Ruston again into the story. Ruston's farm machinery was becoming well known in Russia, and Bernard Newman tells the story of Ruston being summoned to come up with a scheme to drain large areas of land to reclaim for farming. Ruston & Proctor steam-driven pumps were perfect for the job.

The story goes that, whilst in Russia, Ruston heard of developments in the Caucasus in southern Russia where the need was for pumps to extract oil from the ground.[3] Needless to say, his pumps were equally suited to this task.

The first commercial oil well was drilled in Pennsylvania, USA, by Edwin Drake in 1859 and so began 'Big Oil' in America. In 1865, John D. Rockefeller founded the Standard Oil Company. It wasn't until 1907 that William Knox D'Arcy discovered oil in Iran, leading to the founding of the Anglo-Persian Oil Company, which would later become BP – thus, in a nutshell, the means by which vehicles could be powered by internal combustion.

For some decades, engineers had been exploring ways of using the steam engine to power carriages running on roads. The early results had been sufficiently worrying for Parliament to enact legislation to protect other road users from these dangerous vehicles; this included the requirement for a man to walk in front of any powered road vehicle with a red flag. It was probably the absence of similar legislation in Germany and France which encouraged engineers in both countries to explore the possibility of an engine with combustion of fuel contained within the engine, thus reducing the risk of fire. Another possible reason was that in both Germany and France formal education in engineering and science was far advanced of that in Britain, as indeed it had been from the mid-nineteenth century.

Whatever the reason, the evidence is that it was in Germany that the first internal combustion engine appeared. Carl Benz is credited with the first four-stroke engine that actually powered a vehicle. Steven Parissien in his book, *The Life of the Automobile: A New History of the Motor Car*, suggests that Benz had built on earlier work by Belgian Etienne Lenoir and, in 1880, had patented 'a reliable, two stroke, gasoline-powered engine'.[4] In 1885, another German, Gottlieb Daimler, used a four-stroke engine made by his partner, Wilhelm Maybach, to power a bicycle of his own design. In 1890, Daimler and Maybach formed a public company, Daimler-Motoren-Gesellschaft to manufacture to their design. It was such a Daimler which wealthy Englishman, Evelyn Ellis, imported into England in full view of the *Hampshire Chronicle and General Advertiser* of 13 July 1895. The article recording the event went on to say that Ellis was accompanied by Frederick Simms whose company, the Daimler Motor Syndicate Limited, had bought the patent rights for the United Kingdom and Colonies, adding that the vehicle had been made in France by Panhard & Levassor. This switch of focus from Germany to France reveals that, whilst the invention may have been German, the early development was indeed French, with companies such as Panhard & Levassor, but also De Dion-Bouton and, later, Renault.

The British Motor Car Industry

It is at this point that Britain, in the larger-than-life person of Harry Lawson, enters the story. Parissien describes him as 'the crooked entrepreneur Harry Lawson'; the records do indeed show that he was prosecuted for fraud on at least two occasions. However, Lawson was perhaps the unlikely founder of British motor manufacturing, which, in turn, sowed the seeds for motor manufacturing in many countries of the world. As I tell in this chapter, Lawson was far from alone, but part of a network of intriguing men who would together create something truly remarkable: a brand-new and massive manufacturing industry.

In March 1896, Lawson set up the Daimler Company with fellow director, Gottlieb Daimler, and bought the Daimler patents from the Daimler Motor Syndicate Limited; Frederick Simms became a director as consulting engineer. The new company took a lease on a fourteen-acre site in Drapers Field, Coventry, and began production. The site had belonged to Coventry Cotton Mills, and Lawson renamed it Motor Mills. It was the first motor car factory in Britain and would house, in addition to Daimler, the other motor and motor-related companies Lawson owned.[5] By 1897, it employed 223 people and exhibited at the Stanley Cycle Show.

Frederick Lanchester was probably the opposite of Harry Lawson. He was born in 1868, son of an architect, and had a formal mathematical and scientific education before moving to Finsbury where he learned workshop practice. We know this from a detailed and admiring obituary written in 1946 by Harry Ricardo, himself a celebrated motor engineer who, amongst much else, designed the engine which succeeded the 105hp Daimler engine that had powered the first tanks. The obituary appeared in the *Journal of the Royal Society*.[6] Ricardo explains how the early 'horseless carriages' from the continent were just that, carriages with internal combustion engines rather than horses. They were noisy, vibrated uncomfortably and had suspension unsuited to the faster vehicle. Lanchester began his career in 1895 in Birmingham working on gas engines, and there began to build his first car, the first all-British four-wheeled vehicle. He formed the Lanchester Engine Company and produced two more models. Ricardo wrote how he had driven one of these early models and could therefore vouch for their quietness, lack of vibration and smooth ride. He puts it that Lanchester had the remarkable combination of mathematical, scientific and engineering skills. Lanchester wrote two seminal works on aircraft and many learned papers. The third model he made went on to sell well and was widely respected for the quality of design and manufacture. Ricardo explains that Lanchester carried a heavy burden, since, not only was he managing director, he was designer and works manager. He puts flesh on this by adding that every part, except for tyres, had to be made, and, since the technology was new, even experienced mechanics had to be taught new skills. Probably because of all of this, the company was not a commercial success and a receiver was appointed. In 1905, Lanchester started again with the Lanchester Motor Co. Limited and production and indeed development continued. In 1909, Frederick Lanchester fell out with his fellow directors and become a consultant, and, at the same time, became a consultant to the Daimler Company.

The Birmingham Small Arms Company, which was manufacturing bicycles in addition to guns, at their factory at Small Heath in Birmingham, was, in September 1910, rumoured to be in discussions with Daimler with a view to an amalgamation. The *Truth* journal for 7 September 1910 noted that Daimler had twenty-seven acres of land in Coventry on which BSA could expand from their crowded Birmingham site; also, it was thought that BSA would be better able to exploit some of Daimler's patents. Percy Martin, who was then managing director of Daimler, would become managing director of the combined company.[7] The newspapers contained reports of the respective shareholder meetings approving the amalgamation. BSA had suffered from low orders for guns, but had done well in bicycles and was planning a motor cycle. Daimler reported annual profits of £100,000, a little above that of BSA. An article in the *Westminster Gazette,* on the Olympia Motor Show of November 1910, was full of praise for Daimler engines. The combination seemed to be winning approval.

Ricardo's obituary of Lanchester casts some doubt over the boasts in the article, as he tells how Lanchester laboured long and hard to make the engine, which he had inherited from other designers, live up to the advertising hyperbole. He tells also how Lanchester struggled with some of the other far-fetched ideas of Daimler's management, how he eventually persuaded them to form a subsidiary, Lanchester Laboratories Limited focused on research, and how they eventually let him, and it, go. His versatility is evidenced by this company, in 1928, producing radio equipment, an acoustic tube moving coil loudspeaker. In 1928, he also became consulting engineer to Beardmore working with their locomotive diesel engines. The Lanchester Motor Company, then run by Frederick's brother, George, was bought by BSA in 1931.

Thomas Humber had been manufacturing bicycles in his factory at Beeston near Nottingham and had expanded to occupy factories also in Wolverhampton and Coventry. He was near retirement and M. D. Rucker had joined as general manager. He linked with the 'arch-entrepreneur' E. T. Hooley, and a massive expansion took place, with the company setting up subsidiaries in the USA, Russia, Portugal and Denmark. It was huge, yet in 1898 Hooley went bankrupt and Rucker fell from grace, and a new board was appointed under Edward Powell. The overseas entities were closed, as was the Wolverhampton factory. For a few years the company turned to motor cycles, but it was the motor car that was its true destiny. It is here that H. J. Lawson also enters Humber's story. Interestingly, Demaus and Tarring in their book, *The Humber Story 1868–1932*, are more generous to Lawson than was Parissien when they quote 'Bunty' Scott-Moncrieff with the words with which I began this chapter.

Humber took out licences from Lawson's company to produce cars under the patents taken out by the Pennington company of the USA. The designs turned out to be failures and were discontinued. 1900 saw the company become Humber Limited, with the overseas ventures and relationships with Lawson and Hooley left behind. They began building motor cars under licence from the British Motor Traction Company with engines built by De Dion.

In 1901, another famous name, Louis Coatalen, enters the story. Coatalen had studied engineering at the Ecole des Arts et Métiers at Cluny in France. After working for De Dion-Bouton, and Panhard-Levassor, in 1901 he had left France to join Humber in Coventry. He began designing first an 8hp then a 12hp and finally a 20hp model. These were then succeeded by the Humberette, some 500 of which were made in Beeston and Coventry. The company was successful, making an astonishing profit of £154,537 in 1907. As has often been the case in this story, boom was followed by depression and Humber found themselves with too much stock, which then had to be sold at a considerable discount.[8] In the run-up to the First World War, the company branched out first into aviation, under the guidance of aviator Ballin Hinde, and then into building a team of specialist cars for the Tourist Trophy on the Isle of Man. Whilst neither venture was a success, Demaus and Tarring suggest that they offered valuable experience for the war years which were to follow.

William Hillman had also been producing bicycles in Coventry for some years, but in 1907 he set up the Hillman Coatalen Company, when Louis Coatalen left Humber. Coatalen was clearly a man uncomfortable in the same place for too long, and, in 1909, the partnership with Hillman was dissolved and he went to join Sunbeam and its founder John Marsden. Sunbeam was building cars in Wolverhampton under works manager Sydney Guy who would go on to found Guy Motors. He had previously worked at Vickers, Sons & Maxim, at General Electric Company and at Humber. Guy thus links the world of heavy engineering, motor vehicles and electricity. An early Sunbeam was reputedly the first car ever to be driven at more than 200 miles per hour. The Hillman Company continued to prosper, itself winning a number of awards. It would join Humber, Sunbeam & Singer which made up the passenger vehicle side of the Rootes Group.

Vauxhall entered motor car manufacturing by a rather different route. In 1857, Scottish engineer, Alexander Wilson, founded the Vauxhall Ironworks in that area of London that had for many years been the Vauxhall Pleasure Gardens, but was becoming industrialized with the building of Vauxhall Junction railway station. By 1904, the Vauxhall Ironworks was employing some 180 people, with cars being made alongside the marine engine business in a four-storey building that had originally been a brewery. With the lease of the site running out, the decision was taken to move to a thirty-acre site in Luton in Bedfordshire.[9]

We can now move west to Oxford where, in 1893, William Morris set out on his career, first repairing bicycles.[10] I know rather more about him than the others, probably because of his later fame as Lord Nuffield. One byproduct of this is an engaging biography of him written in 1955 by P. W. S. Andrews and Elizabeth Brunner which I think my father bought when it was first published. In this, they offer revealing anecdotes about the man and his business, but also valuable reflection on the business of making motor cars from very nearly the start.

Oxford was probably a good place to set up in business to repair bicycles, given their popularity among young men and the number of wealthy young men in the Oxford colleges. If it was true of bicycles, it was all the truer of motor bikes and motor cars. It didn't take Morris long to begin experimenting with motor bikes. Andrews and Brunner relate the story of the two bikes he made for the Stanley Show of 1902 at the Agricultural Hall in London. The story goes that he was trying to make the bikes while continuing with his business of cycle repair, essentially working all hours. Things became tense when parts for the new bikes were late arriving. When eventually they appeared, he worked non-stop for four days and nights before taking the bikes to London. When he arrived at Paddington, he arranged for horse transport to take the bikes, and he followed on the steam underground railway. He made the mistake of sitting down, for he fell straight to sleep. The train guard woke him only just in time to get to the show. The bikes were well received, but, soon after Morris's businesses partner left, and Morris had to start again.

Motor bikes, however, were not where Morris saw the future, and so he set about designing a motor car. He had been running a business both repairing and hiring cars, and this had taught him a massive amount about what worked and what didn't. His reputation had also attracted other manufacturers to appoint him as their sales agent in Oxford, and he was selling cars for well-known motor car makers such as Arrol-Johnson, Belsize, Humber, Hupmobile, Singer, Standard and Wolseley and motor bikes for Douglas, Enfield, Sunbeam and Triumph.

I have already written about Humber, Singer & Sunbeam. The Wolseley Company brings in the name of Herbert Austin who would be Morris's rival over many years. The Wolseley Company had begun as a manufacturer of sheep-shearing machinery in Australia. Herbert Austin became involved after he had spent a highly constructive 'apprenticeship' with a number of engineering companies around Melbourne where his uncle had persuaded him to move. In 1890, the head office of the firm moved to London. Austin followed and developed further the machine technology, also branching out into machine tools and parts for cycles. It was probably in about 1895 that the first 'Austin' car appeared, branded, of course, as a Wolseley. Austin was clearly a great innovator, but seemingly was held back by the other Wolseley directors.

Towards the end of the century, Vickers and Sir Hiram Maxim were exploring the possibilities of motor car-related inventions and made an investment in Wolseley. In 1901, Vickers registered as a subsidiary, the Wolseley Tool & Motor Car Company Ltd., and moved production to the Adderley Park Works in Birmingham with factory floor space covering seventeen acres. Roy Church suggests that Austin's commitment to his side-valve engine held the company back, with the result that Austin left in 1905 to pursue his own business. Austin's departure coincided with the arrival of rival engineer John Siddeley but it seems with no immediate greater commercial success[11]. Herbert Austin set up the Austin Motor Company in 1905 in a former printworks at Longbridge near Birmingham.

Siddeley had chosen a Daimler car to promote his Clipper motor tyres and, through that connection, realized the commercial potential of the motor car. In 1902, he had set up Siddeley Autocars and imported Peugeot mechanical parts, 'clothing them with his own British built car bodies'. He went on from there to design his own entire car, having the components made by Wolseley and the whole assembled by Vickers, Sons & Maxim.[12] It was after this, that he joined Wolseley, first as sales manager and, following Austin's departure, also as works manager. John Siddeley was, I suspect, also a restless man for he left Wolseley two years later to join the Deasy Motor Car Manufacturing Company, which went on to produce quality cars under the Siddeley-Deasy mark.

Morris's involvement with motorbikes began with Reginald Maudslay, great-grandson of Henry Maudslay. Reginald founded the Standard Motor Company in 1903, producing a single-cylinder car from premises in Coventry. The company expanded under the influence of its distributor, Charles Friswell. The motor cycle connection came when Friswell sold his shareholding to Siegfried Bettmann the founder of the Triumph Motor Cycle Company, which had its origins in the bicycle boom of the 1880s. It had been founded as a wholesale business of bicycles manufactured in Birmingham. It prospered, and began manufacturing in its own premises in Coventry. It was there that it attracted investment from Harvey du Cros, who had earlier provided financial backing for John Boyd Dunlop and the Dunlop company. Du Cros made an investment in Triumph and the manufacture of a motor cycle began in 1902.[13]

The Douglas Company was founded in Bristol in the latter part of the nineteenth century as a boot machine repairer. It progressed into foundry work, and, in the first decade of the twentieth century, made initial forays into motor cycles. The design skill came from Joseph Barter, who had developed a small machine known as the Fairy. Willie Douglas and Barter were true motor cycle enthusiasts, participating in the early years of motor sport. By the start of the First World War, they had produced some 12,000 machines.[14]

The Royal Enfield story began in 1891, when Bob Walker Smith and Albert Eadie bought George Townsend & Co., a Redditch needle manufacturer which had turned its hand to bicycles. The company then won a contract to supply parts to the Royal Small Arms Factory at Enfield. They renamed themselves the Enfield Manufacturing Company, and produced the Enfield Bicycle soon itself to be renamed the Royal Enfield, with the trade mark 'Made Like A Gun'. The motor cycle followed five years later, powered by a De Dion 1½hp engine.[15]

One make of motor cycle not mentioned by Morris was Norton. This company began life in 1898 as a manufacturer of parts for the two-wheel trade. By the turn of the century, they were producing bikes with French engines, which achieved success in the first Isle of Man TT race. In 1909, they added their own engine.[16]

Morris had already built a good working relationship with Coventry carburettor manufacturer, White & Poppe. In 1912, he collaborated with them, and, in particular, their chief draughtsman, H. Landstad, in the design of the engine. He obtained the axle from E. G. Wrigley and pressed steel wheels from Sankey, which would later become part of GKN. The design was a success, but slow in reaching fruition and, so, he had to attend the 1913 Motor Show with only blueprints. Such was his reputation and presence, that Mr Gordon Stewart of London ordered 400 cars then and there. Stewart & Arden would become the sole distributor for Morris in the London district.

He began to think of a larger model, the Morris Cowley, but, conscious of costs, he looked this time to suppliers in the USA, who were benefitting from longer manufacturing runs made possible by the larger American market. Ford, for example, was producing the Model-T in high volume at a low price. He visited the States in early 1914 with Landstad, and, together, they explored what suppliers could offer. In particular, they decided upon an engine from the Continental Motor Company which could be supplied to the UK at under half of what White & Poppe would charge. Morris returned to Oxford, but Handstad remained working at

Continental until later in the year when he too returned to England and joined the W. R. Morris Company. All was set for the production of the Morris Cowley when the First World War intervened.

The First World War is a subject on its own, so for this chapter, what of other manufacturers? What, for example, of Rolls-Royce? Henry Royce had run an electrical and mechanical business since 1884, and in 1904 met Charles Rolls, an old Etonian car dealer. Royce had made a car powered by his 2-cylinder engine, which greatly impressed Rolls. The two agreed that four models would be made under the Rolls-Royce brand and that Rolls would have the exclusive right to sell them. The car was revealed at the Paris Motor Show of 1904. The two men needed to find a factory in which to make them. Derby offered them cheap electricity, and so they selected the site at Sinfin Lane where a factory was built to Royce's design. I write in the next chapter of the revolution that electricity brought about.

Charles Rolls was an aviation enthusiast, and, in 1910, made the first non-stop double crossing of the Channel. Tragically, only one month later, he was killed in a plane crash. I write below on the development of aviation. American academic, Peter Botticelli, writing in *The American Scholar*, tells rather more about Rolls-Royce.[17] In particular, he names two of the early employees of the company, Claude Johnson, who would become general manager, and Ernest Hives, who joined as a boy but who would later become general manager and eventually chairman. Johnson's view of the company was that it should build on its reputation of serving the aristocracy whose cars were nearly always driven by chauffeurs. Thus, if a customer wished to test drive a car, he would be driven by a Rolls-Royce chauffeur who had been schooled in the etiquette of service. Royce demanded the highest possible standards in engineering, as Johnson did in customer service. In those early days, the company would provide the engine and chassis, and a coachbuilder would build the body to the customer's specification. They were aiming high.

What of Other Manufacturers?

David Napier & Son, the precision engineers, had re-emerged near the beginning of the era of the motor car, as manufacturers of high-quality vehicles. By 1914, they were making 700 cars a year from their

Acton Factory and selling from their New Burlington Street showroom, including many to the London taxi trade. [18]

Albion was proudly Scottish. It was created by two engineers, Thomas Murray and Norman Fulton, and began business at the turn of the twentieth century on the edge of the docklands of the upper Clyde. By 1903, it had expanded and moved into new premises. To them, the outlook seemed dire: British industry, once supreme, was now a laggard. Albion prepared to take up the challenge. By dint of inventive engineering and enthusiastic marketing, by 1912 Albion was producing nearly 500 chassis a year. These were mainly commercials, reflecting the predominant use being made of motor vehicles as delivery vans. In 1913, the company expanded again into a new factory block built with the new technology of ferro-concrete as used, for example, by Ford in the USA.[19]

Motor Components

A motor components industry was growing up alongside the manufacturers, in part like them, following on from bicycles.[20] Harry Lucas was quick to see the opportunities to move into lighting and starting motor cars. There were of course others keen to enter this promising market. Roy Church mentions Rotax in Willesden in north-west London, and the larger CAV in Acton in West London in which Herbert Austin held debentures. Spark plugs came largely from Champion in the USA. Chloride produced batteries under licence from the USA and, before the First World War, Bosch was the only producer of magnetos. Smiths, a company with a long history of clockmaking, was a provider of motor watches but also of mechanical instruments.

Dunlop quickly saw the potential of moving on from bicycles to motor cars, or rather Arthur du Cros did, whilst his father, Harvey, remained sceptical. Arthur won the day and, in 1900, Dunlop began producing car tyres in Birmingham using the American method involving a collapsible mould and high-pressure steam.[21]

Another specialist component was glass, although Reginald Delpech, the founder of Triplex Safety Glass, found himself a rather solitary voice in 1912. His concept was simple: the placing of a layer of plastic between two sheets of glass which would prevent the glass splintering into sharp and dangerous pieces. The value of the idea may not have appealed to the motoring public, but the military would see its value in the coming war.

Diesel

Oil wasn't only powering petrol cars. In 1898, Rudolf Diesel invented the engine known by his name as the culmination of an exploration of internal combustion which he had begun in Paris in 1883. In his book on Rustons, Bernard Newman includes a chapter intriguingly titled, 'Diesel with a small "d"', adding that 'in Lincoln and Grantham diesel is always written with a small "d"'.[22] He goes on to relate the work of Hornsby in developing oil engines, from the patented design by Akroyd Stuart. Production began in 1891, some eight years before Diesel. In 1894, the Hornsby engine won first prize of the Royal Agricultural Society, but commercial success seemed elusive. Hornsby had the wisdom to realize that he needed to appoint a manager with experience of large-scale production, which he did in the shape of David Roberts whom he recruited from Armstrong Whitworth. Under Roberts's management, the Hornsby engine soon won a worldwide reputation, not least in electricity generation. Newman points to the Statue of Liberty being lit by electricity generated by a Hornsby engine. More generally, Hornsby engines would be found generating electricity in country houses, factories, farms and lighthouses.

Slaven also writes of the first diesel engine, but notes that it would be twenty years before it powered ships, when the East Asiatic Co. of Copenhagen commissioned two identical vessels, the *Selandia* built in Copenhagen and the *Jutlandia* built by Barclay Curle on the Clyde. The British licence passed to Harland & Wolff who built engines at both their Glasgow and Belfast yards.[23]

Aircraft

Oil also enabled the first powered flight. Many books have been written on this and so here I will only focus on those aspects necessary for the purposes of this story of manufacturing. A reasonable starting point might be the Society of Arts just to the south of the Strand in London and the date, 27 June 1866. It is the first meeting of the Aeronautical Society of Great Britain with a paper presented by F. H. Wenham.[24] The reference is to the text of his paper which explores in detail the science behind powered flight, some years before the petrol engine became available. The Wright Brothers are, of course, known for achieving the first flight in 1903, and the museum dedicated to their memory takes the enquirer back to 1799 and the scientific thinking of another Englishman, Sir George Caley.[25] A number of attempts at glider flight followed, including one by Sir Hiram Maxim. In the late 1890s, the Wright brothers experimented with a number of variations of the glider, and eventually sought a suitable petrol engine to power their design. Nothing could be found which provided enough power at an acceptable weight, and so one had to be built specially. This engine enabled the aircraft to fly under power on 17 December 1903. It wasn't, though, until 1907 when they demonstrated a Model A in France that the doubting world became convinced.

Interest in flight in the UK was focused mainly around the Army School of Ballooning, first at the Woolwich Arsenal, then at Aldershot and finally at Farnborough in Hampshire. Balloons had been used to some benefit in the Boer War, and it was thought that they added to the military capability in the context of reconnaissance. Rickard, writing on the Royal Aircraft Factory, suggests that the Balloon Factory became interested in powered flight once the Wright Brothers obtained their patent.[26] A larger-than-life character, American ex-pat, Samuel Franklin Cody, had been experimenting with box kites capable of lifting a man, and, inspired by the Wrights, he set about constructing a powered aircraft. On 16 October 1908, he took off in British Army Aeroplane No. 1 but crashed, mercifully emerging unharmed. That winter, a subcommittee of the Committee of Imperial Defence considered the aircraft project and decided it should be discontinued, and it was only after Blériot's successful crossing of the Channel in 1909 that it changed its policy, and respected engineer, Mervyn O'Gorman, was appointed superintendent of the factory. A chance meeting at the Olympia Motor Show of 1910 brought Geoffrey de Havilland to join him.

The Balloon Factory would be renamed the Royal Aircraft Factory and would promote the design of a large number of experimental aircraft. In his book, *British Aircraft Manufacturers Since 1909*, Peter Dancy sets out the history of most of the UK's aeroplane manufacturers and, in particular, details the designs explored by the Royal Aircraft Factory, which would, over its lifetime, become the world-renowned Royal Aircraft Establishment. I draw on Dancy's research to highlight some of the main players, but also links to many of the companies which have already appeared in this story.

First, I draw on research by the de Havilland Museum into one of the most influential British aircraft designers, and begin with a quotation: 'Geoffrey and his colleague, Frank Hearle, had designed and built their first aircraft, powered by an engine designed by Geoffrey, and neither of them had even seen an aircraft before.' This aircraft flew, but crashed. Its engine was saved and powered a successor aircraft which, on 10 September 1910, flew without crashing at Seven Barrows near Newbury. They sold the aircraft to the Royal Aircraft Factory and, as I recorded above, de Havilland joined its staff and developed an aircraft which, with a passenger, flew to a record height of 10,560 feet on 10 August 1912. His story continues with the start of the First World War, but, first, I want to paint a picture of what else was happening in the embryonic UK aircraft industry.

It was Edwin Alliot Verdon Roe who, on 9 June 1908, was the first to achieve a powered flight in Britain with an all-British designed aircraft with a British engine, a 9hp produced by J. A. Prestwich. Roe and his brother formed A. V. Roe & Co. at Brownsfield Mill in Manchester in 1912, and, the same year, flew their own design of the first totally enclosed monoplane. The following year, they flew a plane which was developed into the Type 500 biplane, 'that established the company as a legend in its own right'.[27] Another legendary name in the British aircraft industry was founded on 19 February 1910 by Sir George White at Filton, Bristol. The British & Colonial Aeroplane Co. Ltd. (Bristol) began by building the French Zodiac biplane, but then designed its own Bristol Boxkite powered by a French Gnome engine. The company recruited a number of distinguished designers and this resulted in the Bristol Scout. Yet another legend, Handley Page Ltd., was founded on 17 June 1909 and was the first limited company to build aeroplanes in the UK. In 1911, it began work on the largest aircraft so far made in Britain, the O/100 heavy night bomber.

Short Brothers go back even further to 1898, when three brothers came together to pursue a commercial interest in ballooning. In November 1908,

Short Brothers (Rochester & Bedford) was established and built Wright Flyers under licence. They then built a biplane which was the first all-British aeroplane to fly one mile. This was followed by a series of aircraft which were used to establish the Naval Flying School in 1911.

The Sopwith Aviation Company, perhaps the most iconic from the First World War, was founded at Kingston upon Thames in 1912, and its Sopwith Bat Boat No. 1 was the first flying boat to be built in Britain. Another pioneer, Noel Pemberton-Billing, showed his Supermarine PB.1 at Olympia in March 1914, but it never entered production. The name Supermarine, when associated with its offspring, the Spitfire, would become one of the most loved in aviation in the Second World War.

Vickers perhaps stand alone as a major industrial company becoming involved in the these very early days of aviation. Others followed, but in March 1911, the Vickers Aviation Department began to build aeroplanes on licence to the design of Robert Esnault-Pelterie.[28] Vickers also manufactured the Maxim machine gun and explored ways in which this could arm an aircraft. They built an experimental fighting biplane for the navy, but this vividly called into question the suitability of the Maxim gun. With the coming on war, more problems would be encountered, and overcome.

The decades either side of the dawning of the twentieth century had witnessed an astonishing revolution as a result of the internal combustion engine. Its further development would be seen in all its horror on and above the fields of Flanders and in the cold depths of the world's oceans.

Chapter 11

Electric Power

"'I think not." Questioned further, he said, "I fancy the descriptions we get of its use in America are a little exaggerated; but there are conditions in America which necessitate the use of instruments of this kind more than here. Here we have a superabundance of messengers, errand boys, and things of that kind."'

William Preece

Such was the comment made in 1878 by William Preece, Engineer-in-Chief and Electrician of the General Post Office, when asked if he thought the telephone would be largely taken up by the British public.[1] I explore, later in this chapter, the advances in communication enabled by electricity. Preece's point, though, does seem to encapsulate the British attitude to electricity, or rather explain why Britain lagged behind in its application.

An electrical development which would, unquestionably, greatly enhance the brightness of the cities was the invention in the 1860s of the dynamo.[2] The discovery of electromagnetic induction by Michael Faraday, Robert Clark Maxwell and others in the 1830s enabled the generation of electricity by magneto-electric machines. The dynamo took Faraday's thinking on electromagnetism and transformed it, so that a powered rotary motion could generate a steady flow of electricity. The power could be from a water wheel, where such was available, or a steam engine which was better suited to most urban areas. The dynamo would be connected to an arc lamp and a bright light was the result. Sir Humphrey Davy features once more, since the invention of the arc light is attributed to him. In a much-developed form, the idea was brought to the eyes of the public outside the Gaiety Theatre in London in 1878 by theatrical entrepreneur, Jonathan Hollingshead.[3] Thereafter it gained ground, with other small-scale generators. The arc lamp remained a problem, since its carbon elements needed frequent replacement. The problem was eventually resolved with the development of the incandescent lamp.

Electric lighting was here to stay. Siemens Brothers provided the generators, wiring and lamps for the lighting of the Savoy Theatre. In 1881, they also installed a small generating station at Godalming in Surrey powered by water from the River Wey. Other names, long associated with electricity, entered the field: Edison set up the Holborn Viaduct scheme in 1882, and, in 1886, Sebastian de Ferranti built the Grosvenor Gallery Station.[4] Ferranti had worked for Siemens in their very new experimental department. By this time, William Siemens had died and his younger brother Alexander was running the firm.

Sebastian de Ferranti was born in Liverpool in 1864, the son of a photographer whose family had come from Bologna. Ferranti's fascination, from a very early age, was with power generation and transmission. He was convinced that power generation did not need to be located near the user, but rather close to the source of energy used. At school in Ramsgate, he had made both an electric light and a dynamo. When he left Siemens, he went into partnership with engineer friend, Alfred Thompson, and lawyer Francis Ince, and they manufactured dynamos to Ferranti's design. The business was spotted by Sir William Thomson, later Lord Kelvin, who had made a similar machine, and they combined their ideas into the Ferranti-Thomson dynamo. The company didn't achieve commercial success, and so closed. Ferranti pressed on, and, in the early 1880s, we come to the Grosvenor Gallery story. This piece of private initiative was a success and, on the back of it, Ferranti embarked on a project of Herculean proportions. The London Electric Supply Company was incorporated in 1887 with a capital of £1 million to build a power station at Deptford. Ferranti, at the age of 23, was appointed chief engineer. He conceived a project of generators producing electricity which would be transmitted at 10,000 volts through cables and switchgear built to his own design. This was a massive project. Ferranti moved his works to Hollinwood in Lancashire, and, by 1897, employed 700 people.

The generation of electricity was happening across the country. For example, in Glasgow the Scottish firm of Mavor & Coulson established a power supply for the city in 1884. The *Engineer* magazine of 31 May 1901 carried an article on the Glasgow steam exhibition of that year and highlighted Robey & Co. of Lincoln, whose horizontal cross-compound engine powered a Mavor & Coulson dynamo producing 350kW at 550 volts.

A related and vital development was the development of the steam turbine by Charles Parsons, mentioned in Chapter 7. As the source of power for a dynamo, it was highly successful, producing 50,000kW. He had established his own company, C. A. Parsons & Co., to manufacture steam turbines and also founded the Newcastle & District Electric Lighting Company, which was the first to generate electricity using steam turbines.

Siemens and others in the youthful electrical industry thus explored with great energy in these late Victorian years. What they didn't do was to apply a coordinated or sufficient approach. The General Electric Company may have taken issue with this, for it is suggested that they built their early fortune on the demand for electric light. The company had started life in Manchester in 1886 by the coming together of Hugo Hirst and Gustav Byng. They produced a catalogue and offered products such as electric bells, ceiling roses and switches.[5] I remember light switches made of brass and pottery: they may well have been General Electric Co., which was the name of the private company they formed in 1889. They began investing in lamp manufacture in 1893; in 1909, this part of their business would become Osram. In 1902, they put up a purpose-built factory at Witton near Birmingham in which they manufactured a large range of electrical machines and appliances.

Crompton Light Bulbs, based in Bradford and tracing their origin back to 1878, may also have taken issue. They have to their credit the first lighting installations at Windsor Castle and Holyrood Palace.[6] Brush Electrical Engineering installed 1,000 lights in Blenheim Palace for the Duke of Marlborough, the chairman of Brush.

The role of the United States in the British electric power industry is writ very large in the shape of two competing companies. The first is British Westinghouse, which was founded by George Westinghouse in 1897. Westinghouse was an electrical engineer from Pittsburgh where his company was making a big name for itself. In 1894, he built a two-million-square-feet industrial complex to manufacture generators, electric motors for trains and trams, and other equipment. He saw the British market, for electrical generation and electrically powered transport, as large and growing, and so a further site was needed in Britain at least as big. Trafford Park in Manchester was a greenfield site next to the newly dug Manchester Ship Canal and so suited perfectly. It is interesting that E. T. Hooley once again enters the story, for it was he who developed Trafford Park.

The digging of the canal itself is significant for many reasons. The catalyst was the damage being caused to Manchester's traditional cotton trade by the cost of rail transport and Liverpool dock fees (I can't help but wonder what George Stephenson would have thought). The answer was to dig a new thirty-five mile-long canal from Manchester to the sea; the existing canal route took some thirty-six hours. The traditional method of digging, by the employment of thousands of navvies, was simply not viable and so an alternative had to be found and it was, in the shape of Ruston & Proctor of Lincoln. Joseph Ruston had, in 1885, delivered a paper to the Institution of Mechanical Engineers in Lincoln on his steam navvy, described as being something between a traction engine and a crane. He had impressed, for the Manchester Canal Company engaged seventy-one of these massive machines. He impressed even more when the many machines, buried by floodwater in 1890, were soon back in full working order and returned to work successfully to complete the canal.[7] The company's workshops covered sixteen acres, and it was selling steam machinery all over the world.

Westinghouse appointed British building contractors, but progress was slow and they were unable to offer a plan to build the complex in anything near the timescale Westinghouse demanded. He therefore took charge of the project and engaged James Stewart from the USA, who had built his Pittsburgh plant. Stewart set up a management team working on site, and engaged subcontractors, where possible, from the UK. For example, 14,000 tons of steelwork came from Dorman Long at Middlesbrough. Brian Bowan, who described the project in a paper, points to Stewart's team-building approach to management, but also his ability to engage with tradesmen. Bowan gives the example of bricklayers, whom Stewart was able to encourage to more than double their daily output. The whole complex of some 1.3 million square feet was built in eighteen months and was manufacturing soon after. Bowan does offer a salutary postscript to the story. Westinghouse in the USA went bankrupt in 1907 as a result of a sharp downturn in the USA capital markets; British Westinghouse also failed to secure the orders for generation and transport which George Westinghouse had anticipated. The British company remained in administration for the next ten years.[8]

Dorman Long, which supplied the structural steel, was the subject of a visit by the *Engineer* magazine in May 1901. It would seem that they were a good match for Westinghouse, for they were one of the first steelworks to introduce electrically powered machinery. They had also pioneered structural steel, and so it is no surprise that they also supplied Westinghouse's rival, British Thompson-Houston.

Westinghouse's great rival in the US was the General Electric Company, which came into existence in 1892 through the merger of the Thomson-Houston Company and Edison. In 1900, British Thomson-Houston acquired a site in Rugby in the English Midlands and began to build a complex to rival that at Trafford Park. One of the arguments which raged between the two companies was whether electricity should be supplied as direct current (DC) or alternating current (AC). Edison was a firm adherent to DC which was suitable where the distance of transmission was not long. Westinghouse favoured AC, and over time won the argument.[9]

A search of contemporary newspapers for both Westinghouse and Thomson-Houston revealed a number of contracts for which they both bid, for example that for the Exeter tram system. The *Devon and Exeter Gazette* for 23 June 1904 has a report of the tenders submitted and orders made. The project was broken down into sections and tenders submitted for each. Both Westinghouse and Thomson-Houston tendered, but both were quite a way above the lowest tender which was from Dick, Kerr & Co. of Kilmarnock, a locomotive and electrical equipment manufacturer that would become part of English Electric.

Exeter was a small contract, but perhaps illustrative of the spread of electric tram systems across the country. The London Underground was a good deal more prestigious. *Scientific America* ran an article on the development of the 'subway' in the London. Of particular interest was the choice of locomotive for, what we now know as, the Central Line. The preference had been for British manufacture, but no supplier could meet the timescale demanded, and so British Thomson-Houston provided machines manufactured by their USA parent, the General Electric Company. BTH also provided the generators powered by Babcock & Wilcox water tube boilers. The braking system for the locomotives was, however, Westinghouse.[10]

There were of course many other companies exploring the application of electric power. One was a collection of British companies brought together by financier Emile Garcke under the banner British Electric Traction. Garcke was a champion of tramways and promoted their operation by public companies. He became manager and secretary of Brush Electrical Engineering Limited which had been formed to exploit the patents for arc lighting developed in the USA by Charles Francis Brush. The British Brush company operated first in London but grew out of its premises and began looking for a suitable place for expansion. The site selected was in Loughborough next to the Midland Railway where the Falcon Engineering Works had been built by Henry Hughes who had begun by building carriages, railway carriages and eventually steam locomotives. The tie-up with Brush was driven by the clear advantage that electricity had over steam as a means of traction in urban areas. Brush Electrical Engineering became a major manufacturer of electric-powered locomotives whilst continuing with steam locomotive particularly for export markets; the last major contract for steam locomotives was for Siamese Railways in 1910.[11]

Another major area of exploration, where Britain was in the slipstream, was the telephone which was invented by a Scot, Alexander Graham Bell, in the USA in 1875. The website www.britishtelephones. com has done a remarkable job exploring the archives of British Telecom in order to compile a detailed timeline. The story it reveals is a tale replicated many times in this book, as inventors build on the work of their predecessors, and, as holders of patents, flex their financial muscles in defending their property. It tells how Bell filed the first patent, only just before Western Union filed theirs. Two years later, Thomas Edison replaced the electromagnet, used by Bell, with carbon. In the USA, the Bell Telephone Company pursued Bell's patents and Western Union championed the American Speaking Telephone Company's patents which included Edison's.

Both types of telephone crossed the Atlantic for use by the British public. Bell demonstrated his telephone to Queen Victoria in 1878, and, later the same year, Edison's equipment was used for a conversation over 115 miles between Cannon Street in London and Norwich. 1880 was a crux point, when the Postmaster General succeeded in court with a ruling to the effect that a telephone conversation was a telegram within the meaning of the Telegraph Act 1869. Independent companies were thereby obliged to obtain licences from the GPO and some thirty-one did.[12] On 13 May, the Telephone Company Ltd. (which held the Bell patents in the UK) and the Edison Telephone Company of London Ltd. amalgamated to form the United Telephone Company of London Ltd.

William Preece, whose words opened this chapter, was Engineer-in-Chief and Electrician of the General Post Office and would receive a knighthood for his services. Reading newspaper articles of the time, it is clear he was well regarded, but perhaps as a champion of the telegraph rather than of the telephone. His obituary, in the *Westminster Gazette* in 1913, hails him as the 'Father of Wireless Telegraphy', pointing to his first 'bridging of the Solent in 1875, the year of Marconi's birth, but also because he made available to Marconi resources to enable him to develop his wireless technology'.[13] The obituary goes on to tell how Preece, as a young man, would attend Faraday's lectures at the Royal Institution. He worked first for the Electric and International Telegraph Company and then for the London and South-Western Railway, thus underscoring the link between telegraph and railways.

The influence of overseas companies in the UK electrical and telephone industry was significant.[14] I have already mentioned BTH and British Westinghouse. In 1903, the Swedish Ericsson entered into a joint venture with the British National Telephone Company; previously it had sold half of its entire output in the UK.

The same was less the case with wireless, although Guglielmo Marconi was from Bologna in Italy. His fascination was with radio waves, and he built on earlier work, by Hertz and others, for his first patent registered in England in 1897. Two years later he founded the Marconi Telegraph Company, again in England.[15] In 1902 in the journal *Science*, W. S. Franklin wrote a letter suggesting very firmly that Marconi's system would not replace submarine cables, and any attempt would lead to 'a state of affairs closely analogous to the confused din of the stock exchange'. Franklin attaches the report in the *London Electrician* journal which recorded the sending of the Morse letter S from Cornwall to St John's Newfoundland on 12 December 1901.[16] Marconi did of course win the argument. Interestingly, the electricity powering the Morse signal was generated by a Hornsby engine.[17]

The way radio developed, following Marconi's patent, makes sense if we realize that the world was already connected, and had been for some decades, by cable. Messages could be sent between inland towns but also overseas, indeed to the other side of the world. The only places that couldn't receive cable messages were ships on the high seas and remote places on land.

Most interesting were ships, especially for the British at that time when the British fleet dominated world trade. Great commercial advantage could be gained by a shipping office being able to contact a cargo ship;

great kudos could be accrued by a transatlantic liner being able to send often trivial messages for its passengers. Marconi realized the potential, and offered a service to ship owners whereby a wireless operator could be provided with full equipment on their ships able to communicate with the shore stations he operated. The perfect monopoly, and, indeed, one initially outside the ambit of the Telegraph Act. The system worked well for larger ships, for the equipment was bulky. It also added to the safety of shipping. In 1912, following the *Titanic* disaster, all British ships over a certain size had to carry radio equipment.[18]

Whilst Britain was dominant in world shipping, it was fast being caught up by Germany who challenged the Marconi monopoly through the merger of two German radio companies into Telefunken. The British and Germans went head to head until eventually a mode of coexistence was found just before the two nations joined in battle. Shipborne radio, though, was here to stay.

Chapter 12

The Great War

'It is safe to say that no English city was so completely absorbed in munitions production as Coventry ... It was not merely a question of adaptability of existing facilities. New factories sprang up in such numbers and on such a scale as to change the whole face of the city in the matter of a few months. New suburbs grew up like mushrooms, thousands of strangers of both sexes flocked to Coventry from all parts of England in answer to the call for munitions.'
The Official Handbook of the City of Coventry,
written shortly after the end of the war

Whilst, in no way wishing to detract from Coventry's proud boast, it is probably true to say that the whole country would eventually flex its muscles in support of the war effort. Perhaps British manufacturing's time had come.

The Britain of August 1914 was worlds apart from that of 1780. There were three very large conurbations: Greater London with 7.2 million people, Manchester and South Lancashire with 2.3 million, and Birmingham and the West Midlands with 1.6 million. It was estimated that over half the towns with more than 50,000 people were near coalfields. A good number were commercial centres, metalworking towns, textile towns or, interestingly, 'resort towns' like Blackpool, Bournemouth, Bath and Brighton, or naval towns like Portsmouth and Plymouth. Some were associated with a particular industry like Stoke-on-Trent with pottery, St Helens with glass, Nottingham with lace, Macclesfield with silk and Burton with brewing.[1] The old staples of textiles, iron and steel, shipbuilding and coal still provided three-quarters of the nation's exports and employed a quarter of the population. The nation was prosperous, but there were warning signs of the progress being made by France, Germany and the USA. Britain's share of world trade had fallen from one-third in 1870 to a seventh in 1914. There was certainly one area in which Britain was emphatically top dog: coal; Britain was the largest exporter of coal in the world – the Saudi Arabia of the early twentieth century, as David Edgerton puts it.[2] As many people dug coal as farmed the land, an astonishing one million in each case. Yet for food, Britain depended on imports brought to these shores on British ships powered by British coal. In contrast, Britain was the biggest importer of oil, having a motor industry second only to that of the USA, which did of course have its own oil reserves. British oil companies came a close second worldwide to those of the USA. We can think of companies such as Burmah Oil, which was the biggest of all British producers, and of course Royal Dutch Shell and the Anglo-Persian oil company which became BP.

Manchester and South Lancashire still had a great many textile mills producing, it was said, enough cloth to clothe half the world's population. In 1913, the industry employed 1.4 million people. The newly built Royal Mill in Manchester alone employed 30,000 and the Calico Printers' Association with 20,000 dominated the market in printed cloth. But there was now more to Manchester: British Westinghouse had a massive presence in Trafford Park by the Manchester Ship Canal, and Ford of America was manufacturing motor cars. There was much else besides. Returning to textiles, it wasn't only home production: Coats, the manufacturer of cotton thread with headquarters in Glasgow, had some 39,000 overseas employees.

Birmingham and the West Midlands still had many small workshops, but also larger plants producing bicycles, motor bikes, and motor cars and lorries. These plants had their suppliers of tyres, engines and electric parts. Aircraft factories were emerging. Rugby had the UK subsidiary of the General Electric of America. A city like Lincoln, with its long agricultural history, had engineers making machinery for the farmers and food producers, although most food was imported.

The coming of war slowly changed this settled scene. Armies needed feeding, not only that of Britain but also the French and Empire soldiers; there was soon a shortage of shipping space. The British government had initially worked on the assumption that the war would be short, but, when it became clear that this was no longer the case, it pushed for increases in home agricultural production, including the 'ploughing up' campaign. Those to suffer were the farmers of South America and Australasia, who had previously supplied so much food, and, in due course, the British domestic consumer faced shortages and eventually rationing. The Ministry of Supply took on the role of ensuring that farmers had the machinery they needed and this had an impact in the factories.

Looking at farm machinery, we are still talking of an agriculture based overwhelmingly on horse power. As I have already mentioned, there was steam power in terms of traction engines and steam-powered threshing machines. The tractor powered by the internal combustion engine was being developed in the USA by Fordson and others.[3] In the UK it was only Sounderson which manufactured such a tractor. These, and imported Fordsons, were put to work in 1917 to address food shortages. Agricultural machinery and motor companies around the country were appointed to distribute and maintain them. The NFU has produced some interesting research on how the nation was fed. From a manufacturing point of view, I noted that by the end of the war, some 6,000 motor tractors were in use.[4]

The war had closed the routes for the importation of German toys, but there were British manufacturers ready to fill the gap, particularly with war-related toys. William Britain had developed a technique for the hollow-casting of toy figures, which lent itself perfectly to all manner of toy soldier. In terms of toy shops, Hamleys had opened their Regent Street store in 1902 and A. W. Gamage in Holborn stocked so many toy soldiers that it became known as the Aldershot of the toy soldier world.[5]

Practically the whole nation became engaged in the war effort one way or another. Women joined the workforce in great numbers, as more and more young men joined the army, all too many going to their deaths. Manufacturing's contribution to the war effort came in essentially four interconnected areas. I put shipbuilding first, but this is followed by a whole raft of industry under the broad heading of the 'controlled establishments' producing literally millions of tons of ammunition and weaponry of all kinds. There are then the aircraft manufacturers and motor companies. Finally, the electrical industry and pharmaceuticals flexed their young muscles in support the war effort.

In the history of shipbuilding in these islands, 1914 marked the end of a remarkably busy and prosperous chapter. Just looking at the transatlantic routes, Swan Hunter merged with Wigham Richardson and, at their Newcastle yard, built for Cunard the *Mauretania* powered by coal but with steam turbines. Not to be outdone, John Brown of

Clydebank built the *Lusitania* and Harland & Wolff in Belfast the trio of the *Olympic, Titanic* and *Britannic*.[6] Alongside this civilian production was the construction of eight dreadnought battleships, giants by any standard with massive 13.5-inch guns. These had been great days for a supremely confident nation.

When war was declared on 3 August 1914, the government published a royal proclamation by which the Admiralty was authorized to requisition any British ship. Shipyards also received notices placing them under Admiralty control for the duration of the war. The impact of this, over the first two years, was an almost complete ending of orders for merchant ships. The *Newcastle Journal* published in the December of each of the war years, and for some years before, a report on shipbuilding undertaken in the North East in the year then ending. The reports for 1914 and 1915 tell how the yards were taken over for navy work but forbidden from publishing the quantity of such work.

As the war progressed losses in the merchant fleet mounted and Lloyd George created the post of Navy Controller to take responsibility for all ship construction. The first holder of the office was Sir Eric Geddes and he, and his successor, Sir Alan Anderson, 'conceived a policy of support for extending shipbuilding facilities'. Slaven puts a figure on this. The number of operational slipways in British yards in 1914 was 580; by 1920 this had increased to 806, a gain of 40 per cent. British yards essentially stopped building for foreign owners, who naturally turned to shipbuilders in non-combatant states, and so the whole British capacity was directed at home consumption whether in the Royal Navy or Mercantile Fleet. This capacity was used to good effect during 1916–18 whilst the Admiralty was still ordering naval ships and the British merchant marine were still replacing ships lost. As I tell in the next chapter, the post-war world was rather different.[7]

In looking at the shipbuilding areas, we should not forget that companies like Vickers, Armstrong, Beardmore and the Coventry Ordnance Works were also making a great many guns for the army. Scott writes, 'Vickers and Armstrongs were gun-makers before they were battleship builders. Whatever may have been the official Admiralty doctrine, a battleship was to them only a means of bringing guns into range, just as her armour was a means of protecting guns and gunners.'[8] Crucially, both companies built 15-inch guns which outclassed the enemy. Vickers built submarines, many heavily armed; Armstrong was the bigger supplier of guns. Their roles were crucial. Nothing though would have been possible without the production of a great deal of steel, and GKN in South Wales was one of the many producers. These were busy places.

Any discussion of British manufacturing and the First World War would be incomplete without the story of the tank. I pondered where to place it in this chapter and decided upon shipbuilding, for it was the Admiralty, rather than the War Office, which championed its development. I, and indeed many others, have written extensively about the tank, so I shall focus here on how its fits within the wider manufacturing story. It begins, I'm pretty sure, in the Lincolnshire town of Grantham. That is of course far from strictly true, since the idea of a military vehicle to carry and protect its occupants is centuries old; the imperative came from the muddy, bloody fields of Flanders where infantrymen were being mowed down in their thousands by machine guns. There were many technical issues to wrestle with, but first and foremost that of just how to navigate muddy land with a heavy vehicle. Hornsby in Grantham manufactured and supplied farm machinery: steam tractors, steam threshers and such like. The problem was that all too often they would get stuck in the mud. The solution conceived by Hornsby was the track, on which the wheels would run, the track being continuously laid and relaid.[9] In 1908, Hornsby produced a 70hp vehicle that ran on chain tracks, and it was demonstrated at the Royal Review showing how well it could cross soft muddy ground; the Prince of Wales was said to have been impressed. This counted for nothing, since the generals did not share his view and declined to take the vehicle any further.

We have to cross the Atlantic to for the next part of the story, since Lincolnshire farmers were possibly too stuck in their ways to see the advantages of tracked vehicles. Not so the Americans and their machinery supplier, Holt. It seems that many engineers in many countries were searching for the truly functional track mechanism. Holt had developed a tracked vehicle and, when this was demonstrated on Thanksgiving Day in 1904, an artist observed that it moved just like a caterpillar. Holt filed a patent with the name Caterpillar and the rest, as they say, is history. Holt still was not satisfied and travelled to England to look at a good number of patents and the one he chose was Hornsby's. Hornsby granted a licence to Holt for the exploitation of their patent in the USA and Canada. Hornsby didn't stop there, but developed their caterpillar track in conjunction with the Lincoln engineer, William Foster, and together made a huge steam-powered tracked vehicle for use in the extreme cold of Dawson City. With the coming of war, Hornsby concentrated on oil and gas engines and left all ideas of the tank to others.

There is a story that Armstrongs were offered the task of developing a tank, but turned it down probably because they were at full stretch with heavy guns. It fell to the talented Lincoln engineer William Tritton to collaborate with the Admiralty to develop a series of tanks, starting with Little Willie and ending up with the Mark VIII which I mention later in this chapter – for which I am indebted to my friend Richard Pullen for his extensive research.[10] Tritton's company, Fosters, was too small to produce all the tanks needed and so production was shared out among a good number of the engineering companies mentioned in this book. It was a British invention and was developed by British manufacturers. As will be seen in the next chapter, it was not then seen as something having much of a future.

The story of the controlled establishments is told by a young American academic, R. J. Q. Adams in his book, *Arms and the Wizard*, the wizard being Lloyd George who set up the Ministry of Munitions which masterminded the whole enterprise.[11] Lloyd George saw, during the winter of 1914/15, that the traditional model of supply for the army through the Woolwich Arsenal was wholly inadequate for a war on an industrial scale. Such a war needed the full power of British industry and people of exceptional ability: Lloyd George's men of 'push and go'. I wrote about the work of the Ministry of Munitions in my book, *Ordnance*. There are, however, two names of particular significance later in this story: Eric Geddes and George Beharrell. Geddes, whom I have already mentioned, was a railway man, as was Beharrell who was also a statistician of great repute. Their contribution to the war effort was immense in munitions but also in transport and the Royal Navy.[12] They undertook vital roles in the Ministry of Munitions.

A key aspect of the work of the ministry was the manufacture of ammunition, and a key part of the process was the manufacture of nitrates needed for explosives. In my earlier research, I focused on shell-filling because my maternal grandfather had worked as a supervisor in the massive shell-filling factory at Chilwell. I had read about Viscount Chetwynd (the founder of Chilwell) and how he had researched various methods of filling shells. In particular, he explored the percentage mix of the constituent parts (ammonium nitrate, or amatol, and TNT).

His research led him to Northwich and the ammonium nitrate factory of Brunner Mond.

Carol Kennedy puts flesh on the bare bones of the story, but begins one step earlier. In my chapter on the home, I noted that Germany, in effect, had a worldwide monopoly on the production of synthetic dyes, crucially khaki dye. Kennedy tells how the government appointed the distinguished scientist and lawyer, Lord Moulton, to bring together such dyestuff manufacturing that there was in Britain to clothe the army. It took until 1919 for British Dyestuffs Corporation to come into being, although in the meantime individual companies had together produced the necessary supplies with one major problem: dyes were made from coal tar, as was TNT and the demand for the latter was insatiable. The alternative mix with amatol solved the problem and Brunner Mond set about producing massive quantities of ammonium nitrate.[13] Another major producer of explosive was the cordite factory specifically built for war production at Gretna just outside Gretna Green on the Scottish border where some 30,000, mainly women, worked.

The young British chemical industry met other needs of the armed forces: chemical weapons themselves, but also chemicals with other uses. The fuselages of aeroplanes were largely covered with fabric which needed to be stiffened and waterproofed by a liquid known as dope. (I am sure that readers will share with me the memory of using dope on model aeroplanes in our childhoods.) Britain was less favourably placed in 1914, for the three dope producers in the world were based in Germany, France and Switzerland. Camille and Henry Dreyfus were persuaded to come over from Switzerland to Spondon near Derby where they set up British Cellulose & Chemical Manufacturing Company. Cellulose acetate (dope) was produced from April 1917.

As to the controlled establishments more generally, their extent was vast, encompassing factories newly built by government and a very great many factories taken over for war production. Millions of men and women worked in them. Shell-filling factories were formed in many parts of the country: Woolwich, Chilwell, Glasgow, Liverpool, Leeds, Banbury, Morecombe, Pombrey, Abbey Wood, Horley, Devonport and Hereford; as were factories producing cartridges: Woolwich, Glasgow, Liverpool, Leeds, Gloucester and Hayes; and fuses and tubes: Woolwich, Perivale, Abbey Wood, Southwark, Hayes, Elswick, Coventry and Cardonald.[14] Elsewhere, as the war progressed, the ministry would arrange to manufacture or would contract for heavy artillery, gauges, optical glass, shell steel, lumber products, anti-personnel chemicals and many other warlike stores. Towns and cities throughout the country joined in the war effort. As I told at the beginning of the chapter, Coventry claims a particular place in this. It had some sixty government-controlled or -owned establishments which together produced 300,000 tons of munitions; the Coventry Ordnance Works alone produced 40,000 tons including sixty-six heavy guns. Daimler put out 100,000 tons of shell castings. Eight hundred new houses and hostels were built.[15]

In relation to British manufacturing more generally, essentially the whole of the controlled establishment infrastructure disappeared with the coming of peace, as women were sent back to their kitchens or poorly paid work and returning soldiers were found jobs in civilian industry. Yet, it would be wrong to say they left no legacy. Women would return to the workplace in greater numbers when the world again went to war, and, thereafter, would take their rightful place in manufacturing. Working conditions had improved; a million workers enjoyed works canteens as a result of the war. Wages had increased. Militancy had found its voice.

Aircraft production was something new, and the war years saw rapid technical advances. The Royal Aircraft Factory (later the Royal Aircraft Establishment) at Farnborough played a key role in design, and also manufacture, but very much alongside private industry. J. D. Scott offers a flavour, when he writes of the 'Factory' at last inviting 'the trade' to come up with designs of aircraft in October 1915.[16] He tempers this by explaining that the Royal Aircraft Factory's early role had been one of desperately trying to impose standards, not least for safety, in a young industry where designers were very much adventure seekers. The Factory had therefore initially taken on itself the job of designing, but allowing some private companies to manufacturer from their designs. At the beginning of the war, it was all about reconnaissance aircraft, but after a year or so, there appeared a specific role for both fighters and bombers.

Like all the companies listed, the Factory produced a good number of experimental designs, only very few of which emerged into long-term production. Throughout the war, German and British engineers were competing, and, with each leap forward in design, many older planes would become obsolete overnight, relegated to training duties. Each company played their particular part, and many of the names we now remember made their claim to iconic status. I am again indebted to Peter Dancy for his extensive research.[17]

Geoffrey de Havilland joined The Aircraft Manufacturing Co. Ltd. (Airco) at Hendon in North London in June 1914, and first designed a two-seater reconnaissance biplane powered by a 70hp Renault engine, which was later replaced by an engine of 120hp made by Beardmore. De Havilland's highly successful twin-engine day bomber, the DH.4, made its first flight in 1916. Altogether, 6,300 were built in the UK and 4,800 were manufactured under licence in the USA where a number were fitted with the American 12-cylinder Liberty engine, which also powered the Liberty tank. This aircraft notched up over 111,000 miles, an astonishing feat. Of interest, in the context of British manufacturing, are the number of companies who were involved in building DH planes under subcontract: Darracq Motor Engineering (London, but which had originated in Paris), British Caudron (Cricklewood and Alloa), Marsh, Jones & Cribb (Leeds), Grahame-White Aviation (Hendon), Gloucestershire Aircraft, Harland & Wolff, Kingsbury Aviation (London), Morgan & Co., Ramsome Sims & Jeffries and Savages.

Avro, in Manchester, built on the success of its Type 500 biplane and produced 8,340 Avro 504 biplanes in the First World War. It was the first British bomber to undertake a bombing raid. In order to meet the volume of production being demanded, Avro built new factories at Miles Platting, Failsworth, Hamble and Newton Heath. The Bristol company's Frank Barnwell designed a two-seat fighter in March 1916. Experiments were made with 120 and 150hp engines, until a Rolls-Royce Falcon of 190hp was tried with excellent results. Some 4,747 examples were built by September 1919. Fairey Aviation, at Hayes in Middlesex, was formed in the summer of 1915 of the war by electrical engineer, C. R. Fairey. It initially produced the Short seaplane and Sopwith Strutter, but then went on to design its own biplanes and seaplanes which would come into their own after the war. The Handley Page pre-war development work on its O/100 bomber continued at Harrow in North London, and found fruition in the O/400 which had two Rolls-Royce 360hp Eagle VIII engines. Some 400 were built and led to the first civil transport planes after the war. From Rochester Short Brothers' most successful aircraft of the First World War was its two-seat reconnaissance bombing and torpedo-carrying seaplane, the type 184. This was powered initially by a Sunbeam 225hp engine, later upgraded to 260hp and finally to a 275hp Sunbeam Maori III. Some 900 of these were built.

Sopwith Aviation, of Kingston upon Thames, is perhaps the most iconic of the First World War aircraft makers, and the Sopwith Camel fighter the most successful fighter, with some 5,825 built. Many were subcontracted, with over 1,000 being built by Ruston & Proctor in Lincoln, with further examples produced by fellow Lincoln engineering companies, Robey & Co. and Clayton & Shuttleworth.[18] Claytons also made the Handley Page O/400. It wasn't only the Camel that Sopwith provided for the war effort, but also seaplanes, the Sopwith Baby, Strutter and Snipe to name but a few.

Ruston & Proctor, along with many engineering companies across the country, set their hands to all manner of war work. These ranged from hydrogen generators for inflating barrage balloons to horseshoes and baling machines for compressing and trussing hay for the millions of horses used by the army. Of more conventional military equipment, they produced wagons and carriages for shells and machine guns, many thousands of wheels, gun mountings and shell cases. They also worked with fellow Lincoln engineer, Fosters, on tank engines, trailers and sponsons.[19] Perhaps their most significant contribution was in the field of mines where their paravane mine-sweeping device enabled the navy, safely, to destroy a great many enemy mines. Possibly more than anything, there was never a question of keeping designs to themselves – they were open for the nation to use.

Turning now to the heavy engineers, Sir W. G. Armstrong Whitworth & Co. Ltd. moved into aircraft production, building Royal Aircraft Factory-designed fighters at the Elswick works. No great volume of production followed. Beardmore became involved in aircraft production when, in late 1914, it acquired the licence to manufacture Austro-Daimler engines. It later worked as a subcontractor for Sopwith Pup biplane fighters.

Vickers built reconnaissance aircraft under contract for the Royal Aircraft Factory. These were followed by fighter scouts. Vickers factories were close to London, and the largest at Weybridge was, in 1917, producing thirty aircraft a week. This was ground-breaking at a time when total aircraft production was also reaching new levels. Vickers accepted with relish the challenge to come up with their own designs. Scott focuses in particular on the problem of synchronizing machine guns with propellers, such that the one could fire through the other. The Germans achieved this with the Fokker, but, in time, Vickers produced a machine gun which was put into production on the Sopwith 1½ Strutter.[20] Vickers' other significant contribution was with heavy bombers, these leading to the design of the Vickers Vimy which was eventually powered by the Rolls-Royce Eagle engine to great effect. Under Vickers' ownership, as well as wheeled vehicles, Wolseley would contribute to the war effort by developing and producing aero engines, most notably the Viper, some three million shells and also firing gear and gunsights for the Royal Navy.[21]

The rest of the motor industry too was to play its part. In the summer of 1914, it had soon become clear that there were insufficient vehicles for the army and so impressment officers were sent out with a list of suitable vehicles to be pressed into service. The motor companies themselves were forbidden to provide vehicles for civilian use, and had instead to concentrate their production on vehicles of approved military types.

D. Napier & Son manufactured some 2,000 trucks and ambulances, but their main focus was on aero engines. They began by building as subcontractors for Sunbeam and the Royal Aircraft Factory, but then pursued their own design which resulted in the twelve-cylinder Napier Lion which went on in the 1920s to power Malcolm Campbell's Bluebird in the land speed record attempts. [22]

Albion, like other British motor companies, had their stock of 32hp vehicles requisitioned and all future production impressed. With the likelihood of further demands, the directors decided on an expansion of their new factory. There were problems ahead. There simply were not enough skilled male engineers to meet the demands of production, and those there were resisted the employment of lesser-skilled workers. Albion thus shared in the industrial unrest that hit Beardmore and other Clyde engineers. Skilled men in the shipbuilding industry were struggling to protect their livelihoods, which they saw as under attack by a government which was seeking to bring in unskilled men and women to replace the men who had gone to fight. The 'Dilution scheme', as it was called, was eventually accepted, with able men released to the colours and women introduced to the workforce. Albion production of War Office vehicles increased each year from 591 in 1914 to 1,843 in 1918, giving a total wartime production of 5,594.[23]

Daimler, under designer Frank Searle, produced a three-ton lorry to War Office specification. The familiar requisitioning of stock and

Right: The Burrell steam engine. (With thanks to Jim Newton)

Below: Derwent Silk Mill. (With thanks to Derby Museums)

Above: Salts Mill.
(With thanks to Salts
Mill Books)

Left: Steam crane.
(With thanks to Jim
Newton)

Right: Weedon Central Ordnance Depot.

Below: Cadbury cricket pavillion at Bourneville.

Lincoln Drill Hall given
by Joseph Ruston.

Statue of Liberty
powered by Ruston
& Hornsby.

Above: Manmade waterfall at Chatsworth, home to the Duke of Devonshire.

Below: Princess Elizabeth visits Norwich as part of the Festival of Britain, 1951.
(With permission of Rootes Archive Trust)

Above: 1907 oil-burning, steam-driven tracked vehicle. (RLC archive)

Below: Chilwell shell filling factory, 1917.

Above: Inside the Chilwell shell filling factory, 1917.

Below: Ruston & Hornsby factories in Lincoln. (With thanks to Phil Crow)

Above: Humber 14/40, 1927. (With permission of the Rootes Archive Trust)

Below: Mk IV tanks being built at Fosters in early 1917. (With thanks to Richard Pullen)

The choice of men who know most about cars **HUMBER**

HUMBER LTD., COVENTRY. London Showrooms and Export Dept., ROOTES LTD., DEVONSHIRE, LONDON, W.1. London Service Depot, Somerton Road, Cricklewood, N.W.2

Right: Humber advertisement.

Below: Geneva Motor Show, 1949. (With permission of Rootes Archive Trust)

Left and below: Blade Cross and Weisse & Son, The Strand. (Both images with kind permission of John Weiss & Son)

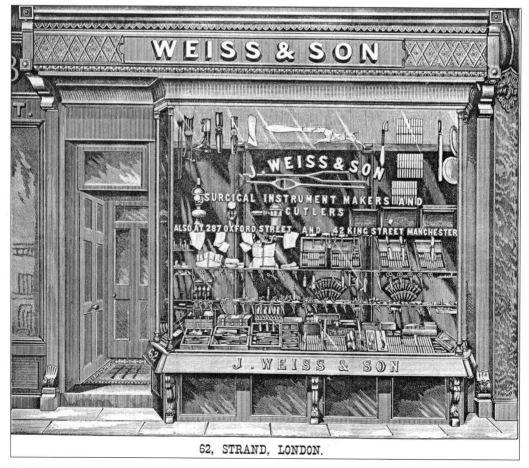

Right: Ruston & Hornsby in
the Bressay Lighthouse.

Below: Mark 1 scout car.
(With permission of the
Rootes Archive Trust)

Bittern (sister of the Mallard) in Lincoln. (With thanks to Jim Newton)

Flying Scotsman. (With thanks to Jim Newton)

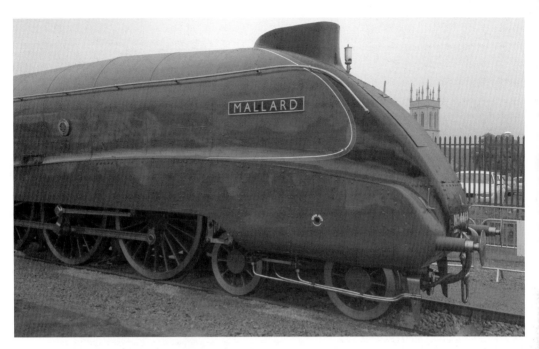

The Mallard at Grantham Station.

A toy First World War tank.

Above: Rolls-Royce used by General Montgomery in Normandy in 1944. (With thanks to the RLC Archive)

Left: Celanese House reproduced from a 1951 desk diary.

BRITISH CELANESE LIMITED
Textiles, Plastics, Chemicals
CELANESE HOUSE · HANOVER SQUARE · LONDON · W.1.

Above: Hillman Minx. (With permission of the Rootes Archive Trust)

Below: Hillman Minx loading at London Docks. (With permission of Rootes Archive Trust)

Central Ordnance Depot Old Dalby, still in use as an industrial estate.

Lincoln Cathedral celebration of manufacturing with a Ruston & Hornsby car.

impressing of future production occurred and Daimler joined in the war effort. Daimler had developed a 105hp engine which had been significantly improved by the skills of their consultant engineer, Fredrick Lanchester, whose former company would produce much for the war effort including the 4x2 armoured car. The Daimler 105hp would go on to power heavy-duty track-laying tractors in conjunction with Fosters of Lincoln, and also the first tank. Frank Searle would serve with distinction in the Tank Corps. Daimler would also produce staff cars and ambulances. The Daimler engine was used in the AEC truck chassis for War Office work.[24]

AEC, in Southall in West London, was another example of the intricate web of the motor industry. The Associated Equipment Co. Ltd. was registered on 13 June 1912 and took over the already busy bus chassis manufacturing business from its then owner, the London General Omnibus Company Ltd. In 1914, LGOC suffered the same fate as other vehicle manufacturers and operators, when 1,185 of its buses were pressed into use and were soon seen transporting troops in France and Belgium. AEC began producing on its own account in June 1916, and, by the end of the war, had supplied 5,200 heavy-duty three-ton vehicles using the Tyler engine.[25]

Thornycroft, in Basingstoke, developed a petrol-driven vehicle, its 'J' type lorry becoming the most popular. This particular type found other uses, including having an anti-aircraft gun mounted on its back.[26] Some 5,000 vehicles were supplied to the army in the war. Crossley was a Manchester company which made high-quality vehicles ranging from saloons used by royalty, to buses and haulage vehicles.[27] In the Great War, it made a name for itself principally with the provision of vehicles for the Royal Flying Corps. Leyland Motors came out of the Lancashire Steam Motor company and, in the Great War, as with Crossley, made most of its vehicles for the Royal Flying Corps. Scammell originated not far from Liverpool Street station in London where its vehicles served the local markets. It manufactured gun carriages and vehicle bodywork for the War Office.[28]

Vauxhall in Luton began the war years with its much-loved 3-litre C-type, a powerful, comfortable and technically advanced car capable also of sporting performance. For war service, though, it was the D-type that was adopted as the staff car of choice and the A-type adapted for field ambulances. The factory was extended and the company also produced shell caps and fuses.[29]

For the Humber Company, the coming of war did 'not immediately bring car production to a halt and full catalogue was produced for 1915'. With the general move away from civilian production, 'warlike' options were produced in the form of delivery vans using the 10hp and 11hp engines and ambulances with the larger 14hp. In Humber's case another iconic name and aircraft production come into play. W. O. Bentley had been working with British engine builder Gwynne who had produced a successful rotary engine, but which was compromised by its propensity to overheat. Bentley proposed the use of aluminium pistons, but Gwynne were unconvinced. Not so Humber who employed him, and with whom they produced many engines for the war effort. Demaus and Tarring reveal a little more of the Bentley/ Humber relationship. In his autobiography, W. O. Bentley recalled that he was summoned by the powers that be because the senior management at Humber were concerned that the war work they had been given did not take advantage of their technical skills or factory facilities. Clearly this worked, for 'under W. O., Humber produced many engines of his rotary design and also complete aircraft including the Avro 504'.[30]

Commercial Cars Limited produced field workshop vehicles, and, for the Red Cross, ambulances. In 1926, The Humber Motor Company would take control of the company and change its name to Commer Cars Limited. Karrier, another of the companies which, with Humber and Commer, would become the Rootes Group, produced a ¾ tonner, and some 3,000 were produced for the services. The Vulcan Motor Company produced some 100 chassis a week for the War Office from their factory at Southport. Vulcan production was eventually taken over by Tilling Stevens at Maidstone whose factory would also become part of the Rootes Group in 1952.[31]

It wasn't just vehicles: during the war the Austin Motor Company produced eight million shells and 650 guns as well as 2,000 aeroplanes, 500 armoured cars and other equipment such as generating sets, pumping equipment, aeroplane engines, ambulances and lorries.[32] William Morris had acquired further premises in Cowley, and built a steel extension giving him a large area in which to assemble cars. Unfortunately, for Morris, the war meant that demand for cars would be strictly limited and so, over the war years, he made only 1,300 cars, yet still honouring his American contract for the supply of engines. This placed him in a precarious position, and he sought War Office work. He was first awarded a contract for Stokes Mortar bomb cases. The success of this led him to be asked to manufacture mine sinkers. Here the space he had available came into its own, and he assembled these devices from parts supplied, and in large numbers, reaching 2,000 per week. The original supplier had offered an upper limit of forty.[33]

Rolls-Royce, which had achieved great success with its Silver Ghost hailed as 'the best car in the world', turned its significant expertise to the production of aero engines, producing the Eagle and the Falcon. The Eagle also powered the first transatlantic flight and the first flight from England to Australia.[34] The superior engineering of the engines enhanced further the company's reputation for excellence. Royce was suffering from ill health and had to remove himself from Derby to his home in the south of England. Here, company engineers would visit him and take instructions. It was clearly an effective way of working, for the chassis of the Silver Ghost proved highly suitable for armoured cars and staff cars. The king also dispensed with the Daimler he had previously used and took to being driven in a Silver Ghost.[35]

Harry Lucas was keen to provide motor companies with what they needed for the war effort. A major problem was that the War Office had specified Bosch magnetos for their vehicles. The components industry pre-war had been content with this, and the ability of British companies to supply magnetos was strictly limited. One company in particular, Thomson Bennett, rose to the challenge. Harry Lucas pounced when, in 1914, the opportunity arose to purchase it. This was going to prove of massive value to Lucas in the years to come, not least in the person of Peter Bennett. During the war, Lucas grew to some 4,000 employees, 1,200 of whom were making magnetos.[36]

Triplex Safety Glass had found few followers among Edwardian motorists. The value of glass that would not shatter was seen more readily when bullets and shrapnel were flying all around. Reginald Delpech therefore found takers for his laminated glass in aeroplane manufacturers for windscreens and airmen's goggles, but also for gasmasks and bulletproof glass.

Dunlop was also a company much in demand and in 1916 completed construction of its iconic factory, Fort Dunlop, in Birmingham. Just six years earlier it had completed the planting of 50,000 acres of rubber plantations in Malaya and had bought cotton mills in Rochdale to bring under single ownership the essentials of tyre manufacture. Under the guidance of Harvey du Cros, it had set up subsidiary and associated companies in a number of overseas territories. At home it was fiercely patriotic and encouraged service in the Territorial Army and, once war was declared, the service of its employees in the army. It prided itself on being a good employer and gained a loyal workforce. It played its part in the development of the tank with rubber for the wheels inside the tank tracks. George and William du Cros served in the army despite being over military age. The company gave fleets of ambulances to the nation.[37]

The motor cycle certainly ranked higher in supply volumes than its four-wheeled counterpart. Its use by the army was principally by despatch riders, but there were others. The Douglas Company manufactured 25,000 motor cycles for army use.[38] Triumph supplied a further 30,000. The Birmingham Small Arms Company had a total involvement in war production, since it produced both the Enfield rifle and the Lewis gun. The company was also producing bicycles, motor cycles and, indeed, a motor car.

The rail network was vital in transporting goods and troops around the country. In 1914, the network comprised over 100 companies and these were brought under temporary government control for the duration of the conflict. Railway locomotive manufacturers rose to the challenge. The Vulcan Foundry had produced 3,000 locomotives by 1914. During the war it turned its attention to shell production, gun mountings and paravanes. The North British Locomotive Company had come into being in 1903 from the combination of the three older companies, and, by 1914, had produced 5,000 locomotives. During the war it would produce a further 1,400. In 1918, it manufactured the prototype of the British/American Mk VIII tank.

The electricity industry in the form of telegraph, telephone and wireless telegraph also had an important role to play. At the start of the war, signals were still the remit of Royal Engineers in their Signal Service, with some 6,000 officers and men. The principal means of communication to begin with was the telegraph, but increasingly this was supplemented by telephone and motorbike despatch riders. It was not just communication between the front line and headquarters, but also the coordination of attacks between infantry, artillery, aircraft and mechanized units.[39] The equipment in use was produced by the Marconi Company but also by British Thomson-Houston, Westinghouse, GEC and others. It was relatively complex, relying on valves and needing two sources of power. At the end of the war there were some 70,000 signallers, and in 1920 the Royal Corps of Signals was formed.

GEC under Hugo Hirst came into its own during the war supplying lamps and motors for ships, arc generators for wireless sets, cables and electrical instruments for telephones and carbons for searchlights. It was also able to acquire the whole of Osram which previously it had only part-owned.[40]

Siemens Brothers at Woolwich had been producing telephone equipment alongside cables and so was likely to be called upon to supply the army. There was a problem. Siemens Brothers and Siemens & Halske in Germany had cross shareholdings, but also a very close working relationship; all this had to come to an end. More than this, there was very public antipathy towards Siemens and the few German nationals it employed. Action was taken and the controlling German interest became the property of the government and a 'supervisor' was appointed to oversee the actions of the board. Scott tells how the person appointed, Frederic Young, 'judged the relationship perfectly' and so the company was able to function without damaging tensions. It produced a large number of field telephones and many miles of cable. The Dynamo Works produced switchgear, but also shell cases. There was also valuable research work including bulbs for the O. L. daylight signalling lamp invented by Oliver Lucas, and bulbs for the lamp invented by A. C. W. Aldis.[41]

A lesson, painfully learnt in the Crimea, was the necessity of proper medical provision. The Royal Army Medical Corps had been formed, and doctors and nurses were trained at the Royal Victoria Military Hospital, yet they needed supplies of medicines. Britain had been importing synthetic medicines from Germany, but now they had to be produced at home. The Boots Company rose to the challenge, and Jesse Boot brought together a team of scientists who produced medicines such as aspirin for the home market but also for the army.[42] Boots became 'the main government supplier for vermin powder, anti-gas cream, water sterilizer, anti-fly cream (flies were a big problem on the front). Also, iodine tubes, matchless tinder lighters, peppermint, compressed medicines, quinine'. Burroughs, Wellcome & Co. supplied 'aspirin, chloroform (from alcohol), cholesterol, cocaine, emetine bismuthous iodide, flavine, hydroquinone, lanoline and phenacetin'.[43]

The provision to the army of appropriate clothing was another huge challenge. Pimlico, near Victorian Station, was where army clothing production and distribution was centralized. In an article on clothing the army, Catherine Rowe-Price makes the important point that the choice of further depots in places like Leeds made sense because they were near Bradford and other places where the cloth was woven and the uniforms made up. The trench coat would become associated with the First World War.[44] For these, Burberry used their patented Gaberdine waterproof material, and Aquascutum, the waterproof cloth that they had patented. The cotton mills of Lancashire maintained their pre-war level of production with a workforce in 1914 of over 600,000. The rationale behind this was that the war was going to be short and Britain's role would be that of armourer funded by its export earnings from textiles. As is clear, this is not what happened. What is odd is that the mills didn't shed labour to where it was needed in the forces and armament factories. This was to be yet another challenge for the post-war world.[45]

The task of feeding the troops was enormous, but, given the static nature of trench warfare, was largely managed by the installation of kitchens behind the lines cooking fresh or frozen meat shipped daily from England. There were large bakeries in Calais and elsewhere. The volume of preprepared or manufactured food was relatively small. There were the biscuit manufacturers, the fabled Machonochie stew, chocolate and cigarettes but little else. Glaxo made its contribution to the war effort by greatly increasing its production of dried milk. It had, by 1914, become the brand leader in the UK, supplying dried milk from their factories in New Zealand but also from one established in the Calvados region of Normandy.[46] At home food was more and more home grown, but food manufacturing was on its way.[47] Elsewhere in the home, Lever Brothers were making 135,000 tons of soap a year, vital for the war effort. The company acquired Pears Soap in 1917. Many Lever employees went to war with the guarantee of a job on their return.

Looking at the nation's account books, in 1914 there were gold reserves, gold mined in colonies and investments overseas. One and a half centuries of industrial growth, when Britain was the workshop of the world, had built up substantial resources. The war came at a great economic and human cost: some £11,325 million was spent, including loans to Russia which were never repaid. About one-third was raised through taxation, £500 million from the sale of investments, but the bulk from borrowing; the national debt increased from £650 million to £8,000 million, and £1,300 million was borrowed from overseas, mainly the USA.[48]

It was a much-weakened Britain that emerged from the war.

Chapter 13

The Aftermath of War

'"Terribly cold," he recorded in his diary. "Frightful landscape of slagheaps and belching chimneys. A few rats running through the snow, very tame, presumably weak with hunger. The mill girls, scurrying to work in their clogs down the cobbled streets, sounded to him "like an army hurrying into battle".'

The diaries of George Orwell, referring to the research
he carried out for his book, *The Road to Wigan Pier*

Thousands of soldiers had come back from the horror of the trenches to a country fit for heroes. Hopes were high. Hopes too for those women who, for the first time, had discovered their own identity in the workplace. They were both met by the Spanish flu which, worldwide, killed more than the trenches had managed. The country they returned to was much as before, or was it?

Industrial capacity had increased, in many cases dramatically. As we have already seen, shipyards had many more births, the new motor industry had built new factories, as had the aircraft manufacturers. Men were de-mobbed and many returned to their old jobs, and the women, who had been doing those jobs so well, had to return to their kitchens.

Looking at the economy, the immediate postwar years witnessed a release of pent-up demand.[2] The shipyards completed ships, the motor companies returned their attention to the domestic market, the aircraft manufacturers looked at what a peacetime market for air travel could be like. The electricity industry witnessed a strong demand for its products. Siemens posted good profits in 1920, demand for cable was strong and they saw growing demand for telephones, certainly in the near future.[3] Even the textile industry, which had languished with wartime restrictions on international trade, saw promise in the post-war world; Lancashire witnessed a 'craze of speculation in cotton', as mills changed hands.[4]

By 1921, the euphoria had died down, demand slumped and companies were laying off workers by the thousand. Cotton exports in 1922 were half of those in 1913, and consumption of raw cotton decreased in line. Coal exports were only a third of prewar levels. By June 1921, two million people were unemployed. The problem was the 'old staples' of textiles, coal, iron and steel, and shipbuilding.

Cotton had maintained a steady level of production during the war, but the 1920s saw a collapse of export markets – India fell by 90 per cent between 1918 and 1939 – and a growth in competition from lower-cost countries, Japan in particular. The Lancashire cotton business still remained fragmented, with merchants, spinners, weavers and finishers. What was needed was rationalization, but the owners were reluctant to act themselves; successive governments didn't want to intervene for fear that subsidies would be demanded.[5] At the initiative of the Bank of England, the Lancashire Cotton Corporation (LCC) was formed in 1929 to try to merge some of the many hundreds of spinning companies operating millions of spindles. It was very much an uphill task and the industry continued to decline. LCC was eventually taken over by Courtaulds in 1962.

One very obvious source of difficulty in the post-war world was what was to be done with the huge armaments industry. The scale of war production had been massive. The demands, particularly of trench warfare, had led to the creation of an astonishing network of companies and works devoted principally to the production of ammunition and all that went with it. There were thus projectile factories, explosives factories, fuse factories and shell-filling factories. Some were privately owned, some in various kinds of partnership with the Ministry of Munitions and some owned and run by the ministry.

The coming of peace meant that the demands on these establishments ceased, and, by 1921, only a handful were still active including the Woolwich Arsenal, the Small Arms Factory at Enfield and the Explosives Factory at Waltham Abbey. Ian Hay, the writer of *R.O.F.: The Story of the Royal Ordnance Factories, 1939–48*, expresses shock at the rashness of this action.[6] When I read it, I found myself nodding, but then it became clear: of course, most would be closed, the need had gone; there would never be another war demanding weaponry on that scale. The factories that remained open ticked over supplying the services with what they needed. This is an important point for, certainly in terms of ammunition, it was all three services which were supplied.

G. I. Brown tells of the possibly even bigger challenge facing explosive manufacturers both in Britain but also in Germany. Britain had fifty-four companies with ninety-three factories and these were all brought together into Explosive Trades Limited which, in 1920, changed its name to Nobel Industries Ltd. In Germany much the same happened with the formation of the gigantic I. G. Farbenindustrie A/G.

It wasn't just the 'controlled establishments', it was also those heavy engineering companies that had thrown their weight into armaments, particularly Vickers and Armstrongs. J. D. Scott describes the attempts the managements of both companies made to address what was a huge hole in their business. In both cases, it was diversification.

Forward-looking companies, including those in the new electrical industries, were looking for strategic partners better to take advantage of the prosperity that peace would bring. The Metropolitan Carriage Company bought, out of administration in 1917, British Westinghouse, which amongst much else produced electric railway locomotives. Metropolitan Carriage, under their charismatic chairman, Dudley Docker, had grown a business, from one which had operated horse-drawn carriages between London and Birmingham, into a significant company manufacturing rolling stock for the railways.

During the First World War, all Britain's rail, rolling stock and staff had been administered as a single unit. The Railway Act of 1921 provided for a rationalization of the railways whereby the 130 or so separate companies were reorganized into four regional groups: Southern, Great Western, London North Eastern, London Midland and Scottish. The names Geddes and Beharrell once again come to be mentioned for it was they who carried out the review that led to this rationalization. Historically, the companies had produced many of their own locomotives and much of their rolling stock in their own workshops.[7] Metropolitan Carriage was an exception in producing passenger carriages both for the home market and for export. Its directors saw a promising future.

Vickers saw the attraction of electrical power, and Docker persuaded Douglas Vickers of the attraction of Metropolitan Carriage. The following year, Vickers bought the business, thereby creating Metropolitan Vickers. This large company had its focus on electrical power generation and electric traction, both perceived to be growth sectors. The problem for Vickers was that they had paid £13 million for a business thought to be worth between £7 and £10 million. The downturn in the economy then prevented the new company from making money, whilst most of Vickers existing businesses, including shipbuilding and Wolseley, were facing empty order books.[8] It was a challenging time.

Armstrongs pursued a different and rather unusual route to diversification in taking on a project to construct the Newfoundland Paper Mills.[9] This project would use the company's capacity in shipbuilding and in the provision of turbines and heavy machinery for the mills. It was, though, all at Armstrongs' risk and demanded the raising of capital. As with Vickers, all this was taking place when the state of the economy was dire. A review was carried out, the outcome of which was a recommendation to merge and create a new company, Vickers-Armstrong, which would carry on the naval shipbuilding and armaments business. The Newfoundland project was sold to International Paper Company. Wolseley was sold to W. R. Morris.

Vickers' controlling interest in Metropolitan Vickers was sold to the American General Electric Company. Metropolitan Vickers then acquired British Thomson-Houston Limited, Edison & Swan Electrical Co. Ltd. And in 1928 its name was changed to Associated Electrical Industries Ltd. (AEI). The name Metropolitan Vickers Electrical Limited continued as a subsidiary company.

The Metropolitan-Cammell Carriage, Wagon & Finance Co. Ltd. was created to take over the rolling stock interests of Vickers and Cammell-Laird and was held equally by Vickers and Cammell-Laird. The English Steel Corporation was formed to take over the Sheffield and Oppenshaw works of Vickers and the stamping department of Elswick. This company was then owned by Vickers-Armstrong with Cammell-Laird holding a significant minority.[10]

The reorganized Vickers/Armstrong companies had rough water to navigate before rearmament brought orders in sufficient numbers. The Barrow yard was fortunate to be considered by the navy as the one yard apart from Chatham where submarines and other major naval vessels could be built, so that, although orders were few, there were orders. Vickers-Armstrong was now unashamedly an armaments company and in the 1920s continued to manufacture tanks, albeit in small numbers. It acquired patents for tracked vehicles from Carden Lloyd, and moved the manufacture of these and the tanks to Elswick. They didn't thrive, but they survived.

Metropolitan-Cammell found that the market for rolling stock had shrunk, both at home and abroad where domestic producers were taking what orders there were. The company was liquidated and a new company formed.

The fate of English Steel was less dramatic, for Charles Craven, already managing director of Vickers-Armstrong, took over as managing director of the Sheffield works and spent £1.5 million on modernization. This had an immediate impact when the market began to recover in 1934. As I say, Vickers-Armstrong had survived and, as I tell below, it also pursued its ambitions in aviation.

Many other companies entered the post-war years with trepidation. Ruston & Proctor and Richard Hornsby & Co had both served their country with distinction. Hornsby maintained its good reputation for its 'diesel' engine, but its management was aware that it needed to find a strong partner, and so they approached Rustons who, at first, were not interested. It seems, though, that the Hornsby reputation and team of skilled engineers appeared increasingly attractive as the reality of the postwar world became clear, and so it agreed to merge: Ruston & Hornsby was born. To begin with, it was busy with Hornsby oil engines, Ruston's own oil engines, but also their traditional steam engines and, of course, road-making and agricultural machinery. The post-war recession then hit hard. At the end of the war, Rustons had employed 10,000 people and Hornsby a further 3,000. In 1921 the workforce of the combined business had shrunk to 4,750.[11] They weathered the economic storm and, at the end of the 1920s, Rustons were expanding their production of earth-moving equipment and saw the need to add to their range, which they did by forming Ruston Bucyrus with the American company, Bucyrus, which had supplied diggers for the Panama Canal. The next alliance was with British engine-builder, Paxman, which built the first diesel engine for use in locomotives in Britain.

Returning to the bigger economic picture immediately post war, as well as unused armament production, there was chronic overcapacity in the shipyards: in 1918, there were 816 berths where new ships could be built, where, in 1914, there had been only 580. In the immediate aftermath of war, this overcapacity was not particularly apparent as yards were already busy completing orders, which contributed to the short-lived post-war boom. Once the ships were launched, the yards fell silent. The reasons were many and interrelated.[12]

Britain's preeminence in shipping had been hit during the war by its need to focus on naval production and replacing ships in the merchant fleet.

127

This focus meant that the worldwide demand for merchant shipping was now being met by yards in what we might view as emerging nations: the USA, but also Norway, Sweden, the Netherlands and Japan. Whilst a huge tonnage of merchant shipping had been lost in the war years, much had been replaced by these overseas yards. These merchant fleets of other flags now carried an increasing share of world trade, reducing the proportion carried by British ships. If foreign buyers approached British yards, those yards, carrying a weighty overhead in excess capacity, would be unable to compete on price and so would fail to win orders. British yards thus saw reduced merchant demand. The post-war treaties on naval power meant that the Royal Navy itself was restricted in the number of ships it could order, and, of course, it would give first option to its own Royal Naval Yards. The net effect was that British yards had both far greater capacity than they needed and very little in the way of orders to fill it.

The result was chronic unemployment. In 1921, when the economy as whole faltered, the shipbuilding and repairing yards were returning figures of 33 per cent unemployment in 1922, rising to 43 per cent in 1926.

The next level of difficulty facing British yards was technological. The world was moving from coal to oil, and British shipbuilding was overwhelmingly geared to coal. It was very good at it. Its marine engineers were top class, especially with steam turbine engines favoured by passenger liners and the Royal Navy. The smaller yards were also very good at building colliers, but with a dramatic reduction in coal exports, these were no longer required. The ships of the 1920s were more and more either oil-burning steam or diesel engined. More so, the colliers had been replaced by oil tankers which not only were about twice the size, but also were diesel powered. It wouldn't be true to say that British yards didn't rise to this challenge because they did, but foreign yards did so more completely.

A third level of difficulty had once been seen as an advantage, and it was the close relationship between British shipbuilders and British shipping lines. It was comfortable. The yard would know what to build and the line would know who could build it. The trouble was that this eliminated technical competition. Foreign merchant fleets were moving to diesel, whilst the British passenger lines and related yards were still content to produce excellent steam turbines. The shipping lines had lost market dominance and so too the shipyards.

The figures for unemployment remained dreadful, in those areas where the old staples predominated, through the mid-1920s, with all the human suffering that went with it. The tragedy is compounded by the subsequent evidence that, despite a century of attempts by successive governments, long-term unemployment has become a way life, or should I say existence.

This is a story of exceptions. GKN emerged from the war years in need of new direction which it found in a roundabout way. Two other steel companies, Joseph Sankey & Sons and John Lysaght & Co. were in discussion with a view to merger. H. Seymour Berry (later Lord Buckland) had built up a profitable coalmining business with his business partner, David Llewellyn, and they had acquired Lysaghts. In 1920, Lysaghts, in turn, acquired Sankeys and Berry and Llewellyn turned their sights on GKN. The combined business had within it the spread of activity that should protect it in depression: heavy steel-making, steel-processing for the electrical industry, fasteners and other steel products, and motor components. It did survive, except that, in 1936, the Dowlais Works closed, bringing to an end 170 years of iron and steelmaking.[13]

In 1920, Dorman Long, the Middlesbrough steel company, bought long-established steelmakers and mine owners, Bell Brothers and Bolckow &Vaughan and embarked on a remarkable period of bridge-building. In the long list of iconic structures attributed to Dorman Long are the Omdurman Bridge over the White Nile (1926), the Tyne Bridge (1928), Sydney Harbour Bridge (1932) and Lambeth Bridge, London (1932).

The aircraft industry was still new and had gone from strength to strength in the war years with many technological leaps forward. With the peace, government support for the aircraft industry evaporated and it was left largely to itself. A number of manufacturers had formed their own air transport operations: Instone Airline Limited, Daimler Airway, Handley Page Transport Limited and British Marine Air Navigation Co. Ltd. In 1924, these came together, with some government subsidy, in Imperial Airways, chaired by Eric Geddes. Several newspapers carried the prospectus for the new company and reported on its progress. This airline proved successful in developing routes to India, the Far East and South Africa, but less so elsewhere, and Britain was being left behind by France and Germany. To address this, in 1935 a new company, British Airways (no connection with the current company), was formed to develop others routes by merging a number of other independent operators. Finally, in the prewar era, in 1939, the British Overseas Airways Corporation was formed from a merger of British Airways and Imperial. All the time, successive governments recognized the need for subsidy.[14]

That was for the future. In the 1920s, the Instone Airline Limited operated eight-seat de Havilland 34s and Daimler hire DH.18s, one of which tragically was involved in the first ever mid-air collision in 1922. Once again, I drawn on the research by Peter Dancy.[15] Geoffrey de Havilland had founded the de Havilland Aircraft Company on 25 September 1920 with financial assistance from his old boss at Airco. The company focused on civil aircraft and, as well as larger passenger aircraft, produced the most popular private aircraft in the de Havilland Moth of which some 8,800 were built. In 1921, Sir W. G. Armstrong Whitworth Aircraft Ltd. was formed in Coventry and became pioneers in the development of all-metal aircraft. It produced Siskin trainer aircraft and commercial airliners for Imperial Airways. Avro built the RAF's standard trainer from their factory at New Hall Farm in Cheshire, where it still manufactures today. Bristol produced some 2,600 aircraft between the wars, including its successful Bristol Bulldog interceptor fighter. The Fairey III series would find its place in the annals of RAF history for its England to South Africa flights. Handley Page built on their First World War production with airliners for Imperial Airways on their European and Eastern routes with the passenger cabin laid out like a Pullman railway carriage. The name of Hawker entered the public records when, in 1920, H. G. Hawker Engineering Co. Ltd. was formed by Harry Hawker to help his friend Thomas Sopwith whose company had been faced with crippling tax demands. This company received the contract from the RAF to repair and rebuild Sopwith Camels. The tragic irony was that Hawker died in a flying accident and Thomas Sopwith stepped in as chairman. Short Brothers refocused their production on boats in the 1920s but then embarked on highly successful flying boats.

Vickers built on the success of their Vimy bomber, exploring the vital question of just who might like air transport and where such people would most likely want to go. One strand of this thinking was taken forward by designer Barnes Wallis, assisted by Nevil Shute Norway who would later be better known as a novelist. Their project was an airship large enough and fast enough to make the trip from England to India and Australia. It was ambitious and controversial, but ended in disaster not of its own making. Two airships, the R100 and the R101, had been commissioned, and the Vickers company worked on the first. The second was built at neighbouring Cardington by different designers and builders. Tragically, the R101 attempted its public test flight before it was ready and crashed in flames in France. The powers that be decided that both project should be buried.

Vickers had been working on civil aircraft, as, indeed, had Wallis. The result was a Vimy adapted to civilian use and it was this aircraft in which Allcock and Brown made their non-stop crossing of the Atlantic.[16] This success, followed by others, gave Vickers the encouragement to develop their designs further with the amphibian Viking powered by a Rolls-Royce Falcon engine. In parallel, Vickers at Weybridge further developed the Vimy for the RAF in the shape of the Vernon and Virginia.

Armstrongs had bought the Siddeley Deasy Car Co. Ltd. in 1919. Siddeley Deasy had manufactured airframes in Coventry during the First World War, its workforce growing from 500 to 5,000 over the war years.[17] This avionics arm of Siddeley Deasy found a home in Sir W. G. Armstrong Whitworth Aircraft Ltd. A move to Coventry and a reorganization gave rise to the Armstrong Siddeley Motor Company with John Siddeley as chairman. The company produced high-quality cars aimed at the aristocracy. The first was 30hp with a 5-litre engine; this was followed by smaller models including a 14hp of which an astonishing 14,000 were sold. Whilst the brand was seen by some as rather staid, in the late twenties they were winning rallies. It wasn't just the engines, the company produced a semi-automatic gearbox designed to overcome the problem of crashing gears, and rival companies such as Daimler were all too happy to buy them; they were also used on tanks. Armstrong Siddeley offered a huge variety of vehicles with the option, also offered by Rolls-Royce, of having the bodywork separately built by a carriage specialist. I write of other developments in the motor car industry in the next chapter.

The wartime industries had largely recovered from the dire years of the early twenties, but then came the Wall Street Crash of September/ October 1929. This triggered a worldwide depression, and even greater unemployment with 64 per cent returned for shipyards and 55 per cent for marine engineers.

These much harder times had the effect of bringing together the leaders of the shipbuilding yards, and, over the next six years, they evolved and carried out a scheme, financed by themselves in conjunction with the Bank of England and Governor Montagu Norman, that would remove yard overcapacity.[18] In it, a new company, National Shipbuilders Security Limited (NSS), was set up 'for the purpose of purchasing redundant and obsolete shipyards, the dismantling and disposal of their contents, and the resale of the sites under restriction of further use for shipbuilding'. Looking down the list of yards thus taken over, it is possible to recognize probably all the major shipbuilding companies. Among the largest were, in 1931, Beardmore on the Clyde which relinquished thirteen berths and 100,000 tons of capacity; and in 1935, Palmers with eighteen berths and 130,000 tons of capacity, mainly at Jarrow. Of the latter Scott observed that 'in the early thirties these derelict yards became a notorious symbol of depression'. Vickers later bought them from NSS for use in repair only. The scheme was remarkably successful; in all, 216 berths were taken out, representing nearly 1,500,000 tons of capacity. In spite of this, by the mid-thirties, prospects were once again looking bleak, at which point the prospect of war once again appeared on the horizon.

Chapter 14

The Interwar Years

'Nothing about it could be bettered. Everything opens and closes like the case of a good watch. The fit of the bonnet sides is a positive sermon. There is nothing to pinch or scratch even the most careless of inquisitors. Yes, a Humber job throughout, amply powered, elaborately equipped and most nicely finished. £645 certainly, which is a lot of money nowadays, but when Humber Ltd. have to fight for business on the basis of price only, Heaven help all that is best [in] the British motor business.'

Edgar Duffield on the 1926 15/40.[1]

This observation about Humber cars, to me, points to a correction of the course that the industrial revolution had been taking in Britain. The early days, with textiles, were all about producing large quantities at low prices. My suspicion is that the experience of precision manufacturing in the Great War had given British engineers renewed confidence that they could produce the best the world had to offer. They may not have the education systems of France or Germany, or the market for mass production that the USA had, but they had supreme skills. The quote is about Humber, but it could just as well have been made about Rolls-Royce, Bentley, Napier or Rover. Equally it could have been made about British ships which were finished to astonishingly high standards. The problem was that the world had moved on, leaving the British behind. As we have seen, the first decade of the interwar years is a story of struggle, although, early on, the signs were promising; it was also a time of sowing seeds for what was to come.

It would be wrong to split the period between the two world wars cleanly between the old staple industries and those new and perhaps more exciting. Coal would remain the main source of power, but much else beside. I write below about the creation of the national grid, the power for which came principally from coal. I write too about the chemical industry which also looked to the byproducts of coal. Its link to precision manufacturing could be found in the cavernous railway company workshops around the land. I write about the growth of the motor industry below, but it would be wholly misleading to overlook the steam railway engine.

The name Sir Nigel Gresley adorns British Railways locomotive number 60007. Nigel Gresley was one of the later railway engineers. He was born in 1876 and educated at Marlborough before taking up an apprenticeship at the Crewe Railway Works. He worked his way up to becoming the chief mechanical engineer of the London and North Eastern Railway whose works at Doncaster built both the Flying Scotsman and the Mallard. The Flying Scotsman was the first steam passenger locomotive to travel at over 100 miles per hour and the Mallard holds the record of 113 miles an hour for the fastest steam locomotive in the world. This was engineering of the highest order.[2]

Turning the focus to electricity, the large generator and cable companies would play fundamental roles in the setting up of the Central Electricity Generating Board in 1926 and the construction of the National Grid. In the aftermath of the First World War, there were many private generation companies providing electricity to their local consumers at a variety of voltages and a few on DC, rather than the majority on AC. Rationalization was vital and took place with remarkable energy, and people witnessed the 'march of the pylons' as electricity was brought to very nearly all parts of the British Isles. John Stephenson in his book, *British Society 1914–1945*, offers some figures: in 1920 there were 730,000 electricity consumers in Britain and by the end of the thirties there were almost nine million.[3] Key for industry was that it could set up anywhere, not just near sources of power.

GEC had prospered during the First World War and was ready to supply a nation hungry for innovation with some of what they craved. It now owned Osram and so could supply electric light. It added to this electric cleaners and cookers and much bigger industrial cooking appliances.[4] In 1918, it bought the heavy engineering company, Fraser & Chalmers and so was prepared to play its full part in the National Grid project. GEC had travelled a long way since its formation and its immediate postwar activity built on its wartime production. In 1920, the company produced a collage of images of its many factories. These included the Conduit

Works, the Carbon Works, the Switchgear Works, and the Engineering Works, all at Witton; the Turbine Works at Erith, the Cable Works at Southampton, the Meter Works at Birmingham, the Accessories Works at Southwark, the Telephone Works at Manchester, the Instrument Works at Salford, the Art Metal Works at Birmingham, the Magneto Works at Coventry, the Glass Works at Lemington, and the Robertson Lamp Works and the Osram-GEC Lamp Works at Hammersmith. In 1923, it set up a research centre in Wembley.

English Electric, formed in December 1918, brought together the electric tram expertise of Dick, Kerr & Company, the electric traction capability of Phoenix Dynamo of Preston, Willans & Robinson of Rugby with their steam turbine engines used for electricity generation and the Coventry Ordnance Works.

Siemens Brothers' main focus was cable and telephones, and so their directors were only too delighted when English Electric agreed to buy their loss-making dynamo business in 1919. The relationship didn't end there, for they also combined their light bulb businesses in the Siemens and English Electric Lamp Company Limited. [5] English Electric would probably become best known for two iconic aircraft which it would later produce. Derek James, in his book on the company, suggests that the seeds of interest in aviation were already present in probably three of the constituent companies when they came together, for they had each produced aircraft as subcontractors.[6] The lack of government spending on aircraft and the depressed economy of the mid-twenties later led to the closure of the English Electric aircraft department. The closure was, however, temporary with much greater things to come in the Second World War and beyond. In 1930, George Nelson was appointed managing director of English Electric and with financial backing from Westinghouse became another major force in the British electrical industry. English Electric supplied the Southern Railway in the electrification of their network in the 1930s.

For domestic consumers, the growing availability of electricity meant a growing market for radio but also for white goods. Charles Belling was born in Cornwall in 1884 and had worked with both Crompton and Ediswan before he started his own business in Enfield just before the First World War, at first, manufacturing water heaters. By 1919, he was making electric cookers and the iconic Baby Belling was launched on a very receptive public in the 1920s. The thirties saw the first all-enamel cooker and a large new factory in Enfield.[7] Elsewhere, Tube Investments brought their domestic appliance businesses together in the Simplex Electric Company Limited manufacturing Simplex heaters and Creda cookers. Donal Morphy teamed up with Charles Richards in 1936 to produce a whole range of electrical products.

Siemens found that their submarine cable business was declining, but not so the demand for telephone equipment. As well as handsets, they supplied their first public automatic telephone exchange in Grimsby in September 1918, handling 1,300 lines. This was followed by exchanges in Stockport, Southampton and Swansea; in all some forty-three out of a hundred exchanges were brought into service by the Post Office up to 1927. It wasn't only the UK: Siemens supplied automatic exchanges to Port Elizabeth in South Africa, Port Adelaide and South Brisbane in Australia and Winnipeg in Canada. Production ran at the rate of equipment for 100,000 lines a year. It wasn't only telephones, as Siemens supplied communications equipment for ships and an increasing number and variety of lamps. It expanded its Woolwich factory and took new space in Hartlepool and Spennymoor.

The market for new submarine cables might have been declining, but the traffic through the cables themselves was not. In 1929, the Cable & Wireless Company was formed by merging the Marconi Company and the Eastern Telegraph Company.

If that was the position with cable, wireless promised yet more. Keith Geddes and Gordon Bussey in their seminal survey of the radio and television industry, *The Setmakers*, make the point that, if you were one of the many radio hams who had taken advantage of the supply of surplus radio parts following the ending the war, you would have enjoyed the broadcasts by the Marconi Company from Chelmsford. In 1922, you would have received the first broadcasts from the British Broadcasting Company.[8] This was formed by leading electrical manufacturers: Marconi, GEC, BTH, Metropolitan Vickers, Western Electric and the Radio Communication Company.

A public hungry for new and exciting technology was, by and large, in for disappointment. Of the leading companies which formed the BBC, only GEC was really involved in consumer products and it was only they who produced reasonably priced receivers for the new broadcasts. It will be apparent that at this stage the wireless was a very small part of a very much bigger and more diverse business.

In wireless, the amateur reigned supreme. Crystal sets, often made from kits, outnumbered the more expensive valve radios even though they had severe limitations of use. The other five companies owning the BBC produced only components, many making valves alongside light bulbs. There was, early on, one exception: Burndept, a small company set up by an amateur enthusiast who produced high-quality but rather complicated receivers. Marconi, through their Marconiphone company, produced valve receivers, but not many. They subcontracted manufacture to the company that would become Plessey, but only for a limited period, and Plessey reverted to component manufacture. Pye was another company involved in a small way in those early days.

Geddes suggests that Marconi's approach was half hearted, and allowed small manufacturers and amateurs to dominate the body of licence fee payers, indeed so successfully that there were many more experimenter licence holders than full licence holders, much to the disadvantage of the BBC and its founders. There were a number of issues that caused problems. Valves radios needed replacement high-tension batteries every three months and charges of low-tension accumulators possibly every week. Valves lasted for only about 100 hours. All this encouraged a network of small retailers/manufacturers/repairers often in conjunction with cycle shops. A radio was something that anyone of moderate competence could take apart. Another later famous name, Mullard, entered valve manufacture and managed to halve production costs. He secretly sold part of his company to Philips of Eindhoven in the Netherlands, thus allowing this other famous name into the fragmented UK market.

It seems that only GEC had any real determination to make this a British business success when they produced their Victor 3 receiver, engineered for mass production and at a very reasonable price. Before this, *Wireless World* described the typical British wireless receiver as 'an aggregate of highly finished units, any one of which could be boxed in an attractive carton and sold as a separate component'. It went on to suggest that 'the Victor 3 may do for wireless reception what the Morris-Cowley had done for motoring'.[9]

There were still problems to be addressed, such as technical drawbacks of the most commonly used valve, and the next challenge for designers was to overcome this. This they did with two advances in design, the first by Metro-Vick and the second by Philips. As important was the adaption of valve sets to mains AC supplies. The 1928 Radio Exhibition showed sets made by Metro-Vick, Pye and GEC; the Philips 2514 was banned by the Radio Manufacturers Association for being not British owned.

In parallel with the development of radio, the record and record-player industry was prospering. In 1929, Decca Dulciphone was floated on the stock market by an ambitious stockbroker named Edward Lewis. Decca had traded successfully as a private company for a number of years as a record wholesaler and dealer. A few months after the successful flotation, Lewis heard that the Duophone Manufacturer of the 'unbreakable record', which had also recently bought British Brunswick, was in trouble. He advised Decca to buy it, but they declined. He therefore formed a new company and took over both Decca and Duophone. He gathered a strong board of directors and the new Decca Record Company prospered. In the thirties, Lewis set up Decca USA, which, by the time the Second World War broke out, had one-third of the US market. Lewis decided to sell his shareholding and focus on the UK. Other players in the UK record industry were Marconiphone and the Columbia Gramophone Company which came together with the Gramophone Company to form Electric and Musical Industries (EMI) with their iconic brand HMV.

Turning attention to the internal combustion engine, many motor companies had produced aero engines and indeed aircraft during the First World War. They could now return to a very different domestic market. The four years of war had taught many more people how to drive and look after motors, and so the industry not unreasonably expected strong demand. It was an industry that attracted new entrants. It was estimated that in 1913 there had been nearly 200 different makes or models put on the market and that about half had fallen by the wayside. In 1919/20 some forty-six newcomers joined those who had remained open for the war years. Demand was strong, prices were good, but costs were high, with labour costs still reflecting the demands of the armament industries. Many components were in short supply, and so the number of cars actually produced at 60,000 was 'not 50 per cent above the peak output of 1913'.[10]

Morris were still the new boys on the block, and had done things differently by sourcing components from other manufacturers and focusing on design and assembly. With the war over, Morris had to reconfirm its supply chain. The American Continental Manufacturing Company had decided to seek no further orders for the 11.9hp engine they had supplied, White & Poppe were still busy on armaments, and so Morris had a major problem. The solution came by serendipity in that the French machine-gun manufacturer Hotchkiss, which had set up in Coventry having fled Paris in 1914, was without work but had space and a skilled labour force. They entered into an agreement to supply Morris with engines. Supplies were also reconfirmed for body and chassis. Importantly for the British motor industry, Morris also gave orders for electric components to two then very small companies, Lucas and Smiths. Morris had the space, which they had built in 1914, and so assembly went ahead and, by mid-1920, they were turning out 280 cars a month. In October, came the first signs of economic slowdown with monthly sales falling to 235, then to 137, 92 and, in January 1921, seventy-four. This was simply a reflection of a rapid fall in demand. For Morris, it meant that cars were being produced since component orders kept arriving, but the cars could not be sold and began to fill every available space; the bank overdraft and suppliers' accounts payable kept increasing.

Morris not only understood how to make motor cars, he also knew how to manage a business and so he cut prices. Actually, he slashed them: the four-seater Morris Cowley was reduced by £100 to £425 and other models by similar amounts. He persuaded his distributors to reduce their sales commission and, where possible, he renegotiated his suppliers' contracts. Sales recovered to 236 in February 1921, 400 in March and on to June with 361 units. In the autumn sales began to fall again and so, once more, he reduced prices. His competitors were open-mouthed. Many disappeared, but the overall result was that the industry had reduced its cost base and so could now supply what the market wanted at a price they were prepared to pay; they could also compete with the likes of Ford. In terms of numbers, total UK motor car production fell by one-third from 1920 to 1921 to 40,000; Morris's output rose from 1,932 to 3,076 and to 6,956 the following year.

In 1919, White & Poppe was acquired by Dennis Brothers, the Guildford bus and fire engine manufacturer. Dennis began life as a bicycle manufacturer and had grown through motor tricycles to produce three-ton trucks in the First World War. Their buses could be seen in most countries around the world, and their fire engines and Black Maria prisoner transports were becoming legendary. In 1933, White & Poppe moved production from Coventry to Guildford.[11]

'The Austin 7 was produced from 1922 to 1939, and was the first truly affordable mass-produced vehicle of British design and manufacture.' Herbert Austin had built his own factory after leaving Wolseley, and had undertaken a good deal of government work during the war. Once peace came, his company was losing money as a result of continuing contracts and so the success of the Austin 'Baby' was timely. [12] The company was no way near as profitable as Morris, and so, in 1924, Austin approached Morris with a view to a merger. In fact, it was to be a three-way combination with Austin's old employer Wolseley now owned by Vickers as the third party. Discussion got under way, but it soon became clear that Morris wanted to retain his independence and so the parties walked away.

Morris was enjoying success. In 1925, he produced 55,000 cars. He had brought some of his suppliers and his sister company, Morris Commercials, into group ownership, and in 1926 formed a public company to bring together his interests under one company. He retained control, but also received a good measure of cash. Barely a year later, some of this cash found a good use when he bought Wolseley from the Receivers who had been appointed following continuing poor results. Wolseley brought to Morris good products and a talented design team.

The very conservative Humber Company returned to domestic production with the same two models it had produced in 1913, the Ten and the Fourteen. Humbers were sold on quality rather than innovation.[13] The twenties saw a series of minor developments steering clear of anything radical, but the result was pleasing to Humber fans such as Edgar Duffield who would write of the 1926 15/40 the words with which I began this chapter.

The later twenties saw a subtle change in Humber design with technical innovation creeping in; a battery and coil ignition replaced the magneto. A name also appeared that would be associated with Humber for many years: the Snipe, and the introduction of the Zenith carburettor. In 1929, Humber acquired the ailing Hillman company, its neighbour in Coventry. In the background two energetic motor car salesmen, William and Reginald Rootes were making a name for themselves. They had formed Rootes Ltd. at Maidstone in Kent in 1920. William had worked for Singer and Reginald had gained a first class pass in the civil service exams and was forging a promising career in public service. They had, however, homed in on what was key to the domestic motor industry:

140

sales and service. With their father, they had worked in the family garage business which had taken large premises by the River Len in Kent. On leaving Singer, William had proved himself as a motor salesman. Their company became distributor of Austin, Singer and Humber cars, and began building a sales network that covered the country. They looked to exports, and built relationships largely with countries within the Empire. They took advantage of falling land prices in the 1920s to buy Devonshire House on Piccadilly which would be the company's prestigious headquarters and main showroom for four decades. The next logical move was into manufacturing, which they did in 1925 by buying the coachworks company, Thrupp & Maberly,[14] which was producing fine bodywork for Humber, but also for Daimler and Rolls-Royce. In 1930, they looked to acquire Humber together with Hillman and so approached Sir George May at the Prudential Assurance Company to invest £1 million 'to foster export trade in motor cars'. Sir George would remain a good friend for many years and, on leaving Prudential in 1931, would advise on the reorganization of the steel industry. The Rootes Group was taking shape.

Spencer Bernau Wilks, born in 1891 and educated at Charterhouse, had joined Hillman after serving as a captain in the First World War, and, when William Hillman died in 1921, he took over as managing director. With the Rootes takeover, he felt increasingly uncomfortable and left to join Rover as works manager. Spencer was soon joined by his brother, Maurice, also from Hillman, as chief engineer. The company didn't prosper and in the early thirties was heading for a financial crisis. Spencer was appointed Managing director and a strategy was adopted to pitch products at a slightly more expensive market than Morris or Austin. This proved successful.

In 1920, the Daimler BSA combine attempted to build on its Daimler wartime experience of aircraft engine and airframe manufacture, when managing director Percy Martin took the decision to buy Airco.[15] The hoped-for success did not materialize, and the group reported very poor results and precious little in the way of dividends.[16] In 1931, BSA bought the Lanchester Motor Company hoping to rebuild their reputation. The reality for the enlarged BSA was continued lacklustre performance until rearmament came in the mid-thirties.

The Swallow Sidecar company was founded by William Lyons and William Walmsley in 1922, and produced coach-built cars. The company moved to Coventry in 1928 and offered stylish saloon cars. In 1935, the name Jaguar appeared for the first time on a new range of cars including the SS Jaguar 100.[17]

Alvis was another motor company founded in the interwar period, in its case 1919. T. G. John, in Coventry, was a naval architect by profession and made mainly stationary engines. He was approached by Geoffrey de Freville with a design for an engine with aluminium pistons. The resulting car became the Alvis and by 1923 the company had produced the iconic 12/50. This was succeeded by bigger 6-cylinder models, all with the emphasis on quality and technical advances.[18]

The US motor industry was vastly bigger than anything the UK could offer. Ford was regularly producing two million cars a year worldwide, with factories in Manchester and Southampton before building their major plant in Dagenham in East London in 1932. Vauxhall had ended the war with larger premises at Luton and a well-regarded, high-end car in the shape of the D-type and a more expensive E-type. Ian Coomber says that Vauxhall had been 'a company run by enthusiasts making cars for enthusiasts'. [19] This was to change, since General Motors planned to bring the tools of mass production to a British mass market. Perhaps to underline this change, they melted down the many trophies Vauxhall had won between 1909 and 1923 and used the silver to produce a single salver on which was engraved all the successes. With American muscle behind them, both Vauxhall and Ford would provide stiff competition to the UK-owned carmakers.

Rolls-Royce emerged from the war with its reputation thoroughly enhanced; however, the demand for aero engines fell dramatically and that for very expensive motor cars did not increase by anything like the same measure. What was more, American companies were producing large luxury cars using the methods of mass production. The saving moment came when Royce was asked to design an 'R' engine for racing and this enabled Britain to win the coveted Schneider Cup in 1929 and 1931 in Supermarine airframes designed by R. J. Mitchell. More importantly it led to the design of the Merlin engine in 1933, which would power the great aeroplanes of the Second World War.[20]

W. O. Bentley, with his brother, formed Bentley Motors in 1920. The *Autocar* magazine reported that he was working on a model 'intended to appeal to those enthusiastic motorists who desire a car which, practically speaking, was a true racing car with touring accessories'. The model, when it emerged, did not disappoint. Its 3 litres finished fourth in the Le Mans 24 hours in 1923. This perhaps spurred Bentley on and he produced the Super Six, which, with its successor, went on to win the Le Mans five times in seven years. His ultimate Bentley was an 8 litre said to be silent at 100 mph. W.O. said, 'I have always wanted to produce a dead silent 100 mph car, and now I think that we have done it.' This verdict was echoed by Captain W. Gordon Aston, reviewing the 8 Litre for *The Tatler*, who said, 'Never in my life have I known a vehicle in which such a prodigious performance was linked to such smooth unobtrusive quietness.'[21] This success coincided with the Wall Street Crash which decimated demand for expensive cars. Bentley was bought by Rolls-Royce in 1930. In their purchase of Bentley, Rolls-Royce pipped at the post David Napier & Son who had ceased car production in 1924 to concentrate on aero engines.

In many ways key to the success of motor manufacturers was the very focused way in which one components manufacturer in particular went about creating a very effective and productive monopoly. Harry Lucas was growing old, and his son, Oliver, entered the business, but was not yet able to run it. Good fortune had provided the company not only with the magneto when they bought Thompson-Bennett, but also a very able and far-seeing manager in Peter Bennett who was able to take up the reins from Harry.[22]

Lucas were growing their business in a number of very focused ways. They accepted offers by the smaller component manufacturers to buy their businesses, and then, a little later, agreed to buy their two larger competitors, Rotax and CAV when the latter experienced harsh trading conditions in the mid-1920s. Lucas was able to do this because they had always pursued conservative financial policies, and so were able to weather storms, but also take advantage of the weakness of others. The expanded company focused individual parts of the business in three locations: Birmingham, Acton and Willesden. At the same time, the company was researching solutions to technical problems, such as the magneto, dynamo and starter motor. None of these initiatives would have been effective were it not for some very focused marketing. Oliver Lucas had developed a very good relationship with William Morris and worked hard to meet all their electrical requirements. It wasn't just Morris, then the biggest UK manufacturer, but also Hillman, Humber, Rover, Triumph, Standard, BSA and Vauxhall. Austin also became customers once CAV had come within the Lucas fold. Interestingly, Oliver Lucas declined the Ford business because he didn't feel confident of fulfilling the large quantities anticipated. The approach to overseas markets was largely to reach agreement with local component manufacturers not to compete, so Bosch kept the European market and Lucas kept the Empire. Lucas became one of the most profitable companies in the UK motor industry in the interwar period.

Certainly as prominent as Lucas, Dunlop faced a wholly different start to the interwar years. James McMillan tells the story of a great company very nearly brought to its knees by greed. The company very nearly sank. Inspectors were appointed under the Companies Acts and produced a thoroughly damning report. Dunlop's most influential investor was a banker, Frederick Szarvasy, who then had the great wisdom to bring into Dunlop's management Eric Geddes and George Beharrell. They proved themselves once again the perfect combination.

In the early years of their reign, Dunlop developed the highly successful wired-tyre and, once it was proved that there was no danger in tyres coming off their wheels, as McMillan puts it, 'the enormously successful Morris Cowley and Austin 7 cars took the market by storm on Dunlop tyres'.[23] They added to this the acquisition of the Charles Macintosh group which made from rubber footwear, cables and clothing. They brought the manufacture of Dunlop golf and tennis balls to the Fort. They made the tyres for Henry Segrave's world land speed record of 1925. In 1929, they introduced Dunlopillo latex foam. They were a company on the move and now soundly managed.

In the late 1920s, the motor companies came round to the idea of safety glass and Triplex grew out of its premises in Willesden and moved to Birmingham with financial backing from Guest, Keen & Nettlefold. In 1927, St Helen's glassmaker Pilkington developed a way of making thin glass and they entered into a joint venture with Triplex to exploit this. In the 1930s, Kenneth Horne joined the company. Horne would serve in the RAF in the Second World War and then write the very popular *Much Binding in the Marsh* with Richard Murdock. He would later present the radio comedy shows *Round the Horne* and *Beyond our Ken*.

The steel industry responded to the changing use of steel, as cars, aircraft and domestic appliances began to take over from ships. In 1932, Stewart & Lloyds, manufacturers of steel tubes, moved, from Dudley where they have outgrown their site, to Corby in Northamptonshire where they used local iron ore for their furnaces. Also in the tube industry, which was supplying pipes for gas and water, Tube Investments (TI) brought together smaller companies in that industry. A key use for tubular steel was the bicycle, and Raleigh in Nottingham saw its business boom.

Raleigh had been another major contributor to the war effort, and, in 1918, had 5,000 employees. This had reduced to 2,000 by 1924 when it was producing 400 bicycles and 100 motor cycles a week. In 1932, it acquired the Humber cycle business. However, by the mid-thirties, it was overtaken in size by the Hercules Cycle Company of Birmingham, which had been founded in 1910 and focused on streamlined production methods which gave it a cost advantage.

Looking at metals more generally, in Ebbw Vale in 1920, the steelworks had employed 34,000 people but had then declined and closed in 1929. As a result of a government initiative, Richard Thomas & Co., the biggest tinplate manufacturer, took over the steelworks and production of tinplate expanded, not least for the growing canning industry. The Metal Box Company in Birmingham had also brought together a number of smaller tinplate box manufacturers. John Summers, at Shotton outside Chester, became the biggest producer of galvanized and painted steel.[24]

The other metal that was increasing in production was aluminium. British Aluminium embarked upon a third major hydroelectric scheme in Lochaber, the first of three phases completed in 1924.[25] In the late nineteenth century, Britain produced one-third of the world's total production, but other countries had caught up. They hadn't quite caught up on aluminium fabrication, which, in the Second World War, would grow to 300,000 tons, not least with the demands of the airframe industry.[26] In 1939, Britain produced 25,000 tons of aluminium.

There was a good deal happening in the 'home' economy.

Lever Brothers under the leadership of Lord Leverhulme had fully shared the optimism of the early twenties; William had been raised to the peerage in 1917. His ambition ran into difficulties as the economy collapsed and there was an urgent need for a management structure to take over from the very direct control he had exercised to such success. In spite of everything, Lever Brothers were by far the biggest exporter of soap in the UK having acquired their older rivals, Crosfield, Gossage & Knight. The first element of management discipline came in the person of Francis D'Arcy Cooper, a member of the accountancy firm Cooper

Brothers whose relationship with Lever went back to the very origins of the company. This financial discipline would hold Levers in good stead as they weathered the interwar years and looked to supply the growing domestic market.[27]

The British chemical industry to emerge from the Great War had a major presence in explosives through the Nobel companies and the demands on soap and textile manufacturers had created two very large producers of alkali. There were in addition producers of general chemicals and, as a result of the cutting off of German supplies, a small but growing dyestuffs industry. The big players were German and American but, oddly perhaps to us, this did not seem to be a matter of great concern. There were market sharing agreements, cartels and all manner of legal devices to share out the world's markets. For the British, there was a problem which carried many echoes from the past: the Germans, and to a lesser degree the Americans, were much more focused on chemistry, invention and innovation. Fortunately for Britain, the leaders of its chemical industries, like so many in the story, had grown up in Germany and so had an almost instinctive bias towards research.

In the autumn of 1926, the leaders of the chemical industries of Britain, America and Germany met in New York to thrash out the arrangements between them. The result of many meetings was that ICI (Imperial Chemical Industries) was formed in 1926 by the merger of Nobel Industries Ltd., Brunner, Mond & Company Ltd., United Alkali Company and British Dyestuffs Corporation. 'The newly formed company was divided into main product areas for alkalis, dyestuffs, explosives, general chemicals (including chlorine, acids, and synthetic ammonia), and metals. It also concentrated on producing cellulose products, fertilizers, lime, and a rubberized fabric known as "leathercloth".' As of 1 January 1927, ICI employed 33,000 people. Along with DuPont of the USA and I. G. Farben of Germany, it supplied the world, carefully divided between the three companies. Carol Kennedy offers a wonderful account of the events that led to the merger. The scene is New York City and we can perhaps imagine the smoked-filled boardrooms in those iconic skyscrapers as these major players divided the world up between them.[28]

G. I. Brown writes of the leaders of the newly formed ICI. Harry McGowan was a Glaswegian, who at age 15 went to work for Nobel's Explosives. Following twenty-six years of service, he was elected a director in 1915 and became managing director and chairman in 1918. Alfred Mond was the son of the co-founder of Brunner Mond and was educated at Cheltenham College before reading science at Cambridge and law at Edinburgh. He was created Lord Melchett in 1910. Mond became the first chairman of ICI until his untimely death in 1930 at age sixty-two. He was succeeded by McGowan who was created Lord McGowan in 1937 and served ICI until 1951. Brown suggests that 'it is probably not too much of an exaggeration to credit him with saving the British chemical industry from collapse in the 1920s and with leading a large part of it through to a bright future'.[29]

Brunner Mond, which had suppled ammonium nitrate to such great effect in the Great War, had invested heavily in a nitrogen plant at Billingham, ready to supply the world's farmers with fertilizer. The problem was that emerging economies also invested in nitrogen production resulting in oversupply which very nearly put an end to the ICI dream. Crucially, Lord Melchett stuck to his vision for ICI as a world leader and so maintained vital investment in research.

The ethos of the giant company strikes me as far sighted really on three counts. In terms of research, the company sought out the most talented graduates to join them but also senior academics to work with them; the managers' club at the major sites like Winnington embraced an informal atmosphere where much creative conversation took place in the bars after dinner. This ran hand in hand with enlightened employment policies which included the formation of works councils far ahead of their time. The third pillar was a commitment to excellence wherever it was to be found. So, for chemical research, where the best laboratory glassmakers and fitters were Dutch, it was from Holland that they were recruited. The result was a working environment highly conducive to invention and innovation.

In the late 1930s, polythene was invented by scientists in the Alkali Division. The process embraced each of the three pillars and is a wonderful example of ICI innovation. The scientists experimented and produced something unexpected. Rather than consigning it to the bin of failures, they kept with it until a use was found and I write of this in the next chapter. It was a revolutionary product, to add to the long list of those created in Britain and employed in the manufacturing world.[30] For ICI it was perhaps the first of a long list of discoveries that would change all our lives.

The housing boom, particularly of the thirties, contributed to the growth of this new chemicals industry which in the later interwar years was operating at twice the rate of the rest of the economy. It wasn't just ICI: Samuel Courtauld, whose family had been in the textile industry since the mid-nineteenth century, produced artificial fibres. Their product was rayon from their Rochdale factory and in thread form was accepted as an alternative to natural cotton by spinners. It brought the company great prosperity and a strong position in the American market, through its subsidiary American Viscose, and in international markets, through its patent and licence agreements. Other companies were developing artificial fibres. In 1923, British Cellulose changed its name to British Celanese and by the 1930s was producing Celanese filament yarn well suited to the fashions of the twenties and thirties. Its acetate drape was being used in competition with silk.

Bakelite, which had been invented in the USA in 1909, was the plastic used in most domestic appliances such as radio. It was produced in the UK by Bakelite Limited which was formed 'from the amalgamation of three suppliers of phenol formaldehyde materials to exploit Baekeland's patents in England'.

On the high street the chain stores were becoming more prominent with Marks & Spencer, the American Woolworths and the Dewhurst chain of butcher shops owned by the Vestey family. Perhaps of equal significance were the cinemas being built in just about every town. Rank, previously known for milling flour, set up J. Arthur Rank to buy films from America to show to British audiences.

The influence of American movies was encouraging young men in particular to take greater care of their appearance, and Brylcreem was one answer. The County Chemical Company produced lubricants and had long held an idea for a hair-grooming product. In 1928, the company's chemist came up with Brylcreem and it was an overnight success. So much so that they couldn't keep up with demand and sold Brylcreem to Beechams.

Beechams was a growing part of the British pharmaceutical industry and had created Beechams Powders, a flu treatment; in the thirties they would add Enos, Venos, Macleans toothpaste and Lucozade. Elsewhere, in 1921, insulin was discovered as means for treating diabetes. It was being manufactured in Britain by Burroughs Wellcome and Allen & Hanburys.

Joseph Nathan had expanded from their Glaxo dried milk and were manufacturing a Vitamin D supplement. In 1935, they formed a subsidiary, Glaxo Laboratories Ltd. In 1924, Henry Wellcome brought together Burroughs Wellcome and his research interests in the Wellcome Foundation owned by the Wellcome Trust. The first chair of the foundation was Nobel prize winner Sir Henry Dale.[31]

Were we to take a very broad brush and a timeline from the formation of ICI to the creation of Glaxo Laboratories, British manufacturing from radios to motor cars was really very successful. It is thus easy to understand, aside from the imperative to avoid another human tragedy on the scale of the Great War, why the government would be passionate about staying on the course of peace rather than being drawn onto that of rearmament.

Chapter 15

Rearmament and the Second World War

'While the E28 taxied to the extreme end of the runway, a group of us went by car to a point about 400 yards along the runway. Sayer was in position at about 7:40pm. He ran the engine up to 16,500 rpm against the brakes. He then released the brakes and the aeroplane quickly gathered speed and lifted smoothly from the runway. After a run of about 600 yards, it continued to the west in a flat climb for several miles and disappeared from view behind the clouds. For several minutes we could only hear the smooth roar of the engine. Then it came into sight again, it made a wide circuit preparatory to landing. As Sayer came in, it was obvious that he had complete confidence in the aeroplane. He approached in a series of gliding turns as though he had flown the machine for hundreds of hours. Those of us who were pilots, knew that he felt completely at home. He made a perfect landing at the far end of the runway and came to stop somewhere short of where we were standing. The flight lasted 17 minutes. He taxied towards us, stopped and gave us the thumbs up sign. We of course rushed up to shake him warmly by the hand.'[1]

Frank Whittle, recalling the first test flight
of his jet engine

I quote Sir Frank Whittle at the start of this chapter since, for me, he epitomizes the very best of inventive British manufacturing which was put to the war effort. He wasn't alone.

The Second World War has been described as 'total war' for the United Kingdom, because essentially the greater part of the population was engaged in it one way or another. A good many were in uniform, but there were also many thousands working in industries providing armaments, those industries working in support of them and industries supplying the essentials of life. For a good number of companies, total war began a long time before the first shot was fired, as the country began, albeit reluctantly, a process of rearmament.

Before looking at rearmament in detail, I wanted to get a better understanding of how the shape of Britain and its manufacturing industries were changing and so looked at population figures in the

Interwar population growth

Borough	1921	1938/1939	Increase %
Dagenham UD	9,096	107,000	1076%
Blackpool CB	73,800	157,000	113%
Barking Town UD	36,250	77,000	112%
Heston & Isleworth	47,290	97,437	106%
Ilford MB	85,500	166,000	94%
Mitcham UD	35,550	66,000	86%
Poole MB	42,900	78,054	82%
Bournemouth	85,127	144,451	70%
Ealing MB	90,633	152,510	68%
Hove MB	45,128	75,337	67%
Luton MB	61,002	100,806	65%
Southgate UD	38,900	61,160	57%
Southend on Sea CB	90,500	138,000	52%
Coventry CD	148,521	224,247	51%
Enfield UD	61,311	92,191	50%
Oxford CB	66,626	98,221	47%
Watford MB	46,408	68,298	47%
Finchley UD	46,680	65,000	39%
Doncaster CB	54,700	73,527	34%
Cambridge MB	58,900	78,711	34%
Edmonton UD	67,800	89,573	32%
Croydon CB	192,180	243,000	26%
Exeter CB	59,500	73,030	23%
Willesden UD	154,214	187,000	21%

census for 1921 and the equivalent survey undertaken in 1938/9. I have then listed the places with largest increase.

Looking at those places, and thinking back to some of the companies I have mentioned, the growth in Barking and Dagenham must surely be to do with Ford, and Luton with Vauxhall; but for Coventry and Oxford the reason for the extraordinary growth was to be found in the indigenous motor industry. Those London boroughs bordering the Great West Road would have been home to some famous inward investment from the USA: Gillette, Palmolive, but also the new electrical industries. Willesden was home to part of Lucas. Enfield and Edmonton were home to small-arms production.

Whilst it had been evident before, the interwar years saw a significant increase in inward American investment; the iconic Hoover building comes from the period. Indeed, it was not only the USA, Electrolux of Sweden was Hoover's main competitor in the domestic white goods market. In photography, Kodak had a very significant UK operation, larger than the native Ilford. Looking at employment figures for 1935, foreign-owned manufacturers ranked among Britain's biggest employers. AEI ranked 11th with 30,000 employees; Singer Sewing Machines, 43rd with 8,103; NCR, 46th with 8,000; STC 52nd with 7,911; Ford, 55th with 7,128; Vauxhall, 64th with 6,726; English Electric, 67th with 6,091; and Kodak, 91st with 4,400. We can put these numbers in context by comparing the largest company overall, Unilever with 66,000. Unilever was of course Anglo-Dutch, having come about through the merger of Lever Brothers with a number of Dutch-owned UK margarine manufacturers.[2]

The presence of so many major foreign-owned companies begs the question as to whether the time had come when Britain ceased its creative contribution to the manufacturing world. Certainly, the work of Whittle and other gifted engineers would offer a stiff challenge to such a suggestion, and there was more yet that Britain would offer. The early thirties was a time of peace and of improving living standards for many people. Lever Brothers had set out their stall with the purchase of Walls sausages and the revolutionary idea of using the summer months, when the demand for sausages fell, to manufacture ice-cream – the first time ice-cream had been mass produced in the UK. Unilever would go on in the 1930s to expand into frozen food by buying Birds Eye, but also promoting the consumption of margarine through their Stork and Blue Band brands.

Unilever, as it had become, joined a grouping of major companies known as Management Research Group No. 1, other members including

ICI, Pilkington, Standard Telephones and Rowntree, to explore modern management issues. The group had been founded by Benjamin Seebohm Rowntree in 1926 to provide a vehicle for the exchange of ideas, the collation of information and the discussion of problems common to member companies in order to promote more efficient management. The group had followed a similar group in the USA, the Manufacturers Research Association of Massachusetts, but was focused on distinctly British management challenges which would benefit, in particular, the supply organization in the coming war. There were eight connected groups outside London drawing together small- and medium-sized companies. Group No. 1 later became the Industrial Management Research Association. In my book, *Dunkirk to D-Day*, I write of particular management initiatives taken at Pilkington by Ronald Weeks who would go on to be Deputy Chief of the Imperial General Staff in the Second World War and then chairman of Vickers.

There were other ways in which Britain was creating manufacturing industry elsewhere. In the mid-1930s, investigations were conducted to assess the possibility of setting up industrial production in Kenya to remove the necessity of importing so many manufactured goods. The place chosen, Nakuru, was conveniently located on the Kenyan communication system both for the collection of raw materials and distribution of finished goods. With the coming of war and the entry of the Italians in 1940, Nakuru was mobilized to produce what was needed to defend the northern frontier. There was a tannery capable of producing five tons of leather a month, a whole plant for the manufacture of blankets plus shoe machinery and a soap plant.

Lever Brothers had acquired the Niger Company in 1920 to secure supplies of palm oil and in 1929 the Niger Company merged with the African & Eastern Trade Corporation Ltd., to form The United Africa Company Ltd. Perhaps in parallel with the initiative in East Africa, from the late thirties through the war and into the later forties, the UAC shifted its focus to providing African countries with what they needed to set up local manufacturing.

Returning to the UK and before looking more closely at specific industries, there are further broad statistics which help to paint the picture. The period between the wars was, as already noted, one of overall economic growth, but uneven and marred by high unemployment. I have shown a comparison of growth and unemployment.

UK economic activity

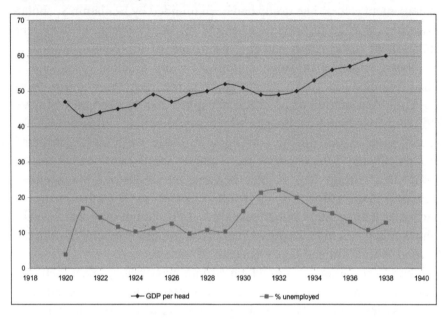

A further look at the census data confirms that Birmingham was huge and growing, having reached a population of one million by the outbreak of the Second World War. It is interesting to look more closely at the second decade of the interwar period and I set out population figures.

Population growth 1930s

Borough	1931	1938/9	Increase %
Ruislip Northwood	16,035	51,001	218%
Hayes & Harlington	22,969	54,770	138%
Chislehurst & Sidcup	27,156	62,620	131%
Bexley	32,652	73,711	126%
Carshalton	28,586	57,375	101%
Harrow	96,656	187,591	94%
Epsom & Ewall	35,231	63,228	79%
Slough	33,612	57,550	71%
Wembley	65,799	112,563	71%
Merton & Morden	41,227	67,622	64%

Borough	1931	1938/9	Increase %
Sutton & Cheam	48,363	73,593	52%
Southall	38,839	51,362	32%
Bedford	42,606	54,572	28%
Beckenham	50,429	63,088	25%

Radio comes first. Further technical advances had made the mains-powered radio set easy to use, and Geddes makes the point that the extension of the national grid meant that, by the end of the thirties, two-thirds of homes had mains electricity. More so, after lighting, the most frequently purchased electrical item was a radio. The industry was set for good times. So, in terms of places and manufacturers, Ruislip and Hayes would be home to employees of EMI. It was the new management of EMI who recruited a young and exceptional research department which powered the company to prominence; they provided the thinking behind the BBC's structure for television broadcasting, some three years ahead of the USA. Their future partner, Thorn Industries, was based in Edmonton in North London. Philips's and Mullard's employees may have lived in Merton and Morden. Philips would dominate the European domestic electrical industry for some years after the war. Cambridge was home to Pye Radio who saw the huge potential of the radiogram, bringing together broadcast and recording. Southend was home to Ecko, which had taken the radical step of using Bakelite for the bodies of their sets.[3] GEC made radio receivers and telephone equipment in Coventry, but these were but part of their overall offering to the domestic market.

An advertisement from 1931, celebrating the centenary of Michael Faraday, stated that GEC was by far the largest electrical manufacturing enterprise in the Empire. Electrical appliances and accessories supplied by GEC included 'Magnet industrial and domestic appliances, OSRAM lamps and valves, Express-SMS lifts, Witton electric motors, Pirelli-General cables, Witton-Kramer tools and hoists, lifting magnets and magnet cranes and Fraser and Chalmers turbines, heavy oil engines, pulverized fuel plant, as well as GEC Bakelite mouldings, radios and instruments'.

Ferranti built a factory in Moston in Manchester which built radio sets from scratch rather than the more common assembling of components.

155

There was Murphy at Welwyn Garden City, and Ultra on Western Avenue in West London, and so probably contributing to the population growth in Southall. Bush was set up in Shepherd's Bush, as a subsidiary of the Gaumont Picture Corporation alongside Baird Television, and produced sets similar to Murphy and with the same flamboyant advertising. Plessey at Ilford had components as their main focus, but their autocratic yet very successful managing director, Allen Clarke, secured a major contract to supply sets under their own brand for the Co-operative Wholesale Society. Towards the end of the thirties, they diversified into telephone, armaments and car components. Brimsdown in Essex was home to valve manufacturers Cosmos and Ediswan who marketed under the brand name, Mazda, both now part of Associated Electrical Industries.[4]

Turning to aviation, certainly Bexley and Chislehurst would be associated with Vickers Aviation, Harrow and Wembley with Hadley Page, Sutton and Merton perhaps also with Vickers. However, all these areas were commutable and were places where building boomed in the thirties and so there is perhaps no need to identify each place with a large company. Southall had AEC and Slough all manner of the new industries. These were the industries where Britain, although perhaps not as leader, was still making a creative contribution to world manufacturing.

The coming of rearmament was a saviour for many areas. Stephenson notes that Cammell Laird at Birkenhead had an order book for 1932 of one solitary dredger, but in 1934 was awarded a contract to build the *Ark Royal*, 20,000 tons of aircraft carrier for £3 million. Between 1933 and 1938 the British government was to spend £1,200 million on military equipment much of which was on aircraft.[5] In the period, before rearmament was accepted as policy, the navy had come first, but, with rearmament being taken seriously, the RAF and aircraft designers were determined that re-equipping should be with modern aircraft capable of competing with the best other countries had to offer.[6] This was really where total war began, and very much with those well-known names long since gone from view.

On 18 May 1933, Hawker Aircraft was formed; the former company, Hawker Engineering under Thomas Sopwith, had been producing aircraft for the previous dozen years. In 1934, Hawker Aircraft was joined by Gloster Aircraft in the establishment of Hawker Siddeley Aircraft, encompassing also Sir W. G. Armstrong Whitworth Aircraft, Armstrong Siddeley Motors, Air Service Training and Avro.

Avro moved its production to a new factory of one million square feet at Chadderton near Oldham, and a new shadow factory at Yeadon in the outskirts of Leeds.[7] Up to 1952, they would produce some 8,000 Ansons with Armstrong Siddeley Cheetah engines, with a further 2,000 in Canada. Avro's first heavy bomber was the Manchester, but the RAF was forced to withdraw it from use, Dancy suggests, because of frequent failures of the underdeveloped Rolls-Royce Vulture engine. The Manchester's successor was of course the Lancaster, and Dancy points out that its designer, Roy Chadwick, went against official policy not to specify Rolls-Royce Merlin engines; the Merlins were intended for fitment to the Supermarine Spitfire. In the event, of course, they powered both. A total of 7,377 Lancasters were built during the war by the production group which comprised Avro itself at Newton Heath (Manchester) and Yeadon; Armstrong Whitworth at Baginton (Coventry), Bitteswell (Lutterworth) and South Marston (Swindon); Austin Motors (Longbridge); Metropolitan-Vickers (Manchester); Vickers Armstrong (Chester and Castle Bromwich); and Victory Aircraft in Canada.

David Napier & Son continued to develop aero engines culminating in the Napier 24-cylinder Sabre, which, at 3,500hp, powered the Hawker Typhoon and Tempest. The company was bought by English Electric in 1942.

Sopwith had designed the Hurricane and produced the first 400 at the company's own risk. Eventually some 14,533 Hurricanes were built, of which Hawkers produced 10,030. The Hurricane was followed by the Typhoon, of which 3,330 were built, and then the Tempest which did battle with the V-2s. In all, the Hawker Siddeley Group provided some 30 per cent of all equipment provided by the British aircraft industry in the Second World War. Factory space increased from two million square feet in 1938 to fifteen million in 1944.

The story of the Bristol Blenheim, like so many stories in this book, is that of the whim of a wealthy man. In 1934, Lord Rothermere, owner of the *Daily Mail*, commissioned Bristol to design a light personal transport. It seems that the Air Ministry was so pleased with its result that it sought permission to develop a light bomber from it. Rothermere gifted the original prototype to the nation. In the course of the war 4,544 Blenheims were built by Bristol, Avro and Rootes. The Beaufort was a development of the Blenheim, and 2,169 were built at Bristol. The third major wartime aeroplane produced by Bristol was the Beaufighter, and 5,600 were manufactured by Bristol at Filton and Whitchurch, Fairey Aviation at Stockport, the Shadow Factory at Old Mixon, Weston-super-Mare, and by Rootes at Blythe Bridge, Staffordshire.

The mention of the Shadow Factory brings into the story a good further tranche of British manufacturing. In his book, *Drive for Freedom*, which I refer to more below, Charles Graves tells the story. In 1936 Lord Swinton, Secretary of State for Air, set up two schemes with the motor industry. One was for airframes, whereby motor companies would set up massive manufacturing facilities to construct Blenheims and Fairey Battles.[8] The other involved five major motor companies producing separate parts of the Bristol Mercury aero engine. The motor industry factories involved were Rootes, Daimler, Standard, Rover and Austin. William Rootes was approached to set up their shadow factory whilst on a tour of the Far East with his son. The Air Ministry very much left the motor companies to make their arrangements for manufacturing, but the government provided the necessary funds. Once the war was underway, further shadow factories were set up in all manner of places, the key being safety from air attack. One such place was the disused quarry at Corsham outside Bath. According to the Dowty Group history, they could have used it, but Bristol got there first. Just how unhappy the Dowty workforce were, I don't know, since a good part of the underground tunnelling was used for ammunition storage. It was close to the Box Tunnel, that brilliant creation of Isambard Kingdom Brunel. Alvis provided their expertise in managing some twenty-one shadow factories as well as producing engines as a subcontractor to Rolls-Royce.[9]

Shadow factories also come to be mentioned in Andrews's biography of Lord Nuffield. William Morris had been created a baron in 1934, from when he became known as Lord Nuffield. In 1936, he sold his interests in Wolseley, MG, SU Carburettors, Morris Commercial and Morris Export to Morris Motors which became a publicly quoted company. He had already delegated day-to-day management and so was largely free to pursue what interested him. Leonard Lord, who had previously worked for Hotchkiss and had remained with that company when it became Morris Engines (Coventry) Limited, now moved to Cowley as managing director of Morris Motors.

Lord Nuffield retained personal ownership of Wolseley Aviation and used his newfound freedom to go ahead with the manufacture of an aero engine for civilian use. This appeared just as government was considering the shadow factory scheme. Nuffield had severe reservations about the scheme, not least because each factory would only produce specified parts for the Bristol engine, making the whole project vulnerable should one factory be bombed. He therefore offered his engine to the Air Ministry, but they declined to take it. To cut a long story short, he ceased production and turned his attention to the tank of which I write more below. In 1938, Nuffield was invited back into the shadow factory scheme on a different basis: to build whole Spitfires. It will come as no surprise that this time Nuffield said yes. A site was found on Dunlop land at Castle Bromwich, and some fifty-two acres of buildings were erected. Again, to cut a long story short, the factory was transferred to the control of Supermarine Vickers Armstrong to run alongside their other Spitfire production. Andrews adds that after the war it did return to the Nuffield fold as Fisher & Ludlow, which was bought in 1953 by the British Motor Corporation.[10]

De Havilland were building Tiger Moths for RAF training squadrons right up until the war. Its famous Second World War Mosquito began as a private venture in October 1938 under the eye of chief designer R. E. Bishop at London Colney in Hertfordshire. This remarkable fighter-bomber achieved 400 mph when the first prototype was flown by de Havilland himself in November 1940. Powered by Rolls-Royce Merlins, some 7,781 of these largely wooden aircraft were built. Fairey Aviation at Hayes in Middlesex designed the last operational biplane, the Swordfish, making 691 themselves with the remainder built by Blackburn Aircraft at Brough in West Yorkshire. Handley Page at Cricklewood produced, first the Hampden bomber and then the more successful Halifax which were manufactured by a production group comprising English Electric, Rootes at Speake (Liverpool) and Fairey in Stockport. Dancy tells that at peak production there were some 660 subcontractors and 51,000 employees completing a new aircraft every working hour, some 6,177 aircraft in all.

Shorts joined with Harland & Wolff in 1936 in a company known as Short & Harland and produced the Sunderland flying boat, and, from this design, the massive Stirling bomber. Production at Rochester became too vulnerable to air attack and so move to Belfast, with Austin also producing a good number.[11] Some 2,375 were produced in all.

In November 1928, Vickers Aviation Ltd. had taken control of Supermarine, but left it largely autonomous and free to pursue its aim of speed. The resulting Spitfire came after a line of fast aircraft designed by R. J. Mitchell. Scott tells how its development was a product of Mitchell's design, McLean's 'tough intransigence' and the vital part played by test pilot Mutt Summers. Sir Robert McLean, a 'man of granite integrity and austere independence' had been appointed by Vickers as chairman of their aviation interests. Mutt had remarkable contacts with his opposite numbers in Germany and so was able to feed in to Vickers thinking developments taking place there.[12] They began production of the Spitfire in 1936, largely using subcontractors, not least Rolls-Royce who built the Merlin engine. With rearmament under way, Supermarine tooled up for a massively increased production of Spitfires. This was not without its challenges, and Dancy tells how the Spitfire might have been dropped had the Hawker Tornado and Typhoon not experienced problems.[13] The total production of Supermarine Spitfires was nearly 20,000, built between Supermarine and Vickers (at the Small Heath Factory) with a small number by Westland.

Vickers-Armstrong Ltd. took over Vickers Aviation, with designer Barnes Wallis, and Supermarine Aviation Works (Vickers) Ltd. in October 1938. Charles Craven became chairman of both aviation subsidiaries. McLean left and later became managing director of EMI and played an important role in radar. Vickers Aviation's first wartime aircraft was the Wellesley, but their best known was the Wellington which first flew in 1936 with a total of 11,461 built at their factories at Weybridge in Surrey and Bexley Heath and Erith in Kent.

Bombers needed bombs, but, more than that, bombs which would destroy precisely what was targeted. In 1940, Barnes Wallis wrote a paper titled, *A Note on a Method of Attacking the Axis Powers*. His thesis was that targets such as factories, coalfields, oilfields, hydroelectric generation facilities and underground storage needed to be attacked with very heavy bombs which would enter deep into the ground and then explode with maximum structural damage. He conceived a ten-ton bomb and asked English Steel to specify the steel required for its aerodynamic body. The problem was to get an aircraft powerful enough to carry such a load. The Wellington wasn't, so he put forward a plan to Lord Beaverbrook that would. As happened so often, the project ran into the sand. It eventually emerged as the Tallboy carried by 617 Squadron Lancasters equipped with H2S radar when they successfully attacked the Saumur tunnel in June 1944. Wallis and 617 Squadron are of course better known for the Dambusters Raid.[14] English Steel also developed vital drop forgings for Rolls-Royce and Bristol engines.

Ruston, of Ruston & Hornsby in its previous incarnation of Ruston & Proctor, had built aeroplanes in the First World War. The contribution of Ruston & Hornsby in the Second World War was no less significant, but perhaps more closely linked to their core business. Hornsby and Ruston engines for electrical generation were used almost everywhere, including, Newman suggests, by the Germans and he tells of one being found in the basement of the Paris HQ of Field Marshal von Kluge.[15] Elsewhere, they made Matilda tanks, Paxman engines for landing craft, generators for searchlights, power for ventilation, air-conditioning and refrigeration for the Ministry of Food, and diesel locomotives for work in depots. They certainly kept an eagle eye on developments elsewhere in engineering, not least the jet engine.

The 1930s is very much the decade of the birth of this wonderful British invention, and so I hope I may be forgiven for devoting some space to it. From the very early days of aircraft, designers had been striving for ever greater speeds. It was thought that the piston-driven engine powering a propeller fell short of what could be achieved and so, in the 1930s, two schools of thought began to emerge. One, pursued by the Royal Aircraft Establishment, was the idea of a gas turbine that would drive a propeller. The other, put forward by a bright young RAF officer, Frank Whittle, was of an aircraft propelled by a high-speed jet using a centrifugal compressor. Gas turbine technology was already in hand in at least two of Britain's large engineering companies: Metropolitan Vickers in Manchester and British Thompson-Houston in Rugby. Work at the Royal Aircraft Establishment advanced slowly, but, in 1930, Whittle filed a patent application for his idea and began to seek backing, which eventually came through two former airmen and a city bank. In 1936, a company, Power Jets Limited, was formed and the idea was progressed. British Thompson-Houston was engaged to produce detailed drawings and then a prototype. The familiar pattern of trial and error followed, with the equally familiar shortage of money. All the while, Whittle remained an RAF officer and received moderate support for his engine. The first breakthrough came when the Gloster Aircraft Company was commissioned to produce an aircraft, known only as E28/39, on which to test the engine, the W.1. Whittle himself recalled the day of the test flight in the words with which I began this chapter.

It was a success but the success was short-lived, and a further period of development followed leading to the W.2 engine. What may only have been a chance conversation introduced the Rover Car company into the mix with chief engineer, Maurice Wicks. Wicks and his design team modified Whittle's plans and the W.2B was the result and was used in the Gloster F9/40 which became the Meteor. Another possibly chance conversation brought in Rolls-Royce, who had been working on the adaption of their piston-driven Merlin engine for use in powering the Cromwell tank.[16] For reasons which have not been recorded, Rover took on the tank engine project and Rolls-Royce began their long relationship with the jet engine. They took the W.2B and developed it into the Welland which then powered the Meteor 1 in the battle against the V-2s. The mention of the V-2s is relevant, since Whittle's patents weren't kept secret and so the Germans were able to learn from him. The W.1 was shared with the USA and developed by General Electric. The Royal Aircraft Establishment collaborated with Metropolitan-Vickers and, in 1941, they succeeded in producing the first axial compressor jet-propulsion gas turbine.[17] Jet power had arrived. From the point of view of British manufacturing, though, it had both arrived and departed, to the USA.

Aircraft production was at the heart of rearmament and may well have taken the lion's share of the £1,200 million. It certainly caught the public's imagination, yet, there was much more going on.

There was little point in having aircraft unless there were airfields from which they could fly. The British civil engineering industry had seen little scope for the earthmoving equipment which had become more common on the other side of the Atlantic, yet for airfields tracked vehicles were essential. The main manufacturer was Caterpillar in the USA, and, in 1935, they appointed two British companies as dealers. Levertons, of Spalding would go on to supply a large number of Caterpillars for airfield building. Jack Olding would, in addition to Caterpillars, set up a factory, commonly known as Tank Central, specifically to prepare tanks for deployment. His main factory at Hatfield had a magnificent Art Deco façade and was known as Caterpillar Corner.

Levertons also sold Caterpillars for agricultural use where tractors struggled, although there were not that many tractors in the early thirties to struggle. The agricultural depression of the 1920s, combined with the conservative view of many farmers, meant that tractors had not come into general use. This was to change, and the change is attributed to an Irishman, Harry Ferguson. The tractors, that were in use before Ferguson came along, were dangerous in that, with only a drawbar to pull implements, should the implement get stuck, the tractor could rear up and injure the driver. Ferguson invented a three-point linkage which addressed the issue. He teamed up with major Huddersfield-based gear-maker, David Brown, and in 1936 they began to manufacture the Ferguson Brown tractor, powered by a 20hp Coventry-Climax engine. Brown and Ferguson fell out, and Ferguson took his ideas to Ford. David Brown modified the design and produced some 60,000 of their own VSK1 tractors by the end of the war.[18]

The contribution of the motor companies, which, in addition to wheeled and tracked vehicles and aircraft, included shells, tin hats and jerrycans, was massive. Andrews makes the important point that with the growth of this new industry aimed at a domestic market, it would form a huge reserve of industrial capacity once the domestic market closed and the demands of war grew. Much the same is true of the radio industry on the basis that many homes already had the sets with which they would listen to Churchill's broadcasts, *Music While You Work* and much else, and so there was expert capacity to address the needs of the armed forces.

Looking first at the motor companies, an early port of call is the remarkable little book, *Drive for Freedom*, written by Charles Graves very soon after the end of the war. It was commissioned by the Society of Motor Manufacturers and Traders and was published by Hodder & Stoughton at two shillings. For me, the most remarkable feature is that it begins with my father, Major-General Bill Williams, who created the army centre for mechanization at Chilwell near Nottingham. I have written about my father in the book, *Dunkirk to D-Day*, but Graves tells the particular story of Chilwell and the engagement with the motor companies. The key point is that Bill Williams saw as vital the expertise of the motor industry in advising how Chilwell should be set up; it was after all a massive motor dealership and maintenance depot. Graves says, and my father's archive confirms, that the industry responded to the approaches with great enthusiasm and generosity. There was, though, a second aspect. Bill saw that the RAOC, which would be responsible for the supply and maintenance of all army vehicles, would need amongst its officer ranks men with business experience. Interestingly, it was not production men that he was seeking, but sales and distribution managers whose skills would be perfect and who would otherwise be redundant in wartime Britain. Graves gives a number of 500 senior motor industry men who joined the RAOC as temporary officers. These would have included those motor engineers who from October 1942 would be part of the Royal Electrical and Mechanical Engineers (REME) providing vital technical back-up to the newly mechanized army. Again, I tell more of them in *Dunkirk to D-Day*, but here is set out a brief summary of what the motor companies produced.

In 1936, Leonard Lord had moved from Morris to Austin where he became managing director and would, during the war years, oversee the manufacture of some 120,000 military vehicles of all kinds, ranging from the 8 hp utility tourer commonly known as 'Tillies', to 3-ton 6x4 trucks, importantly also used as recovery trucks. Tillies were also produced by Morris at Cowley and by Hillman and Standard Cars also in Coventry, based on the Standard Flying 14. In 1939, Austin had planned to re-enter the commercial vehicle market with a 30-cwt truck. With mobilization, this evolved into the Austin 2-ton truck, of which some 27,800 were built during the war, nearly half being ambulances. In addition, Austin produced 1.3 million rounds of 2-, 6- and 7-pounder shells, 3.3 million ammunition boxes, 600,000 jerrycans and 2.5 million steel helmets.

In Coventry, Humber supplied staff cars for all three services.[19] The Humber FWD was a small four-wheel-drive all-purpose vehicle based on the Humber Super Snipe, and the BBC operated a fleet of these for war correspondents.[20] Karrier Motors of Luton was another company within the Rootes Group. Its K6 was a four-wheel-drive 3-ton truck of which 4,500 were produced. This, like many 3-tonners, was adaptable, being also used as a mobile workshop and store. The Humber 8-cwt 4x4 light field ambulance fulfilled a vital role in rescuing the wounded from the battlefields. The Humber scout car, also based on the Snipe, was essential equipment for almost all army divisions. The scout car and staff car were also manufactured by Daimler. Hillman produced a 5-cwt 4x2 light utility based on prewar 10 and 12hp passenger saloons, the Minx, which had been its best-selling model in the 1930s.

Triumph motorbikes had set up a factory in Coventry, but this was destroyed by enemy bombing having produced only fifty bikes. It relocated to Meriden in May 1942, and manufactured 49,700 machines by the end of the war. Another major bike manufacturer was Norton in Birmingham which produce some 100,000 bikes. BSA produced a further 115,000.

AEC turned its wartime production to Matador and Marshall heavy trucks which were used, amongst other things, for transporting pipes for the construction of oil pipelines.[21] They were also used as tractors for medium guns.[22] Albion Motors also manufactured heavy vehicles: an artillery tractor for towing 7.2- or 6-in howitzers, the Albion CX 24S, a 20-ton semi-trailer which could take a Crusader; the Albion BY 1 used to move mobile bridge sections and the Albion CX22 6x4, also a heavy gun tractor.

In 1935, the War Office, aware of developments in the USA, France and Germany in four wheel drive, issued specification for a Q type, 'quad' 3-tonner. Crossley developed a sophisticated version with all-round independent suspension. However, the pressures following Dunkirk meant that sophistication had to be put to one side and a more straightforward version was commissioned and served alongside similar vehicles from Albion, Karrier, Austin and Bedford. Crossley remained principally an RAF supplier.[23]

Sydney Guy had set up his company in Wolverhampton at the start of the Great War, having spent time with Sunbeam and Humber. The coming of peace saw Guy produce a 2½-ton truck aimed at farmers with SPUD wheels capable of being driven over all types of terrain.[24] Guy went on to produce buses, coaches and commercial vehicles, but, in 1935, was invited to take part in army trials. They produced a 15-cwt short wheelbase Ant which ran on low-pressure tyres. Gun tractors offered a link with their living predecessors as having to 'have good cross-country performance, be capable of carrying the gun crew and their equipment, and an initial supply of ammunition to bring the gun into operation'.[25] The tractors' breakdown into uses: field artillery, light anti-aircraft (Bofors) and heavy gun tractors. In 1937, Guy developed its Ant into a 4x4 Quad Ant which, for the duration of the war, would be the field artillery tractor of choice for 25-pounder guns. Derived from the design of the Quad Ant was an armoured car with revolutionary welded armour plate. The demand for this outstripped Guy's capabilities, and Humber took the design and produced some thousands for the War Office. This vehicle fought to great effect in the wide-open space of the desert, but was found less useful in the lanes and built-up areas of northern France.[26]

The planning for D-Day had revealed that a 10-ton truck would be more effective than the smaller-capacity trucks then in use. Accordingly, Leyland adapted its 10-ton Hippo Mk II, but was late on the scene with only 1,000 being in service by VE Day. The Leyland Retriever was adapted as both a machinery and stores truck and as a recovery vehicle. These trucks were of essentially two types, the 'house' version with windows, perhaps too easily identified, and the general service vehicle equipped inside, but looking like any other general service vehicle outside. Like so many motor companies, Leyland also produced bombs, shells and castings

Alfred Scammell had experienced the Great War at first hand, and was definitely on the side of lighter vehicles that could avoid the dangers of mud. He favoured lighter trucks having the ability to tow trailers, thus having the same carrying ability but with a reduced weight on each axle.[27] The idea progressed into an articulated lorry which proved popular in the commercial market. From this came the Scammell Pioneer which performed strongly as a gun tractor or tank or machinery transporter. 'The great thing about the Pioneer was that no amount of mud or sand seemed to bog it down, although it often needed two men to handle the manual steering gear for the big front wheels.' The Scammell 30-ton semi-trailer tank transporter was big enough to carry a Matilda. The Scammell 6x4 heavy breakdown was 'probably the most widely used and longest in service of the British recovery vehicles'. Recovery vehicles came in three types: those with fixed or extendable jibs, those with booms described as 'wreckers' and lastly the gantry type with a rigid steel structure. The other unique Scammell contribution was the three-wheeled mechanical horse.

Many other British motor companies contributed to the war effort. Foden, in Sandbach Cheshire, manufactured a range of heavy trucks. Maudslay, at Alcester in Warwickshire, was known for its Militant 6-ton GS truck. Thornycroft supplied some 20,000 vehicles from mobile cranes to searchlight lorries and machine-gun carriers

Under the management of Oliver Boden, who had succeeded Leonard Lord, and then under Miles Thomas, Morris undertook the manufacture of armoured personnel carriers, then a 15c-wt General Service Truck and power units. Importantly, they also built tanks. Lieutenant-General Sir Clifford le Quesne Martel had seen the speed of Russian tanks in autumn manoeuvres in 1936. He told Lord Nuffield and asked him to assist in producing a similar vehicle for the British Army. This became a collaboration between Martel, Nuffield and the American Walter Christie, who had designed a revolutionary suspension system. The result was the Cruiser tank produced by Morris Commercial and powered by an American First World War Liberty engine build from 'such old drawings that could be found'. Fairfax takes up the tank story by telling how 'when Britain stood alone, Nuffield Mechanizations was responsible for one-quarter of all British tank production'.[28] A total of 22,000 carriers (Bren Gun but also Scout carriers, Universal carriers, Motor Carriers and Lloyd artillery tractors) were produced by Wolseley, including adaptions of carriers originally manufactured overseas.[29] The total workforce was some 30,000 men and women and the overall production vast.

The tank most emphatically brings into the story, once again, Vauxhall, for it was they who were given the task of designing and manufacturing the Churchill tank. I hesitate, though, because they were no longer British owned. Roll the camera forward eighty years to the time when I am writing and there is very little British-owned motor manufacture, but there are many thousands of British workers employed in motor vehicle manufacture. So too with Vauxhall and, indeed, Ford in the Second World War. Vauxhall produced nearly a quarter of a million vehicles for military use in the six years of the war, mainly trucks and lorries. In *War on Wheels*, I tell the story of the painstaking and painful development of the Churchill tank. In the end some 5,600 were manufactured by Vauxhall, but also by Dennis and Leyland.[30]

It wasn't just vehicle manufacturers; subcontractors and component manufacturers played their part. Solex Carburettors, Pyrene Company (fire extinguishers), Firestone, Triplex, Lucas, Lodge, Champion and AC Spark Plugs and Smiths Industries to name but a few. Tecalemit supplied workshop equipment. The car battery to us in the twenty-first century is enclosed, reliable and clean. In the middle of the twentieth century, even though technology had made great strides, the battery, with its elements suspended in acid, was far from simple. Oldham produced a great many batteries for army vehicles in the Second World War, gaining a reputation for reliability. Oldham's traditional business was hats, and from this had come mining lamps, and from these batteries. The depression in coalmining had encouraged a shift towards supplying batteries to the more buoyant motor industry, so Oldham had been well prepared when war came.[31]

Dunlop had grown into a major company under the chairmanship of Eric Geddes with Edward Beharrell as managing director. In 1937, they had added Semtex floor covering to their product range, something that would attract admiration. That same year Eric Geddes died at the age of sixty-two. McMillan rightly laments the loss of such a talent at such a young age. He suggests, not unreasonably that, had he lived, he would be remembered as the 'Churchill of Industry'. In the event, Edward Beharrell took over the chair which he filled with distinction, and, under his leadership, Dunlop's contribution to the war effort was prodigious. In his *History of Dunlop*, James McMillan tells that, 'between 1939 and 1945 the Company produced the vast majority of the 32.7 million vehicle and 47 million cycle tyres manufactured in the UK'.[32] It was though much more than this, as McMillan goes on to write: 'Dunlop made 2.5 million disc wheels, 600,000 aircraft wheels, 750,000 tank wheels (plus a million tank tyres to go with them), 15 million cycle and motor cycle rims, 3,000 miles of rubber tubing, 600,000 pairs of anti-gas gloves and 6 million pairs of rubber gloves.' He adds, 'this is just for starters.' Dunlop desert tyres were so good that General Rommel issued an order only to capture British trucks. The run-flat tyre was particularly important, being able to run for many miles after being shot. Dunlop's rubber decoys – guns, tanks, landing craft – fooled the Germans in the run-up to D-Day. Dunlop barrage balloons were supplied to America as well as being used in our own defence. Dunlop diving suits and rubber dinghies were vital equipment.

The relationship between Dunlop and the RAOC was strong. There is a story of a visit by a senior Dunlop delegation to the RAOC armaments depot at Old Dalby in Leicestershire, and how they took away many new ideas on organization from the techniques developed within the RAOC. The Old Dalby depot was commanded by Bob Hiam, who had come from Dunlop and who would return there after the war as general manager of the tyre division. Charles Graves, in *Drive for Freedom*, avoids mentioning the names of particular companies, but does comment on industries. Where he does so in the case of rubber, it is probably safe to assume that it relates mainly to Dunlop. He highlights some of the products, other than tyres, which the rubber industry produced: de-icing equipment for aircraft and the compressed-air system that fired aircraft machine guns, tyres for desert use with treads mimicking the feet of camels. The industry also found ways round problems of aircraft tyres freezing and tank tyres 'boiling over' (underneath the caterpillar tracks).[33]

The strength of the connection between the motor industry and the RAOC may be further evidenced by two nicknames given to groups of men joining from industry: the Rootes Rifles and the Lucas Light Infantry. I have already looked at Rootes. In *The Times* of 12 December 1945, Peter Bennett chairman of Lucas, gave an account of the remarkable Lucas contribution to the war effort. One million sets of starters and ignition sets, a further million and half spare parts sets, but then technical contributions to the jet engine development, electrically controlled aircraft gun turrets, control mechanisms for tanks, wing assemblies for Spitfires and PIAT anti-tank weapons. Bennett made these remarks in the context of the challenge of returning to peacetime production.

An industry, certainly in my mind closely related to motor vehicle, was toy-making. British toy manufacturers had been encouraged during the First World War, and, following the peace, had reaped benefits both of wartime investment and the absence of German competition. The interwar years saw significant added capacity particularly by those who had established before 1914. G&J Lines had given way to the next generation, three members of which formed Lines Brothers producing toys under the Tri-ang brand. They built the world's most modern toy factory at a forty-seven-acre site in Merton and by the early thirties had over 1,000 employees. The Meccano factory in Liverpool doubled in size and Hornby, which were already producing O gauge clockwork trains, took advantage of the growing number of homes with electric power to bring out their famous OO electric trains. Hornby began manufacture of their Dinky vehicles in 1934. In London, Britains opened two more factories and Chad Valley acquired an additional twenty-acre site. Most of the toys wanted by British children were now being produced at home and at an acceptable price and quality. The toy manufacturers were supplying a hungry market in the 1930s. In the early months of the war, readily available were box sets of soldiers from Britains and Dinky models of army vehicles. With the end of the phoney war, toy manufacturers rolled up their sleeves for the war effort. Britains and Mettoy, who in the fifties would be known for Corgi model vehicles, switched to munition manufacture. Lines Brothers manufactured machine guns, parts of gliders and ammunition magazines and Bassett-Lowke made training models for the forces including Mulberry harbours.[34]

The roles played by the Royal Navy and the Merchant Navy were vital to the survival of the peoples of these islands, and British shipbuilders rose to the challenge of meeting their needs. In terms of numbers, 1,377 merchant ships and 1,148 warships were built by commercial yards during the war. In the same period 2,539 merchant ships were lost to enemy action, leaving the merchant fleet at 12 million gross tons, some 5 million below its prewar level.[35] It wasn't only new production: yards repaired some many thousands of naval and merchant vessels of all sizes during the war. The workforce, which had stood at 175,000 in 1938, increased to a peak of 249,000 in June 1943.

As I explained in Chapter 13, overcapacity as a result of the demands of the First World War had to be reduced and the shipyards themselves took on the task and achieved their objective. So, it was a relatively smaller shipbuilding industry that, in September 1939, came under government control with the Restriction and Repair of Ships Order 1939. This meant that all the anxiety about lack of government support and lack of demand could be forgotten and the tried and tested process of building ships could be restarted. A key issue was always going to be the allocation of capacity between naval and merchant shipping. This was eventually resolved when all shipyards came under the control of the Admiralty, but with strong shipbuilding voices to stand up to those of the Admiralty. The result was an astonishing output of 2.2 million gross tons per annum; indeed, some of the yards previously mothballed were brought back into use.

The dreadful commercial conditions of the interwar years had left yards without financial reserves and with equipment badly in need of replacement. War work was profitable, and Slaven notes that filed accounts not only reported net profits but substantial sums set aside for depreciation and transferred to reserves. Some yards took advantage of opportunities to re-equip. Harland & Wolff took over welding shops provided by the government. Vickers-Armstrong reduced their number of berths to cater for larger ships, and, at the same time, re-equipped with new heavy cranes. Similar action on reducing berths was taken on the Clyde by John Brown, Barclay Curle, Lithgo and Scott, on the Tyne at Swan Hunter, Furness on the Tees and Cammell Laird on the Mersey. Yet the yards, although busy, were not healthy. In a book about Cammell Laird, but referring to British shipbuilding more generally, First Lord of the Admiralty A. V. Alexander observed 'a tendency towards what I may term as fossilization of inefficiency'. This was elaborated upon and at its heart was a mindset that completely failed to embrace modern methods. The workers were undoubtedly skilled, but in old skills and the post-war world demanded new.[36]

Vickers played their part under the direction of Sir Charles Craven, but, as Scott writes, he was not one inclined to take the initiative, but was more used to remain at the bidding of the Admiralty to whom he was always 'Commander Craven'. Nonetheless, the company achieved much in the rearmament period. With the reduction in yards, many workers had left to seek new work elsewhere. Vickers and Armstrongs had, though, with their commercial work and work for foreign governments, managed to keep a workforce and, importantly, an apprentice programme. The demands of rearmament began to show their teeth in 1935, particularly with the need for gun mountings for the massive guns which were to be installed on the new battleships under construction.

Vickers made mountings at Barrow and Elswick. They also worked on new battleships, collaborating with Beardmore, Firth-Brown and English Steel on armour plate. They were working near capacity and, in order to increase it, in 1937 the Admiralty bought and leased to them the Scotstown Locomotive Works owned by Armstrong Whitworth Securities and kept out of the original merger. Vickers entered the war with recruitment in hand at Newcastle, Sheffield, Crayford and Dartford, but with Barrow still 2,000 people short. The total Vickers workforce was by then 64,000.

With the coming of war, Vickers, and the other shipyards geared up to naval construction, expected orders for large battleships. A few came, but the experience of war, particularly the Atlantic convoys, underlined the greater need for smaller, faster ships, but also for submarines and other specialist vessels. The same experience underlined the need for substantial repairs and the Vickers-Armstrong Palmers yard was kept busy. All the time those hoped-for orders for big ships never came. War had changed, as Scott puts it, 'with the advent of radar, the birth of homing devices, rocketry, and atomic warfare ... It was a change from heavy industry in the direction of an alliance of pure science and light industry.'

In the mid-thirties, with a view to the beginning of rearmament, plans had been put in place for the creation of forty-four Royal Ordnance Factories. There would be engineering factories tasked with the manufacture of artillery and small arms. There would then be the manufacture of explosive and the filling of shells. All horribly familiar. Particularly the latter were to be located away from areas of population and the risk of aerial attack.

Priority had been given to the navy and RAF and so progress for the army was slow. As Scott puts it, 'if the re-equipping of the Navy had been slow and hesitant, the rearming of the Army was obstinately reluctant'. He adds that Vickers were probably doing rather more than Woolwich in the development of weapons for the army. They had had the vision to employ the very gifted designer Sir John Carden who had been working on two new tanks: one light and fast and the other heavy and well protected. The heavy tank was given the codename Matilda, which came to be its nickname. A later version of the Matilda was made by the Vulcan Foundry.

Carden was killed in an air crash and tank development slowed, hampered also by the ambivalent attitude of Major-General Sir Hugh Elles, the Master General of Ordnance, who in 1936, 'again changed his mind about tanks'; up to then he had thought them 'useless owing to anti-tank guns, rifles, mines etc', but now he thought they would 'still be of some good to the army but that they would occupy a secondary position to what they had done in the past'. Scott observes that 'Vickers were not encouraged.' As I wrote in *War on Wheels*, there was perhaps more to this. Elles was uncomfortable that Vickers were the only producer of tanks and he approached the Nuffield companies to offer their alternative. I have already described how Nuffield took on tank development. As for Vickers, they pressed ahead with further tank development, arriving at the Valentine. They were also developing a 75mm anti-aircraft gun, but with little interest shown by the War Office. There was a machine gun carrier which would in time become the celebrated Bren Gun Carrier. Their ambition was to have range of armaments which would match those produced by 'Schneider, Bofors or Skoda'. Still, orders in any volume were not forthcoming from the War Office. They were all the time pursuing orders from foreign governments alongside the work they were seeking from the War Office and they did this very much with official blessing; an export drive would help to finance rearmament. None of this was without difficulty.

Vickers returned to profitability in the late thirties, and, by the time war was declared, had capacity for land-based weapons at Crayford, Elswick and Scotstown. Scott gives some figures for orders on hand in 1940. At Elswick, of £22 million orders, £10 million were for the army and, of these, £8 million were for tanks. Of £10 million orders at Crayford, £4 million were for the army; similarly, with Scotstown of £9 million orders, £2.5 million were for the land war. Vickers also took the management of three Royal Ordnance engineering factories at Nottingham, Derby and Manchester. The coming of war massively increased orders. Valentines and Matildas were produced at Elswick, particularly in the first two years, after which tank development passed largely to Nuffield and Vauxhall. Vickers were kept at full capacity with machine and gas-operated guns, field artillery, large artillery pieces and ammunition of all kinds.[37]

Aside from the efforts of Vickers and others, not least Nuffield, by 1939, twenty-three Royal Ordnance Factories had been planned but by the time war broke out, only seven were in production. Four engineering factories were situated at Nottingham, Birtley in County Durham, Blackburn and Dalmuir on Clydeside; an explosives factory at Irvine in Ayrshire; a filling factory at Hereford, with another at Chorley which began production in 1940. Hay makes the point that, at this time, the army numbered 1.5 million men and in addition there was a home guard of 1.2 million to be armed, and most armaments had been left behind at Dunkirk. In April 1939, a Ministry of Supply was set up, but with responsibility only for the army. The Air Ministry, and then in May 1940 the Ministry of Aircraft Production, dealt with supply for the RAF. The navy was dealt with by the Admiralty, but the Royal Ordnance Factories supplied all three certainly with ammunition. Hay adds that the whole of the Royal Ordnance Factories didn't come fully into production until the time of El Alamein in October 1942, three years into the war and an equivalent stage to that reached in the First World War in July 1916, the Battle of the Somme.

Ian Hay visited a number of the factories and provided a wonderful view in the booklet he produced for the Ministry of Supply.[38] Here is some of what he discovered.

The engineering factory at Dalmuir was on the site of Beardmore which had supplied so much in the First World War. It had 2,500 skilled and unskilled workers producing gun barrels, anti-aircraft guns and other heavy armaments. Nottingham, which I would drive past for many years on my way to work, made some 13,000 guns, 23,500 gun barrels and 60,000 spare parts. ROF Cardiff produced 21,200 guns including 7,250 tank guns and 1,875 anti-tank guns. Patricroft was built on the site of the former Naysmith Engineering Works, originally established in 1834, by the Bridgewater Canal in Eccles on the outskirts of Manchester. Employing 3,000 people, it specialized in welding and fabrication, also making parts for Bofors guns. Of those producing shells, Cardonald produced three and a half million 25lb shells and many thousands of heavy bombs. Wigan topped it by producing five and a half million 25lb shells, with Birtley producing cartridge cases and armour-piercing shells.

The shell filling factory at Chorley was twenty-one miles north of Manchester and had its own railway station with workers arriving daily from Liverpool, Manchester and Blackpool. It was purpose built and covered 1,000 acres and had 1,500 buildings employing 35,000 men and women. Building began in 1937 at one time with 15,000 construction workers on site. It had ten staff canteens and housing accommodation for 2,000 people. The canteens were organized across the ROFs by the Controller of Canteens at the Ministry of Supply and priority was given to the nutrition of the tens of thousands of workers it fed. It was a vast catering operation. Other filling factories were Hereford, Aycliffe and Glascoed. Healey Hall filled 136 million 20lb bombs for the RAF, Risley over half a million HE bombs and Swynnerton over a billion percussion bombs. Elaborate safety precautions were in force, particularly in these shell-filling factories. Notwithstanding this, there were accidents but mercifully no major loss of life although much bravery was displayed. Employee relations mattered, and productivity was encouraged by systems of bonuses based on work study. Employee health was taken seriously, not least knowing, from experiences in the First World War, the dangers of TNT poisoning.

TNT was manufactured at Pembury on the South Wales coast between Llanelly and Kidwelly. Covering 500 acres of dunes, it was originally owned and run by Nobel before being taken over by the War Office in the First World War. It was also produced at Irvine, Drigg and Sellafield with Bishopton, Ranskill, Wrexham and Waltham sources of Cordite. Bridgewater produced RDX.

In terms of small arms, the Royal Small Arms Factory at Enfield produced the most, including the Lee-Enfield rifle and two other guns picking up the letters EN from Enfield: the Bren gun and the Sten gun. Fazakerley near Aintree was purpose built, opening in 1941 with a workforce of 12,000, 70 per cent of whom were women, made nearly half of the five million small arms produced during the war. It produced three-quarters of a million No. 4 rifles which replaced the Lee-Enfield. Of the others, Blackburn specialized in fuses and Poole produced the Hispano aircraft gun.

My father wrote about the Central Ordnance Depots of the RAOC as the place where components from the motor manufacturers, Royal Ordnance Factories and radio factories were brought together. He emphasized the need for every part to be present, since, if one was missing, the whole delivery would be delayed.

Hay mentions a few of the many other companies which helped the ROFs: Cadburys, Littlewoods, Imperial Tobacco, Lyons, Metal Box, Lever Brothers, the CWS and specialist companies such as Brocks Fireworks.

Littlewoods, the mail-order and pools company, provided floor space and labour for the war effort in the making of parachutes. 'During the Second World War, Littlewoods produced 12 million shells, 5 million parachutes, 50,000 dinghies, 20,000 barrage balloons, and more than 40,000 pontoons and storm boats across its 16 factories and employing 14,000 workers.'[39]

The Times of 9 August 1945 reported that the Metal Box Company had

> made many things for war service including 140 million metal parts for respirators, 200 million items for precautions against gas attacks, 410 million machine gun belt clips, 1.5 million assembled units for anti-aircraft defence, mines, grenades, bomb tail fins, jerrican closures and water sterilization kits, many different types of food packing including 5,000 million cans, as well as operating agency factories for the government making gliders, production of fuses and repair of aero engines.

Cadburys at Bourneville in Birmingham kept morale high through the sale of chocolate although this had to become ration chocolate as food shortages began to hit. It set up a new company, Bourneville Utilities Limited, to make parts of fellow Birmingham company, Joseph Lucas, amongst much else.[40] J. Lyons had grown massively in the interwar years. By the end of the First World War, Lyons was producing tea, coffee, cakes, ice-cream and groceries from Cadby Hall, supplying 190 tearooms across the country. It acquired two further tea brokers and in

1919 built the largest tea-packing plant in the world at Greenford where it also processed coffee and cocoa products. By 1939 it employed more than 42,000 people and was making 3.5 million gallons of ice-cream a year. It supplied the forces, but it too maintained the morale of the nation as well as lending its management expertise to the Royal Ordnance Factories.[41]

Siemens Brothers was, by the time of the Second World War, recognized as thoroughly British, and so there were none of the problems that its management encountered at the start of previous war. It simply faced the same challenges of mobilizing for war that were faced by the rest of British industry. Labour was short, raw materials scarce and, with the Woolwich factory, enemy bombing frequent and damaging, the Woolwich plant was hit twenty-seven times. The first call on Siemens was for telephone and power cable, which it produced at the rate of thirty miles a week. Cable communication bloomed during the war years with Cable & Wireless volumes rising from 231 million words in 1938 to 644 million in 1943 and 705 million in 1944. Scott outlines special projects entrusted to this company of highly skilled people. The Clyde was vital in producing vast tonnages of essential shipping, which the enemy sought to destroy with magnetic mines. Siemens were commissioned to supply not only the five-miles-long loop cable through which high currents would be passed to explode such mines, but to commission and build all the necessary switchgear and power plant. They also supplied equipment for radar and line communications.

I tell in *War on Wheels* how the Pluto pipeline was built. I did, however, omit the vital detail of Siemens involvement. They were of course the perfect company to produce a submarine cable which could contain petrol at high pressure. Scott tells how they were identified by Mr Hartley, chief engineer of the Anglo-Iranian Oil Company, for the HAIS pipeline (Hartley, Anglo-Iranian, Siemens). He offers a fascinating insight into the technicalities involved, no least the sheer bulk of a cable of seventy miles in length; a whole new building had to be constructed to contain it. Elsewhere, lamp production became even more specialized for the war effort, and the research laboratories were kept busy with demands by the British Aircraft Establishment for specialist bulbs for aircraft signalling.

British manufacturers and scientists certainly played their part in the 'secret weapons' of the Second World War. I wrote of 'Hobart's Funnies', those clever adaptions of tanks that were used so effectively on D-Day, in my book, *War on Wheels*. Other pieces of research are covered in many volumes on the war. It is what is probably the most significant that I want to mention here, albeit briefly. H. G. Wells was a man of astonishing foresight and imagination. He had imagined the tank. In his 1914 book, *The World Set Free*, he imagined atomic energy with remarkable accuracy. Atomic research had been taking place in British universities. Rutherford had famously split the atom at the University of Manchester and his research had been carried on by his pupil, Chadwick. At the start of the war the research programme became more formalized and in 1941 was reported on by the Maud Committee whose report made specific reference to both ICI and Metropolitan-Vickers, underlining the role of British manufacturing in the project. The report received Churchill's blessing with the launch of Tube Alloys, the British body responsible for taking forward the research. The Maud Committee had recognized that Britain simply did not have the resources to pursue the research alone and so British joined with the USA in the Manhattan Project which led to the first atomic bomb.[42]

ICI had entered the 1930s shocked by the untimely death of Lord Melchett. However, with Lord McGowan now at the helm, research continued and the company prospered. ICI was approached in the mid-1930s to increase capacity in all its product areas with the growing possibility of war. 'Almost every industry in Britain required ICI chemicals: 25 plants produced materials ranging from light metals and guns, to mustard gas, detonators, and alloys.'[43] We can add to this explosives but also the production of fertilizer for agricultural use and the development of weedkillers.

In 1937 the complete patent specifications for polythene were filed and each of the Plastics, Dyestuff and Alkali divisions pursued research into its possible uses. Carol Kennedy tells the full and fascinating story including that it was Metropolitan-Vickers which carried out research into its electrical properties. However, it was John Dean of the specialist cable-makers, Telegraph Construction & Maintenance who established the value of polythene as an insulator. From this the developers of polythene discovered that it was perfect insulation, preferable to both rubber and gutta-percha, for the many miles of cable required by the newly invented radar defence system and was put into production just in time for the Battle of Britain.

177

Of equal significance was the invention by ICI chemists of Perspex which was used in the windscreens of aircraft. This had come earlier in conjunction with the development of the Spitfire which incorporated Perspex in its cockpit from 1936.

ICI was far from alone in the British chemical industry. British Celanese at Derby manufactured parachutes and underclothing. By the end of the war, they employed 20,000 people. In conjunction with Courtaulds, ICI formed British Nylon Spinners to exploit the DuPont patent of Nylon for the manufacture of parachutes.

The closely related pharmaceutical industry was much in demand for the treatment of wounded servicemen and civilians. ICI itself discovered Paludrine for the treatment of malaria in its early stages. Penicillin, the discovery of the Scot, Alexander Fleming, had been developed into an antibiotic in the 1930s by researchers at Oxford University and others continuing Fleming's work. In the early 1940s Glaxo as well as Wellcome and Boots began a more active involvement in the Therapeutic Research Corporation and were all exploring the production of the new drug which went into clinical trials in 1943.[44] The Americans provided vital funding to take the idea from the laboratory onto the battlefield where many lives were saved. In Britain, by 1944, Glaxo and Wellcome together were producing 7.5 billion units of penicillin annually.[45]

The radio industry had, by great serendipity, been exploring the new world of television in the five years leading up to the declaration of war, for it would provide the perfect valve technology for radar. Baird had been the trailblazers, but quickly followed by EMI and their remarkable research department who worked with a cathode ray tube with electromagnetic deflection. GEC had favoured the alternative of electrostatic deflection, but, for early television, it was the electromagnetic version that gained favour. Notwithstanding the efforts by Baird, EMI, GEC and Pye, television sets were too expensive, the BBC programmes insufficiently enticing and the sets, with the small bulbous cathode ray tubes, unattractive. All this meant that, before television ceased broadcasting for seven years on 1 September 1939, only 18,000 sets had been sold.

There was another issue which has emerged several times in this story: insufficient attention had been given to educating the workforce. Geddes offers a troubling anecdote: 'A highly respected electronic engineer recalled how, as a young man applying for a job in the prewar industry, he was unwise enough to reveal that he knew some mathematics. He was politely shown the door with the explanation "you see what we want is practical people".[46] Geddes goes on to say that when recruits from the electronics industry joined the armed services, they were found to be in serious need of training.

The manufacturers were nevertheless ready to assist in the production of radar equipment which was being developed by scientists, not least Robert Watson-Watt. The beginnings were rather typical of much of British innovation, for, as Geddes tells, the government researchers were using an EMI set to experiment on, but EMI knew nothing of the experiment and the researchers had no idea where the set had come from. Government was also suspicious of a research team led by a man with a foreign-sounding name which had as members a number of foreign nationals. GEC had no such drawbacks, and possibly for that reason, their electrostatic technology was the first to be used in radar. EMI were, however, soon centrally involved in the development of H2S radar and other projects including infrared image convertor of which 250,000 were made.

Pye at Cambridge devised a set which government scientists thought perfect for an airborne radar receiver and a great many were made. Pye's owner, C. O. Stanley, argued strongly against setting up a shadow factory to manufacture these sets, and instead set up a whole string of small production units in Cambridgeshire villages and ended up employing 14,000 people. Pye designed and made both an infantry set and tank set.

Ekco's factory at Southend was considered too vulnerable to air attack and so they relocated in part to Aylesbury, and, in part, to a nineteenth-century mansion near Malmesbury in Wiltshire. They made radios for bombers and airborne radars and walkie-talkies for infantry. On a visit by Sir Stafford Cripps, he referred to them as 'one of the best, if not the best units in the country producing wireless apparatus'.

Decca, with interests both sides of the Atlantic, bought the record-making company that made Embassy records. This brought them in contact with a talented radio engineer who introduced them to W. J. O'Brien who had failed to interest any American company in his radio navigation system. The result was the famous Decca Navigation system.

Many other radio companies were involved, including Plessey, Philips (once officials had realized that a Dutch company could be trusted) and Mazda. Geddes tells how Philips only barely managed to ship over components and machinery for their vital EF50 valve just before the German invaded in May 1940. During the war, the industry expanded by a factor of two and a half times. With all the demands of war work, the domestic market suffered as batteries became in short supply and receivers began to need repair and replacement.

Alongside the developments in radio and radar, was the secret codebreaking work at hand at Bletchley Park. The name of Alan Turing is the one than comes most swiftly to mind and, of course, the work carried out at Bletchley Park has been written about extensively elsewhere. In the 1930s, Turing had been exploring at Cambridge University some of the implications of the ideas on logic expounded by Lincoln schoolmaster, George Boole, a century earlier. Turing's paper, *On Computable Numbers*, gave birth to a whole new field of research and expounded many of the ideas implicit in Babbage's work, although Dermot Turing does not believe that his uncle was necessarily aware of Babbage's machine until somewhat later.

In relation to British manufacturing, the codebreaking machine created by Turing and his colleague George Welchman, the Bombe, was manufactured by the British Tabulating Machine Company, which had originally manufactured under licence from the Computer-Tabulating-Recording Company. Over time it developed its own products and in 1949 severed the link with the USA. It would become International Computers Limited (ICL).

The Bombe was an electro-mechanical machine aimed at deciphering the daily key to the German Enigma machine.[47] The Germans developed a yet more complex code machine, the Lorenz, and a more powerful codebreaker was demanded. This came in the form of the Colossus which was electronic and used valve technology. It was the brainchild of Max Newman, who had been Turing's teacher at Cambridge, and was made a reality by Tommy Flowers, a senior engineer of the General Post Office which then had the monopoly of telecommunications in the UK and probably the greatest concentration of electronic engineering expertise.[48]

A paper entitled *Blood, Sweat and Tears: British Mobilisation for World War 2*, written by academics Stephen Broadberry and Peter Howlett at the University of Warwick and the London School of Economics, gives a flavour of the scale of war production. From the start of the industrial revolution Britain had created its wealth by exporting and, if anything, had trouble importing enough to balance the books. Suddenly this changed. The early plan for paying for the cost of the war was to have an export drive, but this fell to a trickle by 1941. Thereafter it was the Lend-Lease programme with the USA that saved the nation from bankruptcy. Behind this, massive efforts were made in increasing home production. So, the production of grain, which in 1939 was 4.2 million tons, increased to 7.7 million by 1943, and that of potatoes from 4.3 to 8.5 million tons. Coal production fell and iron increased, with steel staying steady at 13 million tons a year. Aluminium production doubled to 55,000 tons, but with aluminium fabrication growing sixfold. Looking at employment, the workforce grew by over two million between 1939 and 1943 to twenty-two million of which seven million were women. Some 4.7 million people were in the armed services, with 5.1 million working in heavy industry, 5.5 in agriculture, mining and services with the remainder in consumer and distributive trades, which, before the war had accounted for a half of the workforce. Unemployment, which had fallen to 6 per cent in 1939, was eliminated.[49] David Edgerton underlines the significance of Lend-Lease when he writes of the nation's energy needs. Although coal production fell, the nation remained self-sufficient merely by reducing exports. Oil of course was another matter. ICI chemists had worked at the holy grail of extracting oil from coal, but without major success. The Middle East oilfields were largely dedicated to the war in the Middle and Far East and so it was to the USA that Britain looked for its wartime oil supplies, and these supplies were massive. As Edgerton puts it, 'without oil the bombers, the tanks, the warships with which British forces were lavishly equipped could not have been sustained'.[50]

As I did with my chapter on the First World War, I will end this with another look at the nation's account books. In the six years of the war, spending on defence had amounted to £23 billion out of total public expenditure of £28 billion. This was financed by taxation and borrowing largely from the domestic population meaning that, in 1945, government debt had increased by £15 billion. Of crucial importance was the mutual aid rendered under the Lend-Lease arrangements with the USA. Some 65 per cent of what was provided were armaments, including a great many vehicles, as I tell in *War on Wheels*; the number of British men and women in uniform was simply far larger than could be supported by domestic industry. The accounting was not straightforward, as becomes clear in R. G. D. Allen's paper from 1946. In it he sets out in detail what was provided by the US to Britain and Empire nations and also what they provided in return. A grand reckoning was made which showed that the USA had provided US$ 27 billion and in return Britain had contributed £1.2 billion. He looked at the figures in relation to the size of the respective economies and, at around 4 per cent, the contributions match quite closely. In any event the USA demanded payment of only a small fraction. Allen makes the point that the balance was paid in blood, sweat and tears.[51] The debt owed did add seriously to the economic challenge that faced the post-war government and, as part of the deal, Britain lost the right to exploit a number of valuable patents, not least the jet engine, radar and antibiotics.

In fighting the Second World War, Britain had made a prodigious contribution to world manufacturing in a great many ways, as well as bearing the brunt of countering Nazi aggression. The accompanying cost was huge and probably sounded the death knell to Britain's leadership in manufacturing, but not quite its end.

Chapter 16

The Postwar Export Drive

'Out of this war will come great good. It has blown the cobwebs out of us and has given us a much needed spring cleaning. To my mind the broom has not yet swept clean enough. It has only started. Its handle has to be much, MUCH longer. People do not yet perhaps, realize how clean it must still sweep. We are a great people. But we are still a little slow to change.'

Sir William Rootes, *Scope* magazine
interview, September 1944.[1]

The Britain that woke on the morning of 15 August 1945 was exhausted from six years of total war. Every sinew of manufacturing industry had been strained to the limit in aid of the war effort. Now came the massive task of rebuilding, hardly a conducive atmosphere for the country which had shaped so much of the manufacturing world. Yet, in spite of all the hardship that the British people would face over the coming few years, manufacturing industry and government were up for the challenge.

The Attlee government, which came to power just over a month before the war ended, had, in its manifesto, declared that 'only if public ownership replaces private monopoly can industry become efficient'. It inherited a good deal of government control of the economy and was determined to use it to restore the country to prosperity.

It didn't start well, for on 24 August 1945, President Truman announced that Britain's Lend-Lease arrangements with the United States would come to an immediate end . From then on, Britain would have to pay dollars for its imports. The answer was some robust negotiation by economist J. M. Keynes, and then a drive for exports, hand in hand with tough import controls. It wasn't going to be the ad hoc arrangements of 1919; this time there was a governmental infrastructure in place to guide industry. Scott gives a figure of 175 per cent as the increase from prewar volumes in British exports required to maintain the nation's standard of living.[2] Britain had long imported more than it exported, but before the war it had earned from shipping and from overseas investments more than sufficient 'invisible' exports. The war and foreign competition had reduced its shipping fleet and investment had been lost or sold to help pay for the war effort. I come later to how British manufacturing rose to the challenge. The other side of the coin was a severe restriction on imports. During the war Lease-Lend had enabled food supplies; with the coming of peace the British people would have to endure rationing for many more years. Purchase tax was raised to discourage the purchase of items such a motor cars to discourage imports but also to ensure the availability of the maximum number of vehicles for export markets. Raw materials were prioritized for export industries.[3]

The more immediate issue was there for all to see: towns and cities devastated by enemy bombing with the associated acute shortage of housing. In a book on manufacturing, the first focus must be the machinery required for building. In a fascinating paper entitled 'Landscape bulldozer: machines, modernity and environment in post-war Britain', Ralph Harrington paints a vivid picture.[4] He begins by writing of the massive impact of the American bulldozer, and not only for military purposes (many thousands crossed to Normandy in support of the D-Day landings and the advance into Germany). They had also been used, as previously noted, on the push to build airfields, but also and importantly on clearing bombsites. He offers a comparison between two sites in East London, one with American soldiers and bulldozers clearing land ready for temporary housing and the other with British workmen with only a concrete mixer in support. In the years before the war, British builders hadn't seen bulldozers as suitable for British conditions and so British companies hadn't been attracted into manufacturing them in any quantity. Jack Olding and Levertons imported Caterpillars, but that was largely that. In the aftermath of the war, the British government persuaded the Americans to leave behind the thousands of machines they had brought over, and these were purchased both by local government and building companies. In this way the British construction industry moved into the era of mechanization. One name that appeared in a very small way in the later 1940s was that of Joseph Cyril Bamford who began by making trailers from army surplus. He went on to fix a loader to a Fordson tractor. That company, JCB, would go on to become one of the success stories of postwar Britain. There was of course Ruston & Hornsby with their digging and roadmaking equipment, to say nothing of their diesel engines, famous worldwide. But they weren't bulldozers.

Jack Olding had worked closely with the army during the war handling many thousands of British and American tanks before they were issued to units. He would have got to know the powers that be, not least the Deputy Chief of the Imperial General Staff whose responsibilities included equipment, General Sir Ronald Weeks. After the ending of hostilities, Weeks, who before the war had been a director of Pilkington, joined Vickers as a non-executive director, becoming chairman of its English Steel subsidiary. Vickers had played major role in supplying the army with all manner of equipment, including tanks, and, so, had long experience of tracked vehicles. In an effort to diversify from military equipment, it took up the government's challenge of producing a British tracked tractor to take the place of Caterpillar. It would be powered by a brand-new Rolls-Royce 6-cylinder supercharged 12-litre diesel engine.

Jack Olding was approached by Vickers, and was offered the sole worldwide marketing rights for this new crawler, the Vickers Vigor VR180. This crawler's tracks, drive and suspension were based upon the configuration of those of a tank. This meant that the four wheels each side, allowed it to manoeuvre quickly and easily, even over rough ground at speeds of up to 10 miles per hour, twice as fast as a comparable Cat D8 could manage. The deal, Vickers offered, promised huge financial rewards, pending, of course, the subsequent success of the Vigor. Nonetheless, the prospect prompted Olding into the decision of relinquishing his Caterpillar franchise in readiness for the Vickers Vigor. His company went on to sell the Vigor, but it was unsuccessful, as the machines were not as good as the tried-and-tested Caterpillar tractor.

Building materials were an issue. Although steel was in short supply, building in reinforced concrete became more common; the first forty-storey block of flats was finished in 1951. Elsewhere in the new towns, it was low-rise building with an emphasis on space. The Marley tile company originated in Kent and in the postwar period built a number of new factories to meet the huge demand. New building materials were appearing: Formica, plywood and plastics and I write more about them in the following chapter on the Festival of Britain where architecture and design took pride place. The Attlee government had yet more immediate concerns: their manifesto commitments.

The targets for nationalization were Cable & Wireless, the Bank of England and BOAC; the railways and road haulage; coal, gas and electricity; iron and steel, but not shipbuilding. It represented a massive task, but one that was not to be from a standing start. There had been a good deal of governmental control during the war and in the interwar years attempts had been made to rationalize railways and the coalmines.

The Cable & Wireless Act 1946 took into public ownership the Cable & Wireless Company which owned and operated the submarine cables between the dominions, colonies and India.

The Civil Aviation Act of 1946 split the 1939 BOAC into three publicly owned corporations: British Overseas Airways Corporation (BOAC) for Commonwealth, Far East and the North Atlantic routes; British European Airways (BEA) for domestic and European routes; and British South American Airways Corporation (BSAA) for South Atlantic routes. The corporations were to be subsidized for the first ten years, after which time they were expected to be self-financing. In 1949, BSAA was incorporated into BOAC.

Rather more radical was the Coal Industry Nationalization Act 1946, which set up the National Coal Board and took into public ownership the 950 or so pits then being worked. The principle of nationalization had been advanced by coal unions as far back as 1892 and in 1918 the possibility had been actively explored. In 1930, the Coal Act imposed on the industry a degree of coordination. The industry was inefficient and suffered from industrial unrest to a far greater degree than any other; the National Strike of 1926 was followed by the miners staying on strike for a further seven months, reducing coal production for that year by one half, to say nothing of the suffering endured by the mining communities.[5] A committee was set up in 1945 to explore the inefficiencies and came up with proposals that included the need for the industry to work in larger units.[6] Nationalization achieved this by dividing the working mines into eight areas which would operate under divisional boards reporting to the national board.[7] In 1947, there were 726,000 employees, 610,629 of whom became members of the National Union of Mineworkers.[8]

The Electricity Act 1947 brought into full public ownership those private and local authority generation and distribution companies that were not already part of the Central Electricity Generating Board. It was a move that had been expected and did not excite much controversy except, inevitably, for compensation.[9] Also in relation to energy, the Gas Act 1947 brought all the local gas companies into public ownership.

The Transport Act 1947 brought into public ownership the private rail companies, the canal companies and long-distance road haulage.[10] The railway companies had, during the war, been under government control. With the passing of the Transport Act, they were re-organized into six regions: London Midland, Southern, Eastern, Western, North Eastern and Scottish.[11] For the remainder of the forties and well into the fifties, steam would reign supreme with each region's workshops maintaining locomotives and rolling stock and making new when needed. Importantly, Metropolitan-Cammell were manufacturing both locomotives and rolling stock for British Railways, but also export markets and London Transport, where aluminium was used for body work given the shortage of steel.[12]

Work was being done in preparation for the introduction of both diesel locomotives and electrification, and a name from the past emerges, Napier. This old motor engineering company had become part of English Electric in 1942, and, shortly after the war, had been requested by the Admiralty to develop a diesel engine for fast patrol boats. Its engineers rose to the challenge and the Deltic was born.[13] It was the Deltic which would go on in the fifties to power diesel locomotives for British Railways. The engine had many other uses including power generation in remote locations. The Deltic, though, did not power the first diesel locomotive to run on the British rail network. This achievement fell to Paxman and also English Electric and their diesel electric for London, Midland and Scottish, numbers 10000 and 10001.[14]

Another target for nationalization was Power Jets Ltd., the company formed to exploit the jet engine. The management at Ruston & Hornsby was keen to keep at the forefront of technology and saw, in the jet engine, huge potential aside from aviation. Managing Director Victor Bone asked Chief Engineer Oswald Wans, to investigate the potential for gas turbines using jet technology. Wans's report was presented to the board and two Ruston engineers were sent to Power Jets to learn more. A gas turbine division was set up under Bone's son and work was started on a prototype for a 750kW gas turbine. There were inevitable teething troubles, but an engine was ready for the Olympia exhibition in 1953. The company had planned a bit of theatre by rigging up the engine with an electrical generator. A strike by London Electricity Board employees made the theatre all too real, as the Ruston Gas Turbine powered the lighting for the whole of Olympia.[15] Rustons would go on to develop gas turbine technology.

I look at the final leg of nationalization, steel, below, particularly in the context of Vickers and English Steel.

The armament factories did not fall silent as they had in the 1920s; the Labour government was committed to a really quite large army, navy and air force. A core of Royal Ordnance Factories were kept open and, some which had closed, reopened in 1951 in response to the Korean War. Following the war, a British military presence was maintained in Germany (the British Army of the Rhine), in the Middle East and Asia. In addition, NATO was formed in 1949 with Britain as a key participant. All this needed supplying and the many factories which had supplied so well during the war maintained their production. Possibly the most iconic product was the Centurion tank, which had been designed during the war, but only entered service shortly after. It was still in service some fifty-eight years later in Iraq. It was manufactured by the Royal Ordnance Factories, Vickers and Morris.

A good number of the Royal Ordnances Factories were turned over to other uses. For example, after the war, Chorley employed 5,000 in the manufacture of clothing. Arthur Marwick, writing in *British Society Since 1945*, identifies the re-use of Royal Ordnance Factories and wartime shadow factories as drivers of employment, particularly to areas which had suffered declines of industry.[16] An example he gave was of potteries where some 37,000 jobs had been lost, and where Ordnance factories were put to use by Rists (a subsidiary of Lucas), AEI and Simplex (the domestic appliance subsidiary of Tube Investments which included Creda cookers). One particular example of re-use would have ramifications for decades to come. A factory for the production of TNT had been built at Sellafield in 1942, well away from possible German air attacks. In 1947 the site was repurposed by the building of a plant to produce plutonium for the British nuclear deterrent.

As to the export market for armaments, Scott recalled the public hostility to Vickers in the 1930s when it was seen as a warmonger whilst the nation was seeking peace. Since then, it had become known as the builder of the Spitfire, Wellington and Valentine as well as the ships *King George V* and *Illustrious*. Scott then adds the commonly held view that one reason for the warmth of public feeling toward Vickers, of course, was that 'the international armaments business was dead and gone'.

I paused when I read that, noting that at the time of writing Britain is second only to the USA in global defence exports. In business terms in the immediate aftermath of the war, the armament orders to private companies such as Vickers-Armstrong tumbled. Vickers had been preparing itself and was ready to meet the challenge. Its story is illustrative of much else that was going on in postwar British manufacturing. Its biggest business was shipbuilding at Barrow and the Naval Shipyard in Newcastle, plus ship repairing at Palmers in Jarrow. Before looking at Vickers in detail, I shall draw on Slaven to paint an overall picture which the shipbuilding industry faced in August 1945. The government had decided against the nationalization of shipbuilding and, indeed, in the wake of the war, shipyards remained busy. Employment was at an historic peak, at 300,000 in 1950.

British merchant marine had lost 2,539 ships of nearly twelve million gross tons as a result of enemy action, plus a further 226 ships as a result of marine risk losses. These figures include three-quarters of the prewar deep sea tramp fleet and half of prewar liner and tanker tonnages.[17] The problem the government perceived was not how to keep the shipyards in work, but how to share out their limited capacity in the face of demands by British shipowners as well as those of allied countries. The prevention of Germany and Japan restarting their shipyards exacerbated the shortage of supply. Slaven, again, offers some numbers.

The annual tonnage launched in British yards in 1946 was 1.1 million, but this represented 53 per cent of world launches, with the USA second at 24 per cent. In 1947, UK launches were closer to 1.2 million and its share had increased to 57 per cent, with the USA falling back to 8 per cent. 1948 had the UK still at 1.1, but its share was beginning to fall, to 51 per cent that year and to 40 per cent in 1949. The backlog of orders was still large at 8 million in 1948, of which British yards had 56 per cent. Thereafter, the order books increased massively to 27 million in 1958 with Britain's share falling to 20 per cent with each of Germany, Japan and Sweden close behind. Annual launches increased to 9 million with the British share falling to 15 per cent, to the benefit of Sweden, Germany and Japan. Slaven explores in some detail the reasons behind the figures.

British output remained pretty steady at 1.2 million which meant yards were employed but not growing. There was a clear and painful memory of the interwar years of overcapacity and the yards naturally wanted to avoid this. Yet, with the government desperate for exports, why didn't the yards increase production? Slaven repeatedly quotes industry leaders maintaining that an annual output of 1.75 million was entirely possible.

Slaven notes the shortage of steel; Scott is much clearer that this truly was a serious constraint. Government allocated what steel production there was to uses with the best export-earning potential and, I guess, motor cars won. Slaven points out that imports of steel were not prevented and so steel could be had, had yards wanted it. The next hurdle was the system of licences which the Admiralty and Ministry of Supply used to allocate orders to yards. Scott quotes Vickers management and, indeed their shipowner customers, as arguing vehemently against this. Slaven then points to a lack of investment in capital equipment by yard owners, but he acknowledges that Vickers were among the exceptions along with Harland & Wolff. Vickers embarked on substantial re-equipping at both Barrow and Newcastle where they wanted, in particular, to be able to demonstrate to the shipping lines that the Naval Yard could build large first-class ships.

In the same way as he had been in the interwar years, Slaven was convinced that the close relationship between British shipbuilders and British shipowners did neither a favour, effectively removing competition, in particular in relation to innovation, from the market. This lack of innovation or technical development, Slaven saw as perhaps *the* major problem. For example, wartime experience had demonstrated the benefit of welding, as opposed to riveting, as well as prefabrication and batch building, none of which were embraced by British yards or their workforces. There was undoubted reluctance on the part of the skilled riveters to allow lower-skilled welders to invade their workplace. Slaven is reticent to point too much of a finger at the workforce. However, one significant factor counting against British yards was the time lag between taking the order and starting work and then the time actually spent on the berth. The first was often a year and the second seldom better than eighteen months. With the lifting of restrictions on Japan and Germany, these were offering one year from order to completion. The reason for the very long times taken by British yards were frequent stoppages but also the difficulty in operating in crowded and old-fashioned yards.

The market had also changed. Tankers were in huge demand as oil was being moved around the world in ever greater quantities. Ships, not only tankers, were getting bigger and yards needed to invest in order to deal with them. British yards were at heart conservative, preferring a mix of ships to build. Many yards preferred liners, where they could make much more money from skilled fitting-out compared to the essentially all-steel tanker.

Vickers were ahead of the pack, but still operated at less than full capacity. They invested £5 million at Barrow and £8 million at Newcastle where one improvement to facilitate welding was to pipe oxygen throughout the yard instead of using cylinders. Liquid oxygen was delivered by road to an oxygen-evaporating set from where the gas was conveyed not only to the assembly shop, but to the blacksmiths', sheet-metal working, plumbing, copper-smithing and fitting shops and to the electricians' and millwrights' shops.[18] In spite of this investment, even Vickers had orders well in excess of their annual production and, in time and especially when overseas alternatives came available, the previously loyal customers began to drift away. Vickers had addressed the tanker problem and Barrow was producing big tankers, in 1948, two 31-tonners for Stavros Niarchos. The Greek shipping lines would become powerful players.

Turning to the other Vickers businesses, in heavy engineering they reverted to their prewar products of cement-making machinery, big presses and petrol pumps and won good orders from the USA. They still had capacity, but needed orders which matched it with a necessary diversity of work which occupied manpower and used available space – not a simple matter. There was then the question of design staff. Vickers had traditionally had a large staff to deal with armament development. As that diminished and as government scientists took over much of the invention, what would be needed? The Korean War and the fresh demand for both shipping and armaments delayed any big decisions. In terms of new products, 'clearing' presses became very important for the motor industry with orders from Morris, Pressed Steel, Rootes, Vauxhall and Ford. Another important area was printing presses, and Vickers eventually bought George Mann & Co., manufacturers of offset litho presses. In a related area, they bought Powers-Samas accounting machine manufacturers. I have already mentioned the other intriguing departure for Vickers: their entry into the world of track-type tractors.

At English Steel, Vickers found an imaginative and effective managing director, Frederick Pickworth, who was forward looking and adaptable. However, the nationalization programme and the Iron and Steel Act 1949 would divert attention from the business. Sir Ronald Weeks had become a non-executive director of Vickers and chairman of English Steel. I shall quote what Scott had to say about him. 'By the end of the second world war Week's brilliance as an administrator had become recognized as something of a phenomenon. If his career and his personality had been specially designed to fit him for the chairmanship of Vickers they would have differed very little from the actuality.'[19] Weeks would take the chair of the main board in the fifties. For now, though, it was the business of nationalization. English Steel was much more than a steel company: it was really an engineering company that also made steel. Ronald Weeks was appointed chairman of English Steel in 1945 and for the next two years led the argument that most of the company's production were not 'scheduled products' for the purposes of nationalization, but rather engineering products made from steel. Nevertheless, eventually the government argument prevailed and the company was sold into public ownership for, it was said, a fair price. The Conservative government was returned to power in 1951, and by 1953 the necessary structures had been put in place to return the steel assets to private hands. Weeks was again involved and set up a committee to carry out a cold financial appraisal of the part of the business that had been English Steel to see if Vickers wished to buy it back and, if so, at what price. Again, a good price was eventually achieved, and ownership returned in time for an upturn in demand for steel.

The biggest question for Vickers was aircraft production since, with peace, the frenetic building of aircraft came to an end. They wanted to remain in the aircraft industry, but were well aware of the massive costs inherent in developing the next generation of aircraft. They had ended the war and started the peace with the well-regarded Viking, but it was only a stop-gap and something new was needed. The aircraft industry was reviewed by the Brabazon Committee and it was suggested to Vickers that they might develop a twenty-four-seater aircraft powered by four gas-turbine engines driving airscrews. The new chief designer at Weybridge, George Edwards, set to the task of the VC (Vickers Commercial) 2. He favoured the Rolls-Royce Dart engine. Fundamental was the need for the new BEA, soon to be under the direction of Peter Masefield, to select it over its competitors. It was not an easy ride. The engine experienced problems, and BEA seemed to be favouring the Airspeed Ambassador which was conventionally powered by a piston engine and could carry forty passengers. The Vickers aircraft was to be called the Viceroy, but, with an eye to the Indian market this was changed to the Viscount. BEA placed their first order on 3 August 1950.[20] The Viscount went on to win worldwide acceptance and played its full part in the export drive.

Staying with aviation, but moving on from Vickers, de Havilland designed the first commercial jet aircraft, the Comet. It suffered from design issues, but once resolved, provided vital experience for future jet designs.[21] English Electric designed and built the Canberra as a turbo-jet successor to the Mosquito. It would, through many iterations, serve the RAF for decades. Handley Page built the Hermes, Britain's first four-engined airliner, after the war. Hawker focused on military requirements, designing in the 1940s the Sea Hawk, from the company's first jet, and the Hunter, a day interceptor fighter. Shorts produced further variations of their Sunderland flying boat. Westland, who had built a large number of aircraft for other companies, in 1947 focused on rotor craft and built the Wyvern, the first Westland aircraft to enter service with Fleet Air Arm.

Aluminium had come into its own during the war, but, with the peace and a shortage of steel, its uses would be explored further. The war had taught the industry how to use low-grade ore, how to experiment with alloys and how scrap might be used. Aluminium Almin Ltd. was set up in 1947 as a research body to explore further this most useful metal. The UK production of aluminium ingot was lower than that of Canada which also had the benefit of great hydroelectric power.[22] What Britain had done was to create an aluminium fabrication industry of some size, producing sheet and wire for use in aircraft, but also for example the new trains for the London Underground. Manufacturing plant built for wartime production had been sold to private companies and was ready to supply the postwar market, provided it could do so more cheaply than Canada. The largest company, British Aluminium, had formed a joint venture with Hawker Siddeley Aircraft Company and Tube Investments to form the Cable & Wire Company to pool their resources. British Aluminium's major competitor, was Aluminium Ltd. of Canada, which we now know as Alcan.

Turning now to the motor industry, in his seminal book, *The Car Makers*, Graham Turner wrote, 'when the [second world] war ended, the motor manufacturing industry stood helpless before an unparalleled situation: there was a raging demand for cars in a world where there were few cars to be had.'[23] Turner gives the figure for total production of cars in 1943 as 1,649. However, the motor industry had been massively busy during the war with all manner of armaments and had both workforce and factories ready to make for the civilian market. But that was not what happened; the government had other priorities and engaged the motor industry as possibly the key element in its drive for exports.

Geoff Carverhill in his book, *Rootes Story: The Making of a Global Automotive Empire*, gives some statistics of UK car production for 1950 once it had come back up to speed. There were some twenty-seven companies producing thirty-six different makes. Top was Ford with 185,000 vehicles per year, then came Austin with 166,000, followed by the Nuffield organization with 150,000, then Standard-Triumph with 112,000 and Rootes with 90,000 and, finally of the larger companies, Vauxhall (General Motors) with 89,000.[24] Graham Turner highlights the success stories. Some 75 per cent of production went to export markets, amounting to 400,000, with strong sales in Australia and New Zealand but also in the USA, particularly with sports cars such as the Mark V and XK120 Jaguars, the MG and Austin Healey and Sunbeam Talbot 90. In terms of total popularity, the Austin A40 was a winner and in three years sold 250,000. The same was true with the Morris Minor, but so too the Standard Vanguard, which sold 300,000, and Hillman Minx. Carverhill includes photographs of Humber Pullmans produced for Royal Tours. At Rover, Spencer and Maurice Wilks conceived the idea of the Land Rover, based on the design of the Willys Jeep, and taking advantage of aluminium for its bodywork. This, too, proved a popular export as well as finding a ready market among Britain's farmers and in the military. Notwithstanding the challenges and shortcomings, the motor industry played its major role in restoring the nation's finances.

The figures did mask underlying problems. Labour relations have been written about extensively, but here it is appropriate to quote Turner's view that the push for exports did mean that management tended to do anything to keep production moving, including conceding to unions' demands. The push had another downside in terms of quality, with cars being rushed out the factories too quickly.

Looking at the industry more widely, UK companies became increasingly conscious that they had to adopt American methods of the production line, but also increase volumes to benefit from economies of scale; for this, exports would continue to be important. William and

Reginald Rootes made a long trip to the USA in 1947 to assess the market but also to learn from American companies. They had been selling in the US for some time, selling also Rover and MG cars. They set up their own US operation under Brian Rootes and this proved very effective. My father joined the Rootes Group in 1946 with the task of setting up a bespoke servicing depot at the former Sunbeam-Talbot factory in West London. I write about this in *Dunkirk to D-Day*, but in essence he was drawing on his experience of supplying and maintaining the many thousands of vehicles used by the army. Once this was up and running, he became export director with a focus on the Middle Eastern market. In 1951, he was part of a government export mission to the Middle East. The focus on selling overseas is clear from his archives. *Scope*, the magazine for industry, published an interview with Sir William Rootes in its September 1944 issue, an extract from which I began this chapter. The piece shows him as an impatient man advocating buying British because it would lead to full employment. He was passionate about exporting but also apprenticeships; he valued skills but also planning.

A further issue, in terms of achieving economies of scale, was the need to reduce the number of different companies. Carverhill writes that, in 1950, Reginald Rootes had discussions with Reggie Hanks of the Nuffield Organization with a view to a merger. What Rootes didn't know was that Leonard Lord, then managing director of Austin, was in discussions with Lord Nuffield and this resulted in the formation of the British Motor Corporation in 1952.

Another issue was the sheer number of different designs of parts. Lucas had been arguing since 1947 that standardization was needed, if costs were to be reduced. They cited 133 headlamp types and 98 different windscreen wipers. Manufacturers were resistant; they prided themselves on the individuality of British; even at BMC, an Austin was an Austin and a Morris a Morris.[25] I mentioned in the previous chapter the report in *The Times* of Sir Peter Bennett's address to Lucas shareholders in December 1945. Factories had been built or at the very least adapted to wartime production. There was both a cost and a loss in production as the adaptions were reversed. Bennett adds that the burden of high taxation simply made the task all the more difficult. Turner really underlines the point by his exasperation at the frequent changes to purchase tax and its impact on planning.

Dunlop emerged from the war years firmly as part of the British establishment. They had done more than their bit in the war, their products were thoroughly British and loved, and they were good employers. It was not really surprising that the government asked them to take on the former Rootes shadow factory at Speke just outside Liverpool. They brought there the manufacture of a range of products: footwear, tyres, belting, precision instruments and sporting goods under the benign eye of a talented young manager, David Collett. He built on the Dunlop tradition of good employee relations and public service, and his factory, with 7,000 employees, was very much the centre of the community.[26] Elsewhere the company had resumed control of its subsidiaries in France, Germany and Japan. France, though, greeted the postwar world with a revolutionary product that would present a massive challenge for Dunlop: the radial tyre, marketed as the Michelin X. This tyre offered better wear and better road handling and would not be matched until the Pirelli Cinturato (I remember getting a set of 'cints' for my Mini).

There might have been trouble brewing for the motor industry, but there was also great success. Aston Martin had started to make motor cars when Lionel Martin and Robert Bamford set up a small London workshop in 1913. The name derives from their victory in the renowned Aston Clinton Hill Climb. They had made a debut in the French Grand Prix in 1922. The story goes that tractor and gear manufacturer, David Brown, spotted a small ad in *The Times* in 1946 offering a sports car company for sale. He made an offer and, in 1947, bought the company. The following year the iconic DB1 won the Spa 24-hour race.[27]

The toy industry that emerged from the war, in a sense, had all the benefits and none of the disadvantages of its full-size counterparts. Germany and Japan were prevented from supplying toys, leaving the UK industry, which was already strong, free to supply a market that would grow steadily for the next twenty years. Toy shops began to fill up towards the end of the forties. Frank Hornby, who had launched his 12-volt DC Hornby Dublo in 1938, in the postwar period watched as it gained popularity. Hornby also continued to manufacture Meccano and Dinky toys. The postwar boom encouraged new entrants but few survived, a notable exception being Lesney. Rodney and Leslie Smith set up in a disused pub to manufacture small diecast toys sold in matchboxes. Rosebud was manufacturing some ten million dolls a year, many for export. Export was very much the watchword and thanks particularly to core players like Lines Brothers, by the late fifties, Britain was the largest exporter of toys in the world.[28]

The radio and television manufacturers had played an important role in supplying the armed forces with the equipment they needed, not least radar. Technology had developed and companies had grown. With the coming of peace, they had capacity, were well equipped and had a skilled workforce ready to rise to the export challenge. There was debate within the industry on what the export target should be. The Board of Trade set a figure of 400,000 sets for 1946 and this was met, in addition to a million sets manufactured for the home market. The players were largely as before the war: Murphy, Ekco, EMI and Pye; Cossor was still there, but also with a radar company. Two new entrants deserve mention. Ferguson, backed by Thorn Electrical Industries whose interests also including lighting, and Michael Sobell. Sobel, as he was before he changed his name, was, like Jules Thorn, an émigré from Austria. He had been educated in London and had set up a small radio business in the thirties. During the war he had undertaken contracts for the Admiralty and, with the peace, was given the opportunity to take over a former ordnance shadow factory in South Wales. There he manufactured radios and, in time televisions. Sobell was the father-in-law of Arnold Weinstock, who would join the business and, in 1960, engineer its takeover by GEC of which, later, Weinstock would become chairman, creating an electrical giant. Sir Jules Thorn, as he would become, led the major force in British television manufacture in a group comprising lighting and a whole range of domestic electric equipment.

Design was becoming more important, and Pye took on designer Robin Day, moving away from 'high-gloss finishes, radiused corners and gilt trims that were then general in radiogram and television cabinet design. He moved Pye to an over-all geometry and eventually to a house style recognizable of the best 1950s design evident at the Festival of Britain'.[29]

Television too was edging forward, but with endless technical challenges. In 1949, the BBC launched their first regional transmitter at Sutton Coalfield and Bush produced the first set that could be tuned by the user himself; hitherto sets had been tuned at the factory to the Alexandra Palace transmitter.

J. Lyons offers a fascinating link between electronics and catering! In the late forties, J. Lyons was a big player in the catering industry and as

197

such was processing a huge number of small, low-margin transactions each day, occupying a great many human 'accounting machines'. The Lyons management were aware of developments in the new world of computing and sent two representatives to the USA to find out what IBM could offer. The answer will surely raise a smile for it was to return to England and to Cambridge and Maurice Wilkes.

Wilkes had joined Alan Turing in Cambridge and, whilst Turing was working on the Automatic Computing Engine (ACE), Wilkes was developing the Electronic Delay Storage Automatic Calculator. Turing soon moved to Manchester University, joining Max Newman, but Wilkes worked on in Cambridge under Sir Charles Darwin and the National Physical Laboratory.

The men from Lyons and Wilkes struck up a positive relationship and Lyons put money in support of Wilkes's work. In time, though, it became clear that the needs of Cambridge mathematicians were not those of a business seeking to process a large number of small transactions. Lyons therefore went their own way and this resulted in the Lyons Electronic Office (LEO) which proved effective but once more in this story failed to convince much of the commercial market. LEO was later bought by English Electric from which it would join with ICL.[30]

In the world of chemicals, ICI had played a major part in the war effort not least from its Billingham plant on Teeside, reputed to be the largest chemical plant then in the world. In 1945, the company bought the site on which it would build its other major plant, in the north-east at Wilton. This was not only bigger, but would be home to Britain's major chemicals manufacture for decades. It had its own power plant, with 33MW Metropolitan-Vickers/AEI turbine-generator sets powered by Babcock & Wilcox boilers. It was vast then, but in 2013 boasted sixty miles of road, 400 miles of electric cable and 150 miles of pipework on the 2,000-acre site.[31] In the late forties and fifties, its production included nylon, terylene and Perspex. Nylon and terylene were a godsend to the housewife and put an end to some of the weekly washday, being easier both to wash and dry. Polythene, which had been used almost exclusively by the military, began to appear in the nation's kitchen in colourful moulded products. Elsewhere in the chemical industry, Courtaulds had suffered in the war from the loss of its subsidiary, American Viscose, as part of the price of Lease-Lend. This was partially offset by the formation of British Nylon Spinners as a joint venture with ICI to produce parachutes. The late forties and fifties saw Courtaulds back to its core product of viscose staple fibre.[32]

The pharmaceutical industry built on the progress made during the war, particularly with antibiotics. In 1945 the Beecham Research Laboratories were established and in 1947 moved to a bespoke site opened by Sir Alexander Fleming. That same year, Glaxo Laboratories, which had outgrown its parent company, Joseph Nathan & Co., became a significant business in its own right. It had built a strong balance sheet with production facilities at Greenford but also Barnard Castle, Stratford, and Aylesbury. With the coming of peace and the shift to deep fermentation for the production of penicillin, it bought a derelict 100-acre site from Millom & Askam Haematite Iron Co. at Ulverston near Morecombe. The handsome four-storey offices bore a strong resemblance to the Greenford Headquarters and marked for the surrounding area a move away from the grime of an ironworks.[33] Glaxo was firmly established in pharmaceuticals although it continued it food business. What it lacked was its own discoveries; these would come later.

Looking through an illustrated book on the forties, it is clear there was little joy on the retail front.[34] Rationing continued after the war. I came across an advertisement for Sirdar Wool underlining the probability that many women would be knitting their own. Sirdar was famous not only for the quality of its yarn, but also for its patterns for which it boasted an extensive design department. There was Lyle & Scott for men's underwear. This was traditionally woollen knitted underwear, but the company had branched out into knitted outerwear and in the early fifties its first tie-up with a designer brand, in that case, Dior. Dresses were of the New Look and Gor-Ray pleated skirts. For men, tailoring from Austin Reed and Simpsons and shirts from Viyella House. Men were also paying attention to their grooming as evidenced by an advertisement for Brylcreem. Whilst there were no advertisements for Unilever products the postwar period saw the company launch Birds Eye frozen peas.

In terms of entertainment, there was the Pye radio, but also Decca Records which gained a reputation for excellent classical recordings under the guidance of John Coulson who went on to be head of music at the BBC under David Attenborough. There was also an advertisement for a GEC television and Regal Zonophone records which produced many recordings of Salvation Army Bands. Raleigh had an advertisement showing how it had gathered under its wing other makes such as Rudge, Humber and Sturmey-Archer. In 1952 Raleigh employed 7,000 people.

It wasn't only big industry: the Labour government adopted a key recommendation from the 1931 Macmillan Committee which had looked at the difficulties businesses faced in raising capital. In particular, Macmillan recognized a gap, which came to be known as the Macmillan Gap, of up to £200,000 where raising money was particularly difficult.[35] The Macmillan Committee's report had followed the formation of Bankers Industrial Development Company by the Bank of England to provide finance for basic industries such as iron and steel. The Attlee government created the Finance Corporation for Industry, chaired by Sir Ronald Weeks, to provide larger investments, again mainly for steel but also oil. For the Macmillan Gap, ICFC (the Industrial and Commercial Finance Corporation) was formed under the chairmanship of Lord Piercy to provide finance for small- and medium-sized companies seeking funds in the range £5,000 to £200,000.[36] In the 1950s, ICFC set up offices around Britain with teams who got to know their business communities and who provided vital support to growing businesses. ICFC joined with FCI to become FFI in 1973 and later became 3i and still works with independent businesses. The ethos of ICFC from the beginning was that the investor needed to know well the business in which he was to invest, but also to understand the industry and markets. Investments were intended to be long term.

There were surely promising signs for British manufacturing in this, otherwise very grim, immediate postwar period. It seems to me entirely appropriate that this should have been celebrated in the Festival of Britain which is the subject of the closing chapter of this story.

Chapter 17

The Festival of Britain

'THE AUTOBIOGRAPHY OF A NATION is presented for the first time in this Festival of Britain and millions of the British people will be the authors of it, displaying through every means by which Man expresses his nature how we have honoured our stewardship and used our talents. Conceived among the untidied ruins of war and fashioned through days of harsh economy, this Festival is a challenge to the sloughs of the present and a shaft of confidence cast forth against the future.'

So began the introduction to the festival brochure.

The festival ran through the summer of 1951 and was a great celebration of what being British meant. It was to be a tonic to an exhausted nation, but also a rallying call to a bright future. In the context of this book, it is a fitting way to draw together the many strands and offer a conclusion.

The first record of the idea of a Festival of Britain is to be found in 1943, at the point of the Second World War when victory, although challenging, at last seemed possible. The festival was to mark the centenary of the Great Exhibition, and many had in mind a similar exhibition of the nation's products. This made sense, for a good number of such exhibitions had followed that of 1851 and business liked them.

The festival, as its plans emerged under the directorship of journalist, Sir Gerald Barry, and chairmanships of Churchill's right-hand man, Lord Ismay, looked rather different. I quote from the first of three talks Sir Gerald gave to the Royal Society of Arts in 1952:

We were going to tell a story not industry by industry, still less firm by firm, but the consecutive story of the British people in the land they live in and by ... each type of

201

manufacture and each individual exhibit would occur in the setting appropriate to that part of the story in which it naturally fell, e.g. steel knives and sinks in the home part of the story, steel machines in the industry part of the story, steel chassis in transport, and so on ... each industrial exhibit will be chosen by the exhibition organizers themselves in consultation with manufacturers and trade associations.[1]

A stock list was compiled of some 20,000 items from 5,000 manufacturers, only half of which could be exhibited in the space available. Design was key, and was overseen by the still relatively new Council of Industrial Design (now the Design Council). 'The exhibits ranged from locomotives to lipsticks and in value many thousands of pounds to a few pennies.'

Perhaps because of the way the exhibitions were curated, it is hard to find a list of exhibitors, as was and still is readily available for the 1851 exhibition. However, from a large number of pieces of individual research, including that from the memories of visitors, it is possible to highlight some. Before doing so, I want to outline the overall structure of the festival.

There is no doubting the ambition of the project, nor its significance in a country still scarred by war and suffering the austerity demanded by the need to balance the nation's books. The Great Exhibition of 1851 had been an unashamed showing off of what British manufacturers could make. A century later, the Festival of Britain could have done the same: British manufacturers still made wonderful products. Or did they? A piece from the pen of Old Stager in *The Sphere* magazine of 27 January 1951 asks the question, 'Festival of Shoddy?' In it he suggests that the proportion of British products of 'outstanding merit and finish' had fallen over the past decade. He cites domestic products and clothing, but also motor cars, quoting an oft-repeated comment that 'nowadays nothing works'. The exhibition organizers were undaunted by such views and instead chose to tell the story of these islands and of its peoples, drawing into that story some 10,000 products. I look at some of these below.

The festival as a whole dug deeper. The land was shown with its mineral deposits and, from these, the coal, iron and aluminium that could be used. It showed how coal was mined and ore smelted. Hydroelectricity was very much the rage, and so, in the Glasgow exhibition (as I tell below the exhibition extended across the United Kingdom), the visitor would be met by tumbling water generating electrical power.

Government priorities figured. In Northern Ireland, the focus was on agriculture with visitors being shown the farmhouse of 1851 compared to the farm of the future; the war had massively increased agricultural output and government wanted this to continue. War had robbed the country of lives but also homes. Space was at a premium and visitors were shown small homes making the very best use of the space they had.

As important as the story, was the way it was told. The English language and books featured loudly, but it was in the advertising and interpretative material that perhaps the festival mapped the path ahead. During the war, graphic artists and designers had worked with the Ministry of Information on how messages should be conveyed. The medium of the 'exhibition' was seen as key, as perhaps how we now see social media. Great attention was given to words, typefaces and colours. A story was being told, and this needed to be communicated to as many people as possible in the most effective way it could.

The main festival site was on what we now know as London's Southbank as evidenced by the continuing presence of the Royal Festival Hall. For the five months of the festival, it was divided into three sections: the Land of Britain, which looked at how the land was formed, how it was farmed, how it yielded minerals and how these were transformed by industry; the People of Britain, looking at our origins, character and traditions but also how science and design helped in our homes, schools and hospitals. The third and central pavilion was the Dome of Discovery, a giant steel and aluminium structure telling how 'Britain contributed to the world's enquiry about itself and about the universe and how it has applied this knowledge'. So, there were references to Scott and Cook, but also astronomy and Darwin: 'an exploration of the physical world during five hundred years, a body of sustained enquiry and of scientific imagination which has given us electric power, radio and television, nuclear energy, plastics and synthetic drugs.' This was serious stuff. Many visitors may now remember most of all the Battersea Pleasure Gardens with its six-acre amusement park with echoes of the Pleasure Gardens of Vauxhall. Everyone would remember the Skylon which soared above the Dome of Discovery.

A new block of the Science Museum hosted 'Science at South Kensington' which explored the frontiers of science, giving visitors a sense of wonder. Particular attention was given to the way exhibits were displayed.

The war had destroyed swathes of the capital, and, in the festival, architecture could be seen in the flesh in the new buildings at Poplar in East London. There were real houses and flats, churches and schools, and shops which could be explored and which demonstrated contemporary principles of planning and design.

The Victoria and Albert Museum hosted an exhibition of books, highlighting the importance of the English language.

There were then four exhibitions outside London: a floating exhibition on a converted aircraft carrier, the RMS *Campania*, the contents of which told very much the same as the story on the Southbank. The second was a travelling exhibition that shed light on manufacturing, visiting Birmingham, Nottingham, Manchester and Leeds, over 35,000 square feet featuring 3,000 objects arranged in six sections: Materials and Skills, Discovery and Design, People at Home, People at Work, People at Play and People Travel. It talked of domestic equipment and objects made from plastic; in the Home section, space was at a premium, so it talked of furniture and floor coverings and light fittings; in the Play section it spoke of field sports, camping, indoor and outdoor games and recreations, toys and hobbies and leisurewear; the Work section had a focus on Sir Frank Whittle and the gas turbine jet engine; finally Travel looked at shipping and the railways.

An exhibition of Industrial Power at the Kelvin Hall in Glasgow focused on the power of coal, then, looking at steel, on engines of every kind, and electricity. It looked at water power and had a dramatic demonstration of hydroelectricity with 20,000 gallons of water breaking every minute on the roof of a bright glass tunnel leading into the hall of Hydroelectricity, Civil Engineering and Irrigation. There was then a hall of Shipbuilding and Railways leading to the final hall of Atomic Energy. The latter was tapping into the vision for a future Britain. Shipbuilding was highlighting the variety of ships which British yards were building.

An exhibition of Farm and Factory in Ulster, told the story of farming from 1851 and contrasting the farmyard of the future. It also told of Northern Ireland's industries: shirt-making, poplin, woollens and cotton, rope making, pottery, mineral water, tobacco manufacturing machinery, whiskey, shipbuilding and aircraft production.

What to me is most interesting about the exhibition book is that of the seventy-two pages, over thirty are devoted to the arts festivals running across the country, headed by the Edinburgh Festival in August. There were also mini festivals in towns and villages across the land, not least at the village of Trowell near Nottingham which is featured in the book. Truly this was an exhibition about a whole country.

It was an exhibition where arts and culture mingled easily with manufacturing. The V&A website Festival of Britain section has a fascinating page on posters with iconic designs. Robin Day, who we have seen designing for Pye Radio, designed the Exhibition of Science poster, but also the seating in the new Festival Hall. No less iconic is the section on furnishing which highlights new designers, but also new companies seeking to offer well-designed products for the home.[2] Ernest Race, of Race Furniture, produced Springbok and Antelope chairs for the outside of the exhibition: the company still manufactures eye-catching furniture.[3] Heals provided the festival with stacking chairs designed by Andrew John Milne. Robin Day's designs were also evident in his 658 chair, a winged armchair used in the Festival Hall lounge areas. Textiles by Day's wife, Lucienne, featured in the Homes and Gardens pavilions alongside her husband's furniture. Robin Day went on to design for Hille and many others. He is seen as the most influential furniture designer of his time.[4] Design wasn't new; this was after all the land of William Morris and the Arts and Crafts movement. Indeed, I doubt that I am the only person moved by the beauty of a Victorian steam engine. What was new was the place of design in industry.

The Transport section on the Southbank was perhaps particularly important and attracted press comment, specifically on the railways. *The Sphere* of 27 January 1951 featured the Vulcan Foundry at Newton-le-Willows using Pickfords, then part of the newly nationalized British Road Services, to bring a 660hp diesel-electric locomotive destined for use in Tasmania. The following week, it was the turn of the North British Locomotive Company with an eighty-feet WG class steam locomotive for the Indian Railways. This was set alongside the *Silver Bullet*, a high-speed luxury train for the Cairo–Alexandria line built by the Birmingham Railway Carriage & Wagon Company. This five-coach train with a diesel-electric locomotive either end could carry sixty first-class and 112 second-class passengers at 75 mph. The website of the London Transport Museum highlights the presence of the new aluminium-bodied underground carriages manufactured by Metro-Cammell.[5] Unpainted aluminium was selected because of the shortage of steel. Surely this was a nation supremely confident in its transport manufacturing.

An important strand of the festival was traditional crafts. A google search revealed that Rye Pottery has a page on its website of its presence at the festival.[6] *The Sphere* magazine picks up on the pottery theme by carrying festival advertisements for both Royal Doulton and Wedgwood.

The buildings of the festival celebrated 'new' materials, not least because the building industry was desperately short of those traditionally used. The pavilions were made of canvas where possible, otherwise aluminium was used for the Dome and the Skylon. There was an accompanying advertisement from Almin Ltd., the relatively new light-metal research company. Chance Brothers had begun to manufacture glass fibre in the 1920s. In 1938, Pilkington took an interest in the company, which in 1946 increased to a 50 per cent holding and, in 1951, acquired it in its entirety. Fibreglass was the coming building material. Dunlop produced a diagram of the Southbank highlighting their products used in the various areas: Dunlopillo, Semtex flooring, Semastic Decorative Tiles, as well as tyres and rubber suspension.

Looking at festival advertisements, a number of companies have the distinction of both inclusion in the 1851 catalogue and advertising in the 1951 festival. Doulton were manufacturing ceramic pipes for drainage in 1851, but a hundred years later were advertising fine porcelain. Marshall & Snelgrove as haberdashers both exhibited in 1851 and advertised in 1951. Mulliner, coachbuilders, exhibited in 1851 and are mentioned in a Rolls-Royce/Bentley advertisement in 1951. John Weiss & Son had exhibited their knife with 1851 blades at the Great Exhibition, and, in 1951, a retrospective article in *The Sphere* featured images of that knife. An article on books, published in 1951 with a festival theme, highlighted images of the birthplace of Dalton who discovered the atom, alongside photographs of the nuclear plant at Sellafield. Chance Brothers, glass manufacturers, not only exhibited in 1851 but made the glass for the Crystal Palace, and, with fibreglass, were among the new building materials celebrated in 1951. There were other echoes. The travelling exhibition in 1951 carried with it Stephenson's Rocket. The references to gutta-percha in the 1851 catalogue surely had resonance in the Dunlop advertisements in 1951, and of course ICI and polythene.

I found an account of the travelling exhibition which visited Birmingham: 'The Midlands motor industry in particular was well represented with the latest cars from Birmingham's "Austin Motor Company" and "Singer Motors"; the world's first experimental gas turbine car was displayed by "Rover Company", Solihull.'

Looking at newspapers of the time, it was an Austin A70 Hereford that was advertised in connection with the festival. The Rover gas turbine was featured as powering a naval craft. The *Birmingham Gazette* of 5 January 1951 carried a piece on the planned visit to the Southbank Exhibition of all 10,000 employees of motor accessory manufacturer Rubery Owen:

> Various other Birmingham-based manufacturers contributed exhibits, including the 'B.S.A.' guns; the 'Bulpitt' aluminium hot-water-bottle; 'Chad Valley' chess set, dolls, toy tractor, watering can; the 'Creda Comet' electric cooker, and 'Valor' oil convector heater – all in the Land Travelling Exhibition. In addition, at the Southbank Exhibition, there were 'Alldays & Onions' smithy equipment, 'Dunlop' tyres, bicycles from 'Dawes', 'Parkes' and 'Sunbeam', cricket bats by 'Quaife and Lilley', motor cycles from 'Ariel', 'BSA' and 'James' ('Red Hunter', 'Bantam' and 'Comet' models) plus 'I.M.I.' sporting ammunition.

The Kelvin Hall in Glasgow was home to heavy industry and some recollections of the event have been complied. The exhibition was designed by Alastair Borthwick and Basil Spence and was described in the programme:

> A waterfall forms an entire wall of one hall. A million-volt machine sends flashes of man-made lightning to a domed roof representing the night sky. A 250-foot ship, three decks high, runs the length of another hall. After passing through a full-scale prehistoric coal swamp, the visitor descends in real pit cages to a modern mine.

Notwithstanding this drama, the exhibition failed to capture the imagination of the Glaswegians who attended in fewer numbers than expected.[7]

Northern Ireland presented agriculture and manufacturing and, from the newspapers of the time, received some good publicity, I suspect through the energetic approach of its chairman, Sir Roland Nugent, a leading member of the Northern Ireland Senate. The *Northern Whig and Belfast Post* of 8 August 1951 carried a statement from him and a suggestion of the exhibition's popularity highlighting also a visit from the RMS *Campania*.

The festival closed its doors in September 1951, incidentally the month before I was born. From conversations I have since had with people who attended, it clearly made its mark. Yet, it was not universally supported. My mother kept some remarkable albums of my father's war and these continued through the fifties when he was with Rootes; there is no mention of the festival. The general election following the festival saw the return to power of a Conservative government under an ageing prime minister, Winston Churchill, one of whose first acts was to bulldoze much of the festival site.

The festival may have gone, but I believe left a legacy in the field of design, not least in what became the Design Council. The challenges that faced postwar Britain remained, but the country could, with justification, look back with pride on what it had shaped in the field of manufacturing. Within a matter of months, the country would have new young queen and a future full of possibility.

Notes

Chapter 1: A Great Exhibition at the Crystal Palace

1. C. H. Gibbs-Smith, The Great Exhibition of 1851, *The Sphere*, 2 June 1951 p. 368.
2. David Cannadine, *Victorious Century: The United Kingdom 1800–1906* (London: Random House, 2017) p. 277.
3. https://catalog.hathitrust.org/Record/001511518 accessed 27 May 2020. Great Exhibition London, England. Official Catalogue of the Great Exhibition of the Works of Industry of All Nations, 1851 ... 2nd corrected and improved edition (London: Spicer Brothers, 1851).
4. J. D. Scott, *Vickers: A History* (London: Weidenfeld & Nicolson, 1962) p. 13.
5. J. D. Scott, *Siemens Brothers 1858–1958* (London: Weidenfeld & Nicolson, 1958) p. 17.
6. Brian Leyland, *St Helens: The Great and the Good* (Bowden: Stellar Books, 2018) p. 249.

Chapter 2: Trade, Exploration and Shipping

1. Eric Hobsbawm, *Age of Revolution* (London: Weidenfeld & Nicholson, 1962, Kindle edition) loc.641.
2. Anthony Slaven, *British Shipbuilding 1500–2010* (Lancaster: Crucible, 2013) p. 1.
3. Philip Hamlyn Williams, *Ordnance* (Brimscombe: The History Press, 2018) p. 37.
4. Rebecca Fraser, *The Mayflower Generation* (London: Chatto & Windus, 2017).

5. www.blackpast.org/global-african-history/groups-organizations-global-african-history/royal-african-company-2, accessed 12 June 2020.
6. David Gilmour, *The British in India* (London: Allen Lane. 2018; Penguin, 2019) p. 15.

Chapter 3: Coal and Metal

1. Roger Osborne, *Iron, Steam & Money: The Making of the Industrial Revolution* (London: The Bodley Head, 2013, Kindle edition) loc.248.
2. Robert L. Galloway, *A History of Coal Mining in Great Britain* (London: Macmillan, 1882) p. 4.
3. Ibid., p. 38.
4. www.gknaerospace.com/en/about-gkn-aerospace/history/#timeline-1, accessed 3 May 2020.
5. Eric Hopkins, *The Rise of the Manufacturing Town Birmingham and the Industrial Revolution* (London: Weidenfeld & Nicolson, 1989; Stroud: Sutton, 1998) p. 48.
6. Osborne, loc.3478.
7. Osborne, loc.526.
8. Bernard Newman, *One Hundred Years of Good Company* (Lincoln, Ruston & Hornsby, 1957) p. 63, made available as a pdf by www.britishtransporttreasures.com/product/one-hundred-years-of-good-company-the-ruston-centenary-1857-1957-by-bernard-newman-ruston-hornsby-1957-ebook/.

Chapter 4: Textiles

1. Sarah Levitt in Mary. B. Rose (ed.), *The Lancashire Cotton Industry: A History Since 1700* (Preston: Lancashire County Books, 1996) p. 155.
2. David Cannadine, *Victorious Century: The United Kingdom 1800–1906* (London: Random House, 2017) p. 176.
3. Roger Osborne, *Iron, Steam & Money: The Making of the Industrial Revolution* (London: The Bodley Head, 2013, Kindle edition) loc.2127.

4. Mary. B. Rose (ed.) *The Lancashire Cotton Industry: A History Since 1700* (Preston: Lancashire County Books, 1996) p. 2.

5. Ibid., p. 7.

6. Osborne loc.2431.

7. www.derwentvalleymills.org/discover/derwent-valley-mills-history, accessed 30 May 2021.

8. www.johnsmedley.com/discover, accessed 14 March 2020.

9. Dermot Turing, *The Story of Computing: From the Abacus to Artificial Intelligence* (London: Arcturus, 2018) p. 39.

10. www.inspirepicturearchive.org.uk/image/22613/The_William_Hollins_Mills_at_Pleasley_Vale, accessed 16 June 2020.

11. Robert Poole, *Peterloo: The English Uprising* (Oxford: Oxford University Press, 2019) p. 38.

12. Eric Hobsbawm, *Age of Revolution* (London: Weidenfeld & Nicholson, 1962, Kindle edition) loc.855.

13. Klaus H. Wolff, 'Textile Bleaching and the Birth of the Chemical Industry,' *The Business History Review*, vol. 48, no. 2 (1974) pp. 143–63. *JSTOR*, www.jstor.org/stable/3112839 accessed 13 Aug. 2020.

14. David J. M. Rowe, *History of the Chemical Industry 1750 to 1930: An Outline* (University of York (1998) www.rsc.org/learn-chemistry/resources/business-skills-and-commercial-awareness-for-chemists/docs/Rowe per cent20Chemical per cent20Industry.pdf, accessed 13 August 2020.

15. George I. Brown, *The Big Bang: A History of Explosives* (Stroud: Sutton Publishing, 1998) p. 96.

16. www.saltassociation.co.uk/education/salt-history/salt-the-chemical-revolution/leblanc-process, accessed 15 September 2020.

17. Mary. B. Rose (ed.), *The Lancashire Cotton Industry: A History since 1700* (Preston: Lancashire County Books, 1996) p. 50.

18. Charles Wilson, *A History of Unilever* vol. 1 (London: Cassell, 1954; paperback, 1970).

Chapter 5: Steam and Steel

1. Robert L. Galloway, *A History of Coal Mining in Great Britain* (London: Macmillan, 1882) p. 80.

2. Roger Osborne, *Iron, Steam & Money: The Making of the Industrial Revolution* (London: The Bodley Head, 2013 Kindle, edition) loc.1371.
3. Galloway p. 189.
4. Ibid., p. 199.
5. Charlie Bruce, *Great British Railway Journeys* (London: William Collins, 2015) p. 26.
6. David Cannadine, *Victorious Century: The United Kingdom 1800–1906* (London: Random House, 2017) p. 174.
7. Jerry White, *London in the 19th Century* (London: Vintage, 2007) p. 37.
8. Ibid., p. 38.
9. David Boughey, 'The Internalisation of Locomotive Building by Britain's Railway Companies during the Nineteenth Century', *Business and Economic History*, vol. 28, no. 1, 1999, pp. 57–67. *JSTOR*, www.jstor.org/stable/23703250, accessed 4 June 2020.
10. Anthony Slaven, *British Shipbuilding 1500–2010* (Lancaster: Crucible, 2013) p. 31.
11. Eric Hobsbawm, *Age of Revolution* (London: Weidenfeld & Nicholson, 1962, Kindle edition) loc.781.
12. John W. Frey, 'Iron and Steel Industry of the Middlesbrough District', *Economic Geography*, vol. 5, no. 2 (1929) pp. 176–82. *JSTOR*, www.jstor.org/stable/140509, accessed 24 March 2020.
13. Hobsbawm, loc.923.
14. Karen Farrington, *Great Victorian Railway Journeys* (London: William Collins, 2011) p. 162.
15. Henrietta Heald, *William Armstrong, Magician of the North* (Kindle edition).
16. Frey, pp. 176–82.
17. J. T. Gleave, 'The Tees-Side Iron and Steel Industry', *The Geographical Journal*, vol. 91, no. 5 (1938) pp. 454–67. *JSTOR*, www.jstor.org/stable/1787508 accessed 24 March 2020.
18. Heald, loc.3351.
19. J. D. Scott, *Vickers: A History* (London: Weidenfeld & Nicolson, London, 1962) p. 17.
20. Bernard Newman, *One Hundred Years of Good Company* (Lincoln, Ruston & Hornsby, 1957).
21. Slaven p. 39.
22. Heald, loc.3226.

23. Cannadine, p. 296.
24. www.visitbradford.com/saltaire-history.aspx, accessed 1 June 2021.
25. Galloway, p. 255.

Chapter 6: Communication

1. Aileen Fyfe, *Steam-Powered Knowledge* (Chicago: Chicago, 2012) p. 19.
2. Lewis Evans, *John Dickinson and Company* (1896) p. 8.
3. www.npht.org/about-napier/4577703434 accessed 4 November 2020.
4. Jerry White, *London in the 19th Century* (London: Vintage, 2007) p. 42.
5. White p. 53.
6. www.thehistorypress.co.uk/articles/the-forgotten-men-of-the-london-underground, accessed 4 April 2020.
7. Karen Farrington, *Great Victorian Railway Journeys* (London: William Collins, 2011) p. 179.
8. www.telegraph.co.uk/technology/connecting-britain/first-electric-telegraph, accessed 17 April 2020.
9. J. D. Scott, *Siemens Brothers 1858–1958* (London: Weidenfeld & Nicolson, 1958) p. 44.
10. Ibid., p. 36.
11. Brian Bowers & Margaret Wilson, *Sir Charles Wheatstone FRS: 1802–1875* (London: The Science Museum, 2001) p. 183.
12. www.smithsonianeducation.org/scitech/carbons/typewriters.html, accessed 27 April 2020.
13. Dermot Turing, *The Story of Computing: From the Abacus to Artificial Intelligence* (London: Arcturus, 2018) p. 45.

Chapter 7: Armaments

1. Henrietta Heald, *William Armstrong, Magician of the North* (Kindle edition).
2. Maj-Gen A. Forbes, *A History of Army Ordnance Services* (London: Medici, 1929) vol. 1, p. 191.
3. J. D. Scott, *Vickers: A History* (London: Weidenfeld & Nicolson, 1962) p. 26.

4. Heald, loc 2088.
5. George I. Brown, *The Big Bang: A History of Explosives* (Stroud: Sutton Publishing, 1998) p. 100.
6. Carol Kennedy, *ICI: The Company that Changed Our Lives* (London: Hutchinson, 1986) p. 12.
7. Brown, p. 106.
8. www.gknaerospace.com/en/about-gkn-aerospace/history/#timeline-1, accessed 4 May 2020.
9. David Cannadine, *Victorious Century: The United Kingdom 1800–1906* (London: Random House, 2017) p. 315.
10. Ibid., p. 388.
11. www.royalsignalsmuseum.co.uk/early-communications-pre-corps, accessed 26 April 2020.
12. Anthony Slaven, *British Shipbuilding 1500–2010* (Lancaster: Crucible, 2013) p. 46.
13. https://spectrum.ieee.org/tech-history/dawn-of-electronics/this-british-family-changed-the-course-of-engineering accessed 20 June 2020.
14. Karen Farrington, *Great Victorian Railway Journeys* (London: William Collins, 2011) p. 243.
15. Scott. p. 34.
16. David Edgerton, *The Rise and Fall of the British Nation: A Twentieth Century History* (London: Allen Lane, 2018; Penguin, 2019) p. 110.
17. Heald, loc.5660.
18. Scott, p. 49.
19. Philip Hamlyn Williams, *Ordnance* (Gloucester: The History Press, 2018) p. 42.
20. Slaven, p. 62.
21. Scott, p. 53.
22. www.libertyhousegroup.com/our-businesses/liberty-aluminium/liberty-british-aluminium/history, accessed 12 May 2020.
23. James Ashby, 'The Aluminium Legacy: The History of the Metal and Its Role in Architecture', *Construction History*, vol. 15 (1999) pp. 79–90. *JSTOR*, www.jstor.org/stable/41613796, accessed 13 May 2020.
24. K. J. Lea, 'Hydro-Electric Power Generation in the Highlands of Scotland', *Transactions of the Institute of British Geographers*, no. 46 (1969) pp. 155–65. *JSTOR*, www.jstor.org/stable/621414, accessed 13 May 2020.

Chapter 8: The Home

1. Richard Perren, 'Structural Change and Market Growth in the Food Industry: Flour Milling in Britain, Europe, and America, 1850–1914', *The Economic History Review,* vol. 43, no. 3 (1990) pp. 420–37. *JSTOR,* www.jstor.org/stable/2596941, accessed 26 May 2020.
2. https://everydaylivesinwar.herts.ac.uk/2015/01/food, accessed 24 April 2020.
3. Laura Stearman with Dr John Martin, De Montfort University, *World War 1, The Few that Fed the Many* (NFU), www.nfuonline.com/assets/33538, accessed 24 April 2020.
4. Kenneth D. Brown, *The British Toy Industry* (Botley: Shire Publications, 2011).
5. Charles Wilson, *A History of Unilever* vol. 1 (London: Cassell, 1954; paperback, 1970) pp. 34–8.
6. Derek J. Oddy (ed.), 'Plain Fare: Diet during Industrialization', *From Plain Fare to Fusion Food: British Diet From the 1890s to the 1990s* (Boydell & Brewer, Woodbridge, Suffolk; Rochester, NY, 2003) pp. 1–10. *JSTOR,* www.jstor.org/stable/10.7722/j.ctt7zsvhx.6, accessed 26 May 2020.
7. www.ranktrust.org/joseph-rank.htm, accessed 26 May 2020.
8. Edgar Jones, *The Business of Medicine (*London: Profile, 2001) p. 10.
9. http://letslookagain.com/2014/09/the-rise-and-demise-of-the-j-lyons-empire, accessed 12 March 2021.
10. www.cadbury.co.uk/our-story, accessed 8 April 2020.
11. Sarah Levitt in Mary. B. Rose (ed.), *The Lancashire Cotton Industry: A History since 1700* (Preston: Lancashire County Books, 1996) p. 168.
12. www.the-shoe-museum.org/history-of-clarks-1, accessed 22 May 2020.
13. www.culturenorthernireland.org/features/heritage/shirt-industry, accessed 12 June 2020.
14. Jones, p. 105.
15. www.ncbi.nlm.nih.gov/pmc/articles/PMC128961, accessed 6 May 2020.
16. https://pharmaphorum.com/articles/a_history_of_the_pharmaceutical_industry, accessed 6 May 2020.

17. E M. Tansey, 'Medicines and Men: Burroughs, Wellcome & Co, and the British Drug Industry Before the Second World War', *Journal of the Royal Society of Medicine* vol. 95, no. 8 (2002): pp. 411–6, doi:10.1258/jrsm.95.8.411.
18. T. A. B. Corley, 'The Beecham Group in the World's Pharmaceutical Industry 1914–70', *Zeitschrift Für Unternehmensgeschichte/ Journal of Business History*, vol. 39, no. 1 (1994) pp. 18–30. *JSTOR*, www.jstor.org/stable/40695463, accessed 8 June 2020.
19. www.gsk.com/en-gb/about-us/our-history/innovative-entrepreneurs-1715-1891/.
20. Geoffrey Jones, 'Foreign Multinationals and British Industry Before 1945', *The Economic History Review*, vol. 41, no. 3 (1988) pp. 429–53. *JSTOR*, www.jstor.org/stable/2597369, accessed 11 June 2020.
21. Carol Kennedy, *ICI: The Company that Changed Our Lives* (London: Hutchinson, 1986) p. 13.
22. Charles Wilson, *A History of Unilever* vol. 1 (London: Cassell, 1954; paperback, 1970) p. 141.

Chapter 9: The Sewing Machine and Bicycle

1. Alex Askaroff, *A Brief History of the Sewing Machine* (Kindle edition) loc.42.
2. Kenneth Ullyet, *British Clocks and Clockmakers* (London: Read Books 2011).
3. Askaroff, loc.115.
4. www.hillmanownersclub.co.uk/history, accessed 3 April 2020.
5. Obituary *Coventry Herald*, 11 February 1921.
6. A. E. Harrison, 'The Competitiveness of the British Cycle Industry, 1890–1914', *The Economic History Review*, vol. 22, no. 2 (1969) pp. 287–303. *JSTOR*, www.jstor.org/stable/2593772 accessed 3 April 2020.
7. www.gracesguide.co.uk/Henry_John_Lawson, accessed 10 April 2020.
8. www.gracesguide.co.uk/Thomas_Humber, accessed 10 April 2020; David V. Herlihy, *Bicycle: The History* (Yale: Yale University Press, 2006).
9. James McMillan, *The Dunlop Story* (London: Weidenfeld & Nicolson, 1989) p. 12.

10. David. Rubinstein, 'Cycling in the 1890s', *Victorian Studies*, vol. 21, no. 1 (1977) pp. 47–71. *JSTOR*, www.jstor.org/stable/3825934, accessed 29 May 2020.
11. https://siddeley.org, accessed 15 April 2020.
12. Roy A. Church, 'Innovation, Monopoly, and the Supply of Vehicle Components in Britain, 1880–1930: The Growth of Joseph Lucas Ltd.'. *The Business History Review*, vol. 52, no. 2 (1978) pp. 226–49. *JSTOR*, www.jstor.org/stable/3113036, accessed 1 May 2020.
13. Harrison.
14. Roger Lloyd-Jones & M. J. Lewis with Mark Eason, *Raleigh and the British Bicycle Industry: An Economic and Business History, 1870–1960* (Aldershot: Ashgate, 2000).

Chapter 10: The Internal Combustion Engine

1. A. G. Demaus, & J. C. Tarring, *The Humber Story 1868–1932* (Gloucester: Alan Sutton, 1989) p. 27.
2. www.offshore-technology.com/comment/history-oil-gas, accessed 9 April 2020.
3. Bernard Newman, *One Hundred Years of Good Company* (Lincoln, Ruston & Hornsby, 1957) p. 17.
4. Steven Parissien, *The Life of the Automobile, A New History of the Motor Car* (London: Atlantic Books, 2013, Kindle edition) loc.192.
5. Coventry Transport Museum, *Your Journey Starts Here* (Coventry: Coventry Transport Museum) p. 2.
6. H. R. Ricardo, 'Frederick William Lanchester 1868–1946', *Obituary Notices of Fellows of the Royal Society*, vol. 5, no. 16 (1948) pp. 757–66. *JSTOR*, www.jstor.org/stable/768769, accessed 1 May 2020.
7. *Midland Daily Telegraph*, 26 September 1910.
8. Demaus & Tarring, p. 42.
9. Ian Coomber, *Vauxhall: Britain's Oldest Car Maker* (Fonthill Media, 2017, Kindle edition) loc.427.
10. P. W. S. Andrews & Elizabeth Brunner, *The Life of Lord Nuffield: A Study in Enterprise and Benevolence* (Oxford: Blackwell, 1955) p. 40.
11. Roy Church, *Herbert Austin: The British Motor Car Industry to 1941* (London: Europa, 1979) p. 13.

12. www.siddeley.org, accessed 15 April 2020.
13. Harry Louis & Bob Currie, *The Story of Triumph Motor Cycles* (Cambridge: Patrick Stephens Ltd, 1975, 1983) p. 12.
14. J. R. Clew, *The Best Twin: The Story of the Douglas Motor Cycle* (Norwich: Goose & Son, 1974) p. 50.
15. www.royalenfield.com/in/en/our-world/since-1901, accessed 11 April 2020.
16. www.nortonmotorcycles.com/company/history, accessed 29 June 2021.
17. Peter Botticelli, 'Rolls-Royce: How a Legend Was Made', *The American Scholar*, vol. 66, no. 4, (1997) pp. 501–12. *JSTOR*, www.jstor.org/stable/41212678 accessed 2 May 2020.
18. www.npht.org/about-napier/4577703434, accessed 4 June 2020.
19. Sam McKinstry, *Sure as the Sunrise: A History of Albion Motors* (Edinburgh: John Donald, 1997).
20. Roy A. Church, 'Innovation, Monopoly, and the Supply of Vehicle Components in Britain, 1880–1930: The Growth of Joseph Lucas Ltd.'. *The Business History Review*, vol. 52, no. 2 (1978) pp. 226–49. *JSTOR*, www.jstor.org/stable/3113036, accessed 1 May 2020.
21. James McMillan, *The Dunlop Story* (London: Weidenfeld & Nicolson, 1989) p. 26.
22. Bernard Newman, *One Hundred Years of Good Company* (Lincoln, Ruston & Hornsby, 1957) p. 71.
23. Anthony Slaven, *British Shipbuilding 1500–2010* (Lancaster: Crucible, 2013) p. 49.
24. https://invention.psychology.msstate.edu/library/Wenham/WenhamLocomotion.html, accessed 12 April 2020.
25. www.wrightbrothers.org/History_Wing/History_of_the_Airplane/Century_Before/Powering_up/Powering_up.htm, accessed 12 April 2020,
26. J. Rickard (3 April 2009) *Royal Aircraft Factory (R.A.F.)* www.historyofwar.org/articles/company_royal_aircraft_factory.html, accessed 14 April 2020.
27. Peter Dancy, *British Aircraft Manufacturers Since 1909* (Fonthill Media, 2014, Kindle edition) loc.254.
28. J. D. Scott, *Vickers: A History* (London: Weidenfeld & Nicolson, 1962) p. 74.

Chapter 11: Electric Power

1. www.britishtelephones.com/histuk.htm, accessed 17 April 2020.
2. J. D. Scott, *Siemens Brothers 1858–1958* (London: Weidenfeld & Nicolson, 1958) p. 45.
3. Jerry White, *London in the 19th Century* (London: Vintage, 2007) p. 60.
4. Scott, p. 147.
5. https://collection.sciencemuseumgroup.org.uk/people/ap314/general-electric-company-plc, accessed 21 April 2020.
6. www.cromptonlamps.com/AdditionalDepartments/Header-Content/History, accessed 8 June 2020.
7. Bernard Newman, *One Hundred Years of Good Company* (Lincoln, Ruston & Hornsby, 1957) p. 20.
8. Brian Bowen, 'The Building of the British Westinghouse Electric and Manufacturing Plant, Trafford Park, Manchester, 1901–2: An Early Example of Transatlantic Co-operation in Construction Management', *Construction History*, vol. 25 (2010) pp. 85–100. *JSTOR*, www.jstor.org/stable/41613961, accessed 20 April 2020.
9. David P. Billington, 'Edison, Westinghouse, And Electric Power', *Power, Speed, and Form: Engineers and the Making of the Twentieth Century*, student edition (Princeton University Press, Princeton; Oxford, 2006) pp. 13–34. *JSTOR*, www.jstor.org/stable/j.ctt3fgzd1.8, accessed 21 April 2020.
10. 'London's New Underground Electric Railway', *Scientific American*, vol. 83, no. 3 (1900) pp. 40–1. *JSTOR*, www.jstor.org/stable/24981884, accessed 19 April 2020.
11. www.brushelectrichistory.com/railway-tram-products.
12. www.britishtelephones.com/histuk.htm accessed 17 April 2020.
13. *Westminster Gazette*, 6 November 1913, p. 7.
14. Geoffrey Jones, 'Foreign Multinationals and British Industry Before 1945', *The Economic History Review*, vol. 41, no. 3 (1988) pp. 429–53. *JSTOR*, www.jstor.org/stable/2597369, accessed 11 June 2020.
15. www.biography.com/inventor/guglielmo-marconi, accessed 21 April 2020.
16. W. S. Franklin, 'Wireless Telegraphy', *Science*, vol. 15, no. 368 (1902) pp. 112–13. *JSTOR*, www.jstor.org/stable/1628261, accessed 21 April 2020.

17. Newman, p. 79.
18. Lars U. Scholl, 'The Global Communications Industry and Its Impact on International Shipping Before 1914' in David J. Starkey & Gelina Harlaftis (eds.), *Global Markets: The Internationalization of the Sea Transport Industries Since 1850* (Liverpool University Press, 1998) pp. 195–216. *JSTOR*, www.jstor.org/stable/j.ctt21kk2sh.13, accessed 25 April 2020.

Chapter 12: The Great War

1. John Stephenson, *British Society 1914–1945* (London: Penguin, 1990) p. 22.
2. David Edgerton, *The Rise and Fall of the British Nation: A Twentieth Century History* (London: Allen Lane, 2018; Penguin edition, 2019) p. 78.
3. Benjamin Phillips, *British Tractors: A History of Tractors Made or Used in Britain* (Manchester: Nostalgia Road, 2017) p. 46.
4. www.nfuonline.com/nfu-online/about-us/the_few_that_fed_the_many_web, accessed 8 October 2020.
5. Kenneth D. Brown, *The British Toy Industry* (Botley: Shire Publications, 2011).
6. Edgerton, p. 137.
7. Anthony Slaven, *British Shipbuilding 1500–2010* (Lancaster: Crucible, 2013) p. 67.
8. J. D. Scott, *Vickers: A History* (London: Weidenfeld & Nicolson, 1962) p. 115.
9. Bernard Newman, *One Hundred Years of Good Company* (Lincoln, Ruston & Hornsby, 1957) p. 85.
10. Richard Pullen, *The Landships of Lincoln* (Heighington: Tucann, 2007).
11. R. J. Q. Adams, *Arms and the Wizard* (London: Cassell, 1978).
12. James McMillan, *The Dunlop Story* (London: Weidenfeld & Nicolson, 1989) p. 48.
13. Carol Kennedy, *ICI: The Company that Changed Our Lives* (London: Hutchinson, 1986) p. 15.
14. National Archives, WO 95/60/4 lecture on ammunition supply.
15. *Midland Daily Telegraph*, 30 June 30 1922.

16. Scott, p. 120.
17. Peter Dancy, *British Aircraft Manufacturers Since 1909* (Fonthill Media, 2014, Kindle edition) loc.74.
18. John Walls & Charles Parker, *Aircraft Made in Lincoln* (Lincoln: Society for Lincolnshire History & Archaeology, 2000).
19. Newman, p. 54.
20. Scott p. 121.
21. St John C. Nixon, *Wolseley, A Saga of the Motor Industry* (London: G. T. Foulis, 1949) p. 94.
22. www.npht.org/about-napier/4577703434, accessed 4 June 2020.
23. Sam McKinstry, *Sure as the Sunrise: A History of Albion Motors* (Edinburgh: John Donald, 1997) p. 56.
24. Alan Townsin, *Daimler* (Shepperton: Ian Allan, 2000) p. 23.
25. Alan Townsin, *AEC* (Shepperton: Ian Allan, 1998) p. 17.
26. Alan Townsin, *Thornycroft* (Shepperton: Ian Allan, 2001) p. 24.
27. M. Eyre, C. Heaps & A. Townsin, *Crossley* (Oxford: Oxford Publishing, 2002) p. 7.
28. Pat Kennett & Patrick Stephens, *Scammell* (Cambridge, 1979) p. 5.
29. Ian Coomber, *Vauxhall: Britain's Oldest Car Maker* (Fonthill Media, 2017, Kindle edition) loc.760
30. A.G. Demaus & J. C. Tarring, *The Humber Story 1868–1932* (Gloucester: Alan Sutton, 1989) p. 84
31. L. Geary, *Rootes Commercial Vehicles* (Romford: Ian Henry, 1993) p. 89.
32. Roy Church, *Herbert Austin: The British Motor Car Industry to 1941* (London: Europa, 1979) p. 43.
33. P. W. S. Andrews & Elizabeth Brunner, *The Life of Lord Nuffield: A Study in Enterprise and Benevolence* (Oxford: Blackwell, 1955) p. 80.
34. www.rolls-royce.com/about/our-history.aspx, accessed 15 April 2020.
35. Peter Botticelli, 'Rolls-Royce: How a Legend Was Made', *The American Scholar*, vol. 66, no. 4 (1997) pp. 501–12. *JSTOR*, www.jstor.org/stable/41212678, accessed 2 May 2020.
36. Roy A. Church, 'Innovation, Monopoly, and the Supply of Vehicle Components in Britain, 1880–1930: The Growth of Joseph Lucas Ltd.', *The Business History Review*, vol. 52, no. 2 (1978) pp. 226–49. *JSTOR*, www.jstor.org/stable/3113036, accessed 1 May 2020.

37. James McMillan, *The Dunlop Story* (London: Weidenfeld & Nicolson, 1989) p. 50.

38. J. R. Clew, *The Best Twin: The Story of the Douglas Motor Cycle* (Norwich: Goose & Son, 1974) p. 50.

39. www.royalsignalsmuseum.co.uk/corps-history, accessed 26 April 2020.

40. Stephen Aris, *Arnold Weinstock and the Making of GEC* (London: Aurum Press, 1998) p. 37.

41. J. D. Scott, *Siemens Brothers 1858–1958* (London: Weidenfeld & Nicolson, 1958) p. 230.

42. www.boots-uk.com/about-boots-uk/company-information/boots-heritage, accessed 6 May 2020.

43. E. M. Tansey, 'Medicines and Men: Burroughs, Wellcome & Co, and the British Drug Industry Before the Second World War', *Journal of the Royal Society of Medicine* vol. 95 no. 8 (2002): 411–16, doi:10.1258/jrsm.95.8.411.

44. Catherine Rowe-Price, *First World War Uniforms: Production, Logistics and Legacy (Modern Conflict Archaeology* (Barnsley: Pen & Sword 2018, Kindle edition).

45. John Singleton, 'The Cotton Industry and the British War Effort, 1914–1918', *The Economic History Review*, vol. 47, no. 3 (1994) pp. 601–18. *JSTOR*, www.jstor.org/stable/2597596, accessed 11 June 2020.

46. Edgar Jones, *The Business of Medicine* (London: Profile, 2001) p. 19.

47. Derek J. Oddy (ed.) 'Food and Food Technology in the Interwar Years', *From Plain Fare to Fusion Food: British Diet from the 1890s to the 1990s* (Boydell & Brewer, Woodbridge, Suffolk; Rochester, NY, 2003) pp. 95–112. *JSTOR*, www.jstor.org/stable/10.7722/j.ctt7zsvhx.10, accessed 1 July 2020.

48. Stephenson, p. 105.

Chapter 13: The Aftermath of War

1. The diaries of George Orwell.

2. John Stephenson, *British Society 1914–1945* (London: Penguin, 1990) p. 107.

3. J. D. Scott, *Siemens Brothers 1858–1958* (London: Weidenfeld & Nicolson, 1958) p. 84.
4. Stephenson, p. 107.
5. Julian I. Greaves, 'Competition, Collusion, and Confusion: The State and the Reorganization of the British Cotton Industry, 1931 — 1939', *Enterprise & Society*, vol. 3, no. 1 (2002) pp. 48–79. *JSTOR*, www.jstor.org/stable/23699997, accessed 15 May 2020.
6. Ian Hay, *R.O.F.: The Story of the Royal Ordnance Factories, 1939–48* (London: His Majesty's Stationery Office, 1949).
7. David Boughey, 'The Internalisation of Locomotive Building by Britain's Railway Companies during the Nineteenth Century', *Business and Economic History*, vol. 28, no. 1 (1999) pp. 57–67. *JSTOR*, www.jstor.org/stable/23703250, accessed 4 June 2020.
8. J. D. Scott, *Vickers: A History* (London: Weidenfeld & Nicolson, 1962) p. 140.
9. Ibid., p. 153.
10. Ibid., p. 168.
11. Bernard Newman, *One Hundred Years of Good Company* (Lincoln, Ruston & Hornsby, 1957) p. 117.
12. Anthony Slaven, *British Shipbuilding 1500–2010* (Lancaster: Crucible, 2013) p. 68.
13. www.gknaerospace.com/en/about-gkn-aerospace/history/#timeline-1, accessed 4 May 2020.
14. www.nationalarchives.gov.uk/cabinetpapers/themes/wartime-postwar-developments.htm, accessed 14 May 2020.
15. Peter Dancy, *British Aircraft Manufacturers Since 1909* (Fonthill Media, 2014, Kindle edition) loc.1161.
16. Scott, *Vickers*, p. 175.
17. www.siddeley.org, accessed 15 April 2020.
18. Slaven, p. 98–100.

Chapter 14: The Interwar Years

1. A. G. Demaus,. & J. C. Tarring, *The Humber Story 1868–1932* (Gloucester: Alan Sutton, 1989) p. 114.
2. www.p2steam.com/nigel-gresley, accessed 21 June 2021.

3. John Stephenson, *British Society 1914–1945* (London: Penguin, 1990) p. 110.
4. Stephen Aris, *Arnold Weinstock and the Making of GEC* (London: Aurum Press, 1998) p. 37.
5. J. D. Scott, *Siemens Brothers 1858–1958* (London: Weidenfeld & Nicolson, 1958) p. 88.
6. www.thehistorypress.co.uk/publication/english-electric/9780752411781, accessed 26 April 2020.
7. www.museumofpower.org.uk/Belling.html, accessed 24 January 2021.
8. www.bbc.com/historyofthebbc/timelines/1920s accessed 25 April 2020.
9. Keith Geddes & Gordon Bussey, *Setmakers: A History of the Radio and Television Industry* (The British Radio & Electronic Equipment Manufacturers' Association, 1991) p. 67.
10. P. W. S. Andrews & Elizabeth Brunner, *The Life of Lord Nuffield: A Study in Enterprise and Benevolence (*Oxford: Blackwell, 1955) p. 96.
11. Andy Goundry, *Dennis Buses and Other Vehicles* (Marlborough: Crowood Press, 2020).
12. Roy Church, *Herbert Austin: The British Motor Car Industry to 1941* (London: Europa, 1979).
13. Demaus & Tarring, p. 95.
14. Geoff Carverhill, *Rootes Story: The Making of a Global Automotive Empire* (Crowood Press, 2018) p. 28.
15. Roger Lloyd-Jones, Josephine Maltby, Myrddin John Lewis & Mark David Matthew, *Personal Capitalism and Corporate Governance: British Manufacturing in the First Half of the Twentieth Century* (Modern Economic and Social History, 2011) p. 118.
16. Roger Lloyd-Jones, et al., 'Control, Conflict and Concession: Corporate Governance, Accounting and Accountability at Birmingham Small Arms, 1906–1933', *The Accounting Historians Journal*, vol. 32, no. 1 (2005) pp. 149–84. *JSTOR*, www.jstor.org/stable/40698312 accessed 1 May 2020.
17. Philip Porter & Phil Skilleter, *Sir William Lyons: The Official Biography* (Yeovil: Haynes Publishing, 2001, 2011).
18. www.thealviscarcompany.co.uk/our-heritage, accessed 30 June 2021.
19. Ian Coomber, *Vauxhall: Britain's Oldest Car Maker* (Fonthill Media, 2017 Kindle edition) loc.1100.

20. Peter Botticelli, 'Rolls-Royce: How a Legend Was Made', *The American Scholar*, vol. 66, no. 4 (1997) pp. 501–12. *JSTOR*, www.jstor.org/stable/41212678, accessed 2 May 2020.

21. www.bentleymotors.com/en/world-of-bentley/the-bentley-story/history-and-heritage/historic-people/w-o-bentley.html, accessed 4 May 2020.

22. Roy A. Church, 'Innovation, Monopoly, and the Supply of Vehicle Components in Britain, 1880–1930: The Growth of Joseph Lucas Ltd.', *The Business History Review*, vol. 52, no. 2 (1978) pp. 226–49. *JSTOR*, www.jstor.org/stable/3113036, accessed 1 May 2020.

23. James McMillan, *The Dunlop Story* (London: Weidenfeld & Nicolson, 1989) p. 66.

24. Stephenson, p. 108.

25. K. J. Lea, 'Hydro-Electric Power Generation in the Highlands of Scotland', *Transactions of the Institute of British Geographers*, no. 46 (1969) pp. 155–65. *JSTOR*, www.jstor.org/stable/621414, accessed 13 May 2020.

26. S. Moos, 'The Structure of the British Aluminium Industry', *The Economic Journal*, vol. 58, no. 232 (1948) pp. 522–37. *JSTOR*, www.jstor.org/stable/2226176, accessed 13 May 2020.

27. Charles Wilson, *A History of Unilever* vol. 1 (London: Cassell, 1954; paperback, 1970) p. 257.

28. Carol Kennedy, *ICI: The Company that Changed Our Lives* (London: Hutchinson, 1986) p. 8.

29. George I. Brown, *The Big Bang: A History of Explosives* (Stroud: Sutton Publishing, 1998) p. 109.

30. Kennedy p. 65.

31. www.gsk.com/en-gb/about-us/our-history/building-brands-1919-1949, accessed 4 February 2021.

Chapter 15: Rearmament and the Second World War

1. G. B. R. Feilden & William Hawthorne, 'Sir Frank Whittle, O. M., K. B. E.. 1 June 1907–9 August 1996', *Biographical Memoirs of Fellows of the Royal Society*, vol. 44 (1998) pp. 435–52. *JSTOR*, www.jstor.org/stable/770254, accessed 3 May 2020.

2. Geoffrey Jones, 'Foreign Multinationals and British Industry Before 1945', *The Economic History Review*, vol. 41, no. 3 (1988) pp. 429–53. *JSTOR*, www.jstor.org/stable/2597369, accessed 11 June 2020.
3. Keith Geddes & Gordon Bussey, *Setmakers: A History of the Radio and Television Industry* (The British Radio & Electronic Equipment Manufacturers' Association, 1991) p. 114.
4. Ibid., p. 84.
5. John Stephenson, *British Society 1914–1945* (London: Penguin, 1990) p. 115.
6. J. D. Scott, *Vickers: A History* (London: Weidenfeld & Nicolson,1962) p. 200.
7. Peter Dancy, *British Aircraft Manufacturers Since 1909* (Fonthill Media, 2014, Kindle edition) loc. 312.
8. Charles Graves, *Drive for Freedom* (London: Hodder & Stoughton, 1946) p. 13.
9. www.thealviscarcompany.co.uk/our-heritage, accessed 30 June 2021.
10. P. W. S. Andrews & Elizabeth Brunner, *The Life of Lord Nuffield: A Study in Enterprise and Benevolence* (Oxford: Blackwell, 1955) p. 231.
11. Jonathan Falconer, *Stirling Wings: The Short Stirling Goes to War* (Stroud: Sutton, 1995, 1997) p. 22.
12. Scott, p. 200.
13. Dancy, loc.2951.
14. Scott, p. 278.
15. Bernard Newman, *One Hundred Years of Good Company* (Lincoln, Ruston & Hornsby, 1957) p. 168.
16. Peter Botticelli, 'Rolls-Royce: How a Legend Was Made', The American Scholar, vol. 66, no. 4, (1997) pp. 501–12. JSTOR, www.jstor.org/stable/41212678, accessed 2 May 2020.
17. Lord Kings Norton, 'The Beginnings of Jet Propulsion', *Journal of the Royal Society of Arts*, vol. 133, no. 5350 (1985) pp. 705–23. *JSTOR*, www.jstor.org/stable/41374031, accessed 3 May 2020.
18. Benjamin Phillips, *British Tractors: A History of Tractors Made or Used in Britain* (Manchester: Nostalgia Press, 2017) p. 26.
19. Geoff Carverhill, *Rootes Story: The Making of a Global Automotive Empire* (Crowood Press, 2018) p. 102.
20. Pat Ware, *A Complete Dictionary of Military Vehicles* (Bournemouth: Southwater, 2012) p. 113.

21. A. Townsin & B. Goulding, *80 Years of AEC* (Glossop: Senior Publications, 1992) p. 33.
22. M. P. Conniford, *A Summary of the Transport Used by the British Army 1939–1945* (Bellona Publications, 1969) pt. 2, p. 1.
23. M. Eyre, C. Heaps & A. Townsin, *Crossley* (Oxford: Oxford Publishing, 2002) p. 82.
24. R. Hannay & S. Broatch, *80 Years of Guy Motors Limited* (Glossop: Venture, 1994) p. 14.
25. Conniford, pt. 2, p. 1.
26. I. V. Hogg & J. Weeks, *The Illustrated History of Military Vehicles* (London: Quarto Books, 1984) p. 49.
27. Pat Kennett, *Scammell* (Cambridge: Patrick Stephens, 1979) p. 6.
28. Ernest Fairfax, *Calling All Arms* (London: Hutchinson, 1946) p. 51.
29. J. C. Nixon, *Wolseley Saga of the Motor Industry* (London: Marshall Press, 1950) p. 119.
30. Ian Coomber, *Vauxhall: Britain's Oldest Car Maker* (Fonthill Media, 2017 Kindle edition) loc.1896.
31. www.oldhamcaplamps.com/about-us/full-history, accessed 18 June 2020.
32. James McMillan, *The Dunlop Story* (London: Weidenfeld & Nicholson, 1989) p. 83.
33. Charles Graves, *Drive for Freedom* (London: Hodder & Stoughton, 1946)p. 118.
34. Kenneth D. Brown, *The British Toy Industry* (Botley: Shire Publications, 2011) p. 29.
35. Anthony Slaven, *British Shipbuilding 1500–2010* (Lancaster: Crucible, 2013) p. 114.
36. Kenneth Warren, 'Shipbuilding in World War II and the Postwar World', *Steel, Ships and Men: Cammell Laird and Company 1824–1993* (Liverpool University Press, 1998) pp. 272–92. *JSTOR*, www.jstor.org/stable/j.ctt5vjffv.26, accessed 11 May 2020.
37. Scott, p. 283.
38. Ian Hay, *R.O.F.: The Story of the Royal Ordnance Factories, 1939–48* (London: His Majesty's Stationery Office, 1949).
39. https://homefrontmuseum.wordpress.com/2014/01/03/littlewoods-parachute-division, accessed 12 May 2020.
40. Carl Chinn, *The Cadbury Story: A Short History* (Brewin, 1998).
41. http://letslookagain.com/2014/09/the-rise-and-demise-of-the-j-lyons-empire, accessed 12 March 2021.

42. https://ukdefencejournal.org.uk/britain-and-nuclear-weapons-the-second-world-war-to-the-21st-century, accessed 29 January 2021.

43. Carol Kennedy, *ICI: The Company that Changed Our Lives* (London: Hutchinson, 1986) p. 78.

44. Edgar Jones, *The Business of Medicine* (London: Profile, 2001) p. 69.

45. www.gsk.com/en-gb/about-us/our-history/building-brands-1919-1949, accessed 4 February 2021.

46. Geddes p. 260.

47. www.tnmoc.org/bombe, accessed 12 March 2021.

48. Dermot Turing, *The Story of Computing: From the Abacus to Artificial Intelligence* (London: Arcturus, 2018) p. 75.

49. https://warwick.ac.uk/fac/soc/economics/staff/sbroadberry/wp/totwar3.pdf, Stephen Broadberry (University of Warwick) & Peter Howlett (London School of Economics), *Blood, Sweat And Tears: British Mobilisation For World War* II (16 January 2002), accessed 13 May 2020.

50. David Edgerton, *The Rise and Fall of the British Nation: A Twentieth Century History* (London: Allen Lane, 2018; Penguin edition, 2019) p. 94.

51. R. G. D. Allen, 'Mutual Aid Between the U.S. and The British Empire, 1941–45', *Journal of the Royal Statistical Society*, vol. 109, no. 3 (1946) pp. 243–77. *JSTOR*, www.jstor.org/stable/2981369, accessed 12 May 2020.

Chapter 16: The Postwar Export Drive

1. Olive Moore, *Scope* magazine, September 1944, p. 34.

2. J. D Scott, *Vicker: A History* (London: Weidenfeld & Nicolson,1962) p. 302.

3. David Edgerton, *The Rise and Fall of the British Nation, A Twentieth Century History* (London: Allen Lane, 2018; Penguin edition, 2019) p. 149.

4. Ralph Harrington, 'Landscape with Bulldozer: Machines, Modernity and Environment in Postwar Britain' in Jon Agar & Jacob Ward (eds.), *Histories of Technology: The Environment and Modern Britain* (London: UCL Press).

5. B. L. Johns, 'Nationalisation of the Coal-Mining Industry: The Lessons of British Experience', *The Australian Quarterly*, vol. 30, no. 3 (1958) pp. 71–81. *JSTOR*, www.jstor.org/stable/20694683, accessed 14 May 2020.
6. A. Beacham, 'Efficiency and Organisation of the British Coal Industry', *The Economic Journal*, vol. 55, no. 218/219 (1945) pp. 206–16. *JSTOR*, www.jstor.org/stable/2226081, accessed 14 May 2020.
7. www.nationalarchives.gov.uk/cabinetpapers/themes/interwar-coal-mining.htm.
8. 'Great Britain: Coal Mining Since Nationalization', *Monthly Labor Review*, vol. 70, no. 1 (1950) pp. 19–25. *JSTOR*, www.jstor.org/stable/41831949, accessed 14 May 2020.
9. R. H Coase, 'The Nationalization of Electricity Supply in Great Britain', *Land Economics*, vol. 26, no. 1 (1950) pp. 1–16. *JSTOR*, www.jstor.org/stable/3159326, accessed 3 June 2020.
10. Gilbert Walker, 'The Transport Act 1947', *The Economic Journal*, vol. 58, no. 229 (1948) pp. 11–30. *JSTOR*, www.jstor.org/stable/2226343, accessed 15 May 2020.
11. www.nationalarchives.gov.uk/cabinetpapers/themes/railways-act.htm.
12. http://metcam.co.uk.nstempintl.com/history.htm, accessed 5 June 2020.
13. www.npht.org/about-napier/4577703434, accessed 4 June 2020.
14. www.railwaysarchive.co.uk/docsummary.php?docID=4083, accessed 5 June 2020.
15. Bernard Newman, *One Hundred Years of Good Company* (Lincoln, Ruston & Hornsby, 1957) p. 187.
16. Arthur Marwick, *British Society Since 1945* (London: Pelican, 1962, Kindle edition) loc.459.
17. Anthony Slaven, *British Shipbuilding 1500–2010* (Lancaster: Crucible, 2013) p. 114.
18. J. D. Scott, *Vickers: A History* (London: Weidenfeld and Nicholson, 1962) p. 313.
19. Ibid., p. 308.
20. Ibid., p. 340.
21. Peter Dancy, *British Aircraft Manufacturers Since 1909* (Fonthill Media, 2014, Kindle edition) loc.1350.
22. S. Moos, 'The Structure of the British Aluminium Industry', *The Economic Journal*, vol. 58, no. 232 (1948) pp. 522–37. *JSTOR*, www.jstor.org/stable/2226176, accessed 9 June 2020.

23. Graham Turner, *The Car Makers* (London: Eyre & Spottiswoode, 1963) p. 29.
24. Geoff Carverhill, *Rootes Story: The Making of a Global Automotive Empire* (Crowood Press, 2018) p. 131.
25. Ibid., p. 142.
26. James McMillan, *The Dunlop Story* (London: Weidenfeld & Nicolson, 1989) p. 91.
27. https://magazine.astonmartin.com/heritage/story-behind-db-aston-martins-famous-marque, accessed 8 November 2020.
28. Kenneth Brown, *The British Toy Industry* (Botley: Shire Publications, 2011) p. 31.
29. Keith Geddes & Gordon Bussey, *Setmakers: A History of the Radio and Television Industry* (The British Radio & Electronic Equipment Manufacturers' Association, 1991) p. 301.
30. Dermot Turing, *The Story of Computing: From the Abacus to Artificial Intelligence* (London: Arcturus, 2018) pp. 106–8,
31. www.thejournal.co.uk/business/business-news/the-wilton-power-house-4530291, accessed 7 June 2020.
32. Graham D. Taylor, *The Business History Review*, vol. 55, no. 2 (1981) pp. 287–9. *JSTOR*, www.jstor.org/stable/3114922, accessed 7 June 2020.
33. Edgar Jones, *The Business of Medicine* (London: Profile, 2001) p. 85.
34. Alison Maloney, *The Forties: Good Times Just Around the Corner* (London: Michael O'Mara, 2005).
35. Raymond Frost, 'The Macmillan Gap 1931–53', *Oxford Economic Papers*, vol. 6, no. 2 (1954) pp. 181–201. *JSTOR*, www.jstor.org/stable/2661850, accessed 17 June 2020.
36. David Merlin-Jones, *The Industrial and Commercial Finance Corporation: Lessons from the Past for the Future* (London: Civitas, 2010).

Chapter 17: The Festival of Britain

1. Gerald Barry, 'The Festival of Britain: 1951', *Journal of the Royal Society of Arts*, vol. 100, no. 4880 (1952) pp. 667–704. *JSTOR*, www.jstor.org/stable/41365427, accessed 2 June 2020.

2. www.vam.ac.uk/articles/the-festival-of-britain, accessed 2 June 2020.
3. www.racefurniture.com, accessed 19 June 2020.
4. www.hille.co.uk/robin-day accessed 19 June 2020.
5. https://blog.ltmuseum.co.uk/2017/05/03/the-1951-festival-of-britain-showcase-of-new-london-transport-r49-stock, accessed 2 June 2020.
6. www.ryepottery.co.uk/product/rye-pottery-at-the-1951-festival-of-britain, accessed 2 June 2020.
7. https://kelvinhallproject.wordpress.com/2016/04/07/glasgows-forgotten-exhibition-the-festival-of-britain-at-the-kelvin-hall-1951, accessed 2 June 2020.

Further Reading

Adams, R. J. Q., *Arms and the Wizard* (London: Cassell, 1978).

Andrews, P. W. S. & Elizabeth Brunner, *The Life of Lord Nuffield: A Study in Enterprise and Benevolence* (Oxford: Blackwell, 1955).

Aris, Stephen, *Arnold Weinstock and the Making of GEC* (London: Aurum Press, 1998).

Askaroff, Alex, *A Brief History of the Sewing Machine* (Kindle edition).

Bowers, Brian & Margaret Wilson, *Sir Charles Wheatstone FRS: 1802–1875* (London: The Science Museum, 2001).

Brown, George I, *The Big Bang: A History of Explosives* (Stroud: Sutton Publishing, 1998).

Brown, Kenneth D., *The British Toy Industry* (Botley: Shire Publications, 2011).

Bruce, Charlie, *Great British Railway Journeys* (London: William Collins, 2015).

Burton, Anthony, *The Canal Builders* (Barnsley: Pen & Sword, 2015 Kindle edition).

Cannadine, David, *Victorious Century: The United Kingdom 1800–1906* (London: Random House, 2017).

Carverhill, Geoff, *Rootes Story: The Making of a Global Automotive Empire* (Crowood Press, 2018).

Chinn, Carl, *The Cadbury Story: A Short History* (Brewin, 1998).

Church, Roy, *Herbert Austin: The British Motor Car Industry to 1941* (London: Europa, 1979).

Clew, J. R., *The Best Twin: The Story of the Douglas Motor Cycle* (Norwich: Goose & Son, 1974).

Conniford, M. P., *A Summary of the Transport Used by the British Army 1939–1945* (Bellona Publications, 1969).

Coomber, Ian, *Vauxhall: Britain's Oldest Car Maker* (Fonthill Media, 2017 Kindle edition).

Crickshank, Dan, *A History of Architecture in 100 Buildings* (London: William Collins, 2015).

Dancy, Peter, *British Aircraft Manufacturers Since 1909* (Fonthill Media, 2014).

Demaus, A. G. & J. C. Tarring, *The Humber Story 1868–1932* (Gloucester: Alan Sutton, 1989).

Edgerton, David, *The Rise and Fall of the British Nation: A Twentieth Century History* (London: Allen Lane, 2018, Penguin edition 2019).

Eyre M., C. Heaps & A. Townsin, *Crossley* (Oxford: Oxford Publishing, 2002).

Fairfax, Ernest, *Calling All Arms* (London: Hutchinson, 1946).

Falconer, Jonathan, *Stirling Wings: The Short Stirling Goes to War* (Stroud: Sutton, 1995, 1997).

Farrington, Karen, *Great Victorian Railway Journeys* (London: William Collins, 2011).

Forbes, Major-General A., *A History of Army Ordnance Services* (London: Medici, 1929).

Fraser, Rebecca, *The Mayflower Generation* (London: Chatto & Windus, 2017).

Fyfe, Aileen, *Steam-powered Knowledge* (Chicago: Chicago, 2012).

Galloway, Robert L., *A History of Coal Mining in Great Britain* (London: Macmillan, 1882).

Geary, L., *Rootes Commercial Vehicles* (Romford: Ian Henry, 1993).

Geddes, Keith & Gordon Bussey, *Setmakers: A History of the Radio and Television Industry* (The British Radio & Electronic Equipment Manufacturers' Association, 1991).

Gilmour, David, *The British in India* (London: Allen Lane 2018, Penguin 2019).

Glynn, Sean & John Oxborrow, *Interwar Britain, A Social and Economic History* (London: George Allen & Unwin 1976).

Goundry, Andy, *Dennis Buses and Other Vehicles* (Marlborough: Crowood Press, 2020).

Graves, Charles, *Drive for Freedom* (London: Hodder & Stoughton, 1946).

Hamlyn Williams, Philip, *Ordnance* (Brimscombe: The History Press, 2018).

Hamlyn Williams, Philip, *Charlotte Bronte's Devotee* (Independently published, 2019).

Hannay, R. & S. Broatch, *80 Years of Guy Motors Limited* (Glossop: Venture, 1994).

Harrington, Ralph, 'Landscape with Bulldozer: Machines, Modernity and Environment in Postwar Britain' in Jon Agar & Jacob Ward (eds.), *Histories of Technology: The Environment and Modern Britain* (London: UCL Press).

Hay, Ian, *R.O.F.: The Story of the Royal Ordnance Factories, 1939–48* (London: His Majesty's Stationery Office, 1949).

Heald, Henrietta, *William Armstrong, Magician of the North* (Kindle edition).

Hobsbawm, Eric, *Age of Revolution* (London: Weidenfeld & Nicholson, 1962, Kindle edition).

Hogg, I. V. & J. Weeks, *The Illustrated History of Military Vehicles* (London: Quarto Books, 1984).

Hopkins, Eric, *The Rise of the Manufacturing Town Birmingham and the Industrial Revolution* (London: Weidenfeld & Nicolson, 1989; Stroud: Sutton, 1998).

Hunt, Tristram, *The Radical Potter, Josiah Wedgwood and the Transformation of Britain* (London: Allen Lane, 2021).

Jones, Edgar, *The Business of Medicine* (London: Profile, 2001).

Jones, Edgar *True and Fair: A History of Price Waterhouse* (London: Hamish Hamilton, 1995).

Kennedy, Carol, *ICI: The Company that Changed Our Lives* (London: Hutchinson, 1986).

Kennett, Pat, Stephens, Patrick *Scammell* (Cambridge, 1979).

Leyland, Brian, *St Helens: The Great and the Good* (Bowden: Stellar Books, 2018).

Louis, Harry & Bob Currie, *The Story of Triumph Motor Cycles* (Cambridge: Patrick Stephens Ltd, 1975, 1983).

Maloney, Alison, *The Forties: Good Times Just Around the Corner* (London: Michael O'Mara, 2005)

Manners, William, *Revolution: How the Bicycle Reinvented Modern Britain* (London: Duckworth, 2019).

Marwick, Arthur, *British Society Since 1945* (London: Pelican, 1962, Kindle edition).

McKinstry, Sam, *Sure as the Sunrise: A History of Albion Motors* (Edinburgh: John Donald, 1997).

McMillan, James, *The Dunlop Story* (London: Weidenfeld & Nicolson, 1989).

Miller, Marion, *Cawnpore to Cromar: The MacRoberts of Douneside* (Kindle edition).

Moore, Peter, *The Endeavour* (London: Chatto & Windus, 2018).

Newman, Bernard, *One Hundred Years of Good Company* (Lincoln, Ruston & Hornsby, 1957)

Nixon, St John C., *Wolseley: A Saga of the Motor Industry* (London: G. T. Foulis, 1949).

Nixon, J. C., *Wolseley Saga of the Motor Industry* (London: Marshall Press, 1950).

Orwell, Sonia & Ian Angus (eds.), *The Collected Essays, Journalism and Letters of George Orwell: An Age Like This 1920–1940*, Vol. 1 (London: Secker & Warburg, 1968, Penguin edn.1971).

Osborne, Roger, *Iron, Steam & Money: The Making of the Industrial Revolution* (London: The Bodley Head, 2013, Kindle edition).

Parissien, Steven, *The Life of the Automobile: A New History of the Motor Car* (London: Atlantic Books, 2013).

Phillips, Benjamin, *British Tractors: A History of Tractors Made or Used in Britain* (Manchester: Nostalgia Road, 2017).

Poole, Robert, *Peterloo: The English Uprising* (Oxford: Oxford University Press, 2019).

Porter, Philip & Phil Skilleter, *Sir William Lyons: The Official Biography* (Yeovil: Haynes Publishing, 2001, 2011).

Pullen, Richard, *The Landships of Lincoln* (Heighington: Tucann, 2007).

Rose, Mary B. (ed.), *The Lancashire Cotton Industry: A History Since 1700* (Preston: Lancashire County Books, 1996).

Scott, J. D., *Vickers: A History* (London: Weidenfeld & Nicolson, 1962).

Scott, J. D., *Siemens Brothers 1858–1958* (London: Weidenfeld & Nicolson, 1958).

Slaven, Anthony, *British Shipbuilding 1500–2010* (Lancaster: Crucible, 2013).

Stephenson, John, *British Society 1914–1945* (London: Penguin, 1990).

Townsin, Alan, *Daimler* (Shepperton: Ian Allan, 2000).

Townsin, Alan, *AEC* (Shepperton: Ian Allan, 1998).

Townsin, Alan, *Thornycroft* (Shepperton: Ian Allan, 2001).

Townsin, Alan & Brian Goulding, *80 Years of AEC* (Glossop: Senior Publications, 1992).

Turing, Dermot, *The Story of Computing: From the Abacus to Artificial Intelligence* (London: Arcturus, 2018).

Turner, Graham, *The Car Makers* (London: Eyre & Spottiswoode, 1963).

Ullyet, Kenneth, *British Clocks and Clockmakers* (London: Read Books, 2011).

Upton, Chris, *A History of Birmingham* (Chichester, Phillimore, 1993).

Walls, John & Charles Parker, *Aircraft Made in Lincoln* (Lincoln: Society for Lincolnshire History & Archaeology, 2000).

Ware, Pat, *A Complete Dictionary of Military Vehicles* (Bournemouth: Southwater, 2012).

White, Jerry, *London in the 19th Century* (London: Vintage, 2007).

Wilson, Charles, *A History of Unilever* vol. 1 (London: Cassell, 1954; paperback, 1970).

Index